EGYPTIAN MASONIC RITE OF MEMPHIS

FOR THE INSTRUCTION AND GOVERNMENT OF THE CRAFT.

Published, edited, translated, and compiled by CALVIN C. BURT, 96° A. M.
P. C. K. T., 32° in the A. and A. Rite, and Grand Master General Ad
Vitem of the E∴ M∴ R∴ of M∴, Egyptian year of true light,
000,000,000, York Masonic date, A. L. 5879, and Era Vulgate 1879.

Cornerstone Book Publishers

Egyptian Masonic Rite of Memphis

A Cornerstone Book
Published by Cornerstone Book Publishers
An Imprint of Michael Poll Publishing

Cornerstone Book Publishers
New Orleans, LA

First Cornerstone Edition - 2012

www.cornerstonepublishers.com

ISBN: 1613420455
ISBN 13: 978-1-61342-045-4

MADE IN THE USA

EGYPTIAN MASONIC RITE OF MEMPHIS.

CITY OF CHICAGO, STATE OF ILLINOIS.

June 17, A. D. 1867.

By reason of a notice for a Convention of Masons belonging to the Rite of Memphis, issued May 4th, 1867, the brethren of the Order, representing one Grand Council, 90°; two Senates, 45°; ten Rose Croix Chapters, 18°, and about fifty ninety degree (unaffiliated) members assembled together this day in the Masonic Temple, in Apollo Commandery Hall, or K. T. Room, to organize a Grand Body, and form a Constitution.

On motion, Ill. Bro. B. F. Patrick was called to the Chair, and Bro. Samuel H. Underhill was chosen Secretary.

Bro. Patrick stated the object of the meeting.

The following preamble and resolution were offered by Bro. Blake, 95°:

Whereas, when we received the degrees of the Memphis Rite, we were taught that the Rite contained 96 degrees, and as such, received *our* degrees, and the several bodies in this Rite were formed in this State, and represented here this day, as well as each, all and every member of this Rite heretofore, was so instructed and obligated; all of whom have been made and the bodies formed by H. J. Seymour, 96°, Grand Master, and Calvin C. Burt, 96°, Deputy Grand Master and Grand Representative General at large, as a Rite of ninety-six degrees and no less;

And whereas, we have now been notified by the aforesaid Grand Master, that the Grand Orient of

France has reduced the degrees to 33, and changed the names of some of them, and as we believe unlawfully interfered with the original and ancient work, thereof; greatly in our opinion injuring its beauty usefulness, and antiquity;

And whereas, we are informed that our worthy and and Illustrious Brother and Deputy Grand Master, Calvin C. Burt, 96°, has not accepted of the change, and does not believe that such power exists in the Rite, and that the adoption of such a reduction will be attended with bad results;

And whereas, our former Grand Master, H. J. Seymour, 96°, has abjured, renounced and abrogated the Rite of Memphis, containing 96 degrees, for, and adopted the 33° Rite, and that there is not now, either in this country or in France, any persons working the 96° Rite;

And whereas, we are members of the 96° Rite, and have, by an authority of 96° Rite, issued by the Grand Heirophant, 97°, of France, countersigned, acknowledged, vised, and recognized by all the great and grand jurisdictions of Europe, and all other nations of the world where the work is known;

And whereas, we, as Masons, of our own free will and accord, became so, so we intend to remain, and we do as the entire representatives and representation of the Rite of Memphis in America, in convention assembled, solemnly and firmly

Resolve, That we will not acknowledge or subscribe to any such reduction of degrees, believing as we do, that the Orient of France, nor any other Masonic body in this Rite, can lawfully require us to do so; therefore we conscientiously refuse, and do henceforth, and forever declare ourselves a sovereign grand body for this continent of the Rite of Memphis, of 96 degrees, and do hereby absolve and withdraw from all other bodies of Memphis Masons of less than 96 degrees, and hereby offer this as a proper beginning of a new body in the old Rite.

On motion of Bro. Leonard, the resolution was unanimously adopted.

Whereupon, Bro. Allen offered the following, viz:

That we do declare Bro. Calvin C. Burt, 96°, our Sovereign Grand Master, and that we proceed to place him in the Orient, with a request that he appoint temporary officers, in order that we may proceed to the business of a permanent organization of a grand body.

Which was unanimously adopted, and a committee consisting of Bros. Allen, Patrick, Brierlee, appointed to escort the M. W. Grand Master to the Chair, where he was so placed and declared Grand Master ad Vitem, and so saluted by the whole body.

Whereupon he took the gavel, appointed the officers of the Sovereign Sanctury, and opened the body in due form, which was announced and declared the Sovereign Sanctuary for America, sitting in the valley of Chicago, duly organized by the representatives of one Council, two Senates, and ten Rose Croix Chapters, and the whole 96° representatives in America, in convention assembled.

A record was opened and the foregoing and following record made and entered in due Masonic form, when the following entry on motion was ordered entered, viz: on motion of Bro. Starrett, a committee of three brothers were appointed to submit the names of proper persons to fill the several offices in this grand body, viz, Brothers Gurney, Storey, and Dyche, who retired to consult and report. The committee on nomination and permanent organization reported as follows, viz:

Calvin C. Burt, A. M., 96°, Grand Master, Counselor at Law, Knight Templar, and 32° Scotch Rite; J. Adams Allen, A. B., M. D., A. M., LL.D., 96°, Deputy Grand Master, Professor in Rush Medical College, Chicago, Past Grand Commander, and Past Grand Master of Michigan; Benjamin F. Patrick, 95°, Grand Representative, Gen. Pass. Agent C. & N.

W. R. W., Past Master, Past E. Com. Apollo Commandery, and 33° Scotch Rite; H. N. Hurlburt, M. D., Grand Orator, Past High Priest. Master of Home Lodge, Chicago, and 32° Scotch Rite; T. T. Gurney, 95°, Grand Prelate, Member of Apollo Commandery, Master of Cleveland Lodge, Chicago, and 32° Scotch Rite; H. W. Bigelow, 95°, Grand Senior Warden, Member of Apollo Commandery, and 32° Scotch Rite; George McElwain, 95°, Grand Junior Warden, Member of 32° Scotch Rite, Apollo Commandery; Samuel E. Underhill, 95°, Grand Secretary, Recorder of Apollo Commandery, and 32° Scotch Rite; D. R. Dyche, M. D., 95°, Grand Treasurer, Member of Apollo Commandery; Robert E. Storey, 95°, Grand Conductor, Member of Apollo Commandery; Ira S. Younglove, 95°, Grand Senior Master of Ceremonies, Master of Wm. B. Warren Lodge, Chicago, Member of Apollo Commandery, and 32° Scotch Rite; J. H. Blake, 95°, Grand Organist; Charles E. Leonard, 95°, Grand Junior Master of Ceremonies, Member of Apollo Commadery, and 32° Scotch Rite; Charles H. Brower, 95°, Grand Captain of the Guard, Member of Apollo Commandery, and 32° Scotch Rite; Francis H. Nichols, 95°, Grand Guard of the Tower, Member of Apollo Commandery, and 32° Scotch Rite; L. K. Osborn, 95°, Grand Sentinel, Member of Apollo Commandery, and 32°.Scotch Rite.

The report of this committee was on motion received and entered on the minutes, and the committee discharged. The ballot was then spread and each of the aforesaid brothers reported by the Committee on Permanent Organization was elected, and by the Grand Master duly installed, and took their places in the body.

On motion, a committee was appointed to draft a constitution and laws for the government of the grand, body and the craft throughout the civilized Cosmos. Whereupon, they retired to consult, and the grand body called from labor to meet again at 6 o'clock P. M.

6 O'CLOCK P. M., JUNE 17th, A. D. 1867.

The grand body was opened in ample form by M. W. Bro. Calvin C. Burt, 96°, Grand Master, the Deputy Grand Master and other officers and brethren being present.

The Committee on Constitutions, Resolutions and Laws reported a Constitution, Resolution and Laws, which was taken up by sections and adopted as follows, viz:

ARTICLE I.

SEC. 1. Therefore, be it by this convention duly assembled, enacted, ordained and written, that this, our first constitution for the formation of this, our Grand Jurisdiction, embracing the continent of America, shall commence as follows :

In consideration whereof, we in solemn conclave assembled and duly open on the 95°, as the Supreme Body of the E∴ M∴ R∴ of Memphis, for America, with a constitutional representation of members, and representing one Grand Council, two Senates and ten Rose-Croix Chapters, duly working within the State of Illinois, and other non-affiliated 90° Masons, declare that the Rite of Memphis, to wit : The Egyptian Masonic Rite of Memphis, which grand body we do now here constitute and so name, is the Sovereign Sanctuary of the Egyptian Masonic Rite of Memphis for America, containing ninety-six degrees, ninety of labor, and six official degrees; which it is not in the power of any body of men or Masons to alter, abridge, condense or interpolate to any less number of degrees.

And that no law, constitution, edict or by-law, having such reduction in view, shall ever be made, passed or enacted in this grand jurisdiction. And the Grand Master of this Rite shall declare any and all such enactments, resolutions or motions tending to reduce said degrees or adopt any such measure or law, out of order. And we do hereby and forever absolve ourselves and separate our Masonic Brotherhood from each, all and every, and all bodies or members claiming to be of the Rite of Memphis, of less number than 96°, and refuse to hold Masonic intercourse with any such abridged Memphis Masons in the Rite.

And from this day henceforth and forever consider all such reduction as clandestine Masonry, and no law or constitution shall ever be made or enacted, nor shall this constitution be ever so construed or amended as to reduce the Memphis Rite to less than 96 degrees from the first to the 96th, and not otherwise or different.

ARTICLE II.

SEC. 1. The present proclaimed Grand Master of this Rite, Bro. Calvin C. Burt, 96°, shall hold the office of Grand Master General by virtue of this constitution in this grand body, in addition to his other appointments and this grand jurisdiction, for and during his natural life, and no law or amendment to this constitution shall be offered, passed or enacted, contravening the same or in any way curtailing or abridging his term of office, or his power as Grand Master, without his written consent; and that he shall always possess the right and have the power to make Masons at sight and name his successor, and preside at all meetings during his natural life.

SEC. 2. This grand body shall be called the Sovereign Sanctuary and Grand Body and Jurisdiction of the Egyptian Masonic Rite of Memphis, for the Continent of America, it being the only grand body of the Egyptian Masonic Rite of Memphis of 96° in America or the world, and shall be composed of its officers and members as follows:

Grand Master, 96°; Deputy Grand Master, 96°; Grand Representative, 95°; Grand Orator, 95°; Grand Senior Warden, 95°; Grand Junior Warden, 95°; Grand Prelate, 95°; Grand Secretary, 95°; Grand Treasurer, 95°; Grand Conductor, 95°; Grand Captain of the Guard, 95°; Grand Organist, 95°; Grand Senior Master of Ceremonies, 95°; Grand Junior Master of Ceremonies, 95°; Grand Sentinel, 95°; Grand Guard of the Tower, 95°; such other officers as shall be hereafter chosen and designated, and its members by affiliation and representation, viz: All 90° Masons may become members under such rules and regulations as may hereafter be enacted. And until the formation of a State Council, the three first officers of each chapter and each senate, and also the three first officers of each council during their term of office after they are installed, shall be members *ex officio*, and may also become permanent members, (by affiliation,) if elected after their official representative terms shall expire.

Sec. 3. This grand body shall meet once in each year to elect and install its officers, who shall hold their offices for the respective terms, as follows, (except the present Grand Master, who shall hold his office for life,) Deputy Grand Master, four years, and Grand Representative two years, and each of the other officers for one year, or till his successor shall be elected and qualified or installed. Provided however, the Grand Master shall have power, and it shall be his duty, when in his opinion the interests of the order and body shall be promoted thereby, to omit the regular meeting, and by notices in writing, con-

A*

tinue the offices for such further term as in his judgment shall best promote the interests of the craft.

Provided further, that the meetings of the grand body shall be held at Chicago, unless the Grand Master shall otherwise direct, and

Provided further, that all meetings of this grand body, regular or special, shall be convened by summons and under the hand and seal of the Grand Master or Secretary or both, and

Provided further, that special meetings may be called on ten days notice, in writing, when ordered by the Grand Master, and

Provided further, that the Deputy Grand Master shall be entitled to the 96°, and in case of the death of the Grand Master, shall at once succeed to the office of Grand Master, appoint his Deputy, and invest him with the 96°, and shall hold, each of them, their respective office till the next regular meeting, when a Grand and Deputy Grand Master shall be elected by ballot, and shall at once be invested with the 96°, and be duly installed.

Provided further, that all officers and members, as well as representatives, shall be entitled to the 95°, and all other elective officers of subordinate bodies, when installed, each to the 90°.

ARTICLE III.

Sec. 1. This Rite is divided into four divisions or bodies, as follows:

Rose-Croix, the Chapter, 18°, including the three symbolic degrees, which it explains, illustrates and embellishes; without the possession of which, viz: the symbolic degrees, no person can become a member of the Rose-Croix Chapter of this Rite or Order.

Sec. 2. Second, a Senate of Hermetic Philosophers, (27°,) making 45°, into which no person can be initiated without being in the possession also of the Rose-Croix degrees, making 45°.

Sec. 3. Third, a Grand Council, or Grand Body of a State or Territory, (45°,) making 90, into which no person can be admitted who has not taken the Chapter and Senate degrees, 45, with the Senate, making 90°.

Sec. 4. Fourth, the Sovereign Sanctuary, or Grand Body for the continent of America, or civilized Cosmos, 5 degrees, into which no person can be admitted who has not first taken the Chapter, Senate and Council degrees, and in possession of the 90° perfect pontiff, past master of the great work, 90°, and has also been elected or appointed to some office in this Rite to entitle him to the Sanctuary degrees, 95, and not otherwise.

ARTICLE IV.

· Sec. 1. The time for holding the regular meetings of this grand body, shall be on or before the 27th day of June in the regular or appointed year.

Sec. 2. The times for holding the regular meetings of all State Councils, shall be on or before the 27th day of January in each year, and at such other times as the Sublime Dai shall in writing direct, and of all regular meetings twenty days notice must be given, and ten days notice of special meetings shall also be given when possible.

Sec 3. Rose-Croix Chapters and Senates of Hermetic Philosophers must hold their regular meetings and install their officers on or before the 31st of December in each year, and at such other times as they shall by their By-Laws designate, or such as may be called by the presiding officer of each; but all regular election meetings shall be called by written notice of at least ten days before the regular election meeting day or time.

ARTICLE V.

SEC. 1. The Egyptian Masonic Rite of Memphis, extracts from former constitutions and laws as far as consistent with this constitution, are also adopted, viz :

The Egyptian Masonic Rite of Memphis consists of ninety degrees of Science, and six degrees of Merit and Distinction. The whole are arranged in four series and classes.

These four series comprise all Masonic knowledge.

The Masonic Rite of Memphis possesses five Decorations, viz :

1st. The Grand Star of Sirius.

2d. The Decoration of Alidee.

3d. The Decoration of the Grand Commanders of the Third Series of the Rite.

4th. The Decoration of the Lybic Chain.

5th. The Decoration of the Golden Branch of Eleuisis.

These five Decorations are exclusively official and the Reward of Merit, and are regulated by a programme, deposited in the Grand Body of the Rite.

Series First teaches Morality and Ancient Work, and extends to thirty degrees.

Series Second teaches Science and Morality, and extends to sixty degrees.

Series Third teaches Religion, Mythology, Philosophy, Theosophy, Zoology, Geometry and Astronomy, with its kindred Sciences, and extends to ninety degrees.

Series Fourth, six degrees, from ninety to ninety-six, and are Official, with Decorations of Merit.

No person can be admitted into this Rite who is not a Master Mason, in good standing.

This Rite does not work the first three degrees of Masonry in the first instance, but embellishes the degrees and teaches the Ancient and European work of to-day.

The Bodies of this Rite are as follows:

1.—Chapter Rose-Croix, 18 Degrees.

SEC. 2. Discreet Master, Perfect Master, Sublime Master, Just Master, Master of Israel, Master Elect, Grand Master Elect, Sublime Grand Master Elect, Master of Geometry, Knight of the Royal Arch, Knight of the Secret Vault, Knight of the Flaming Sword, Knight of Jerusalem, Knight of the Orient, Knight of the Rose-Croix.

2.—Senate of Hermetic Philosophers, 27 Degrees.

SEC. 3. Knight of the Occident, Knight of the Temple of Wisdom, Knight of the Key, Knight of Noachite, Knight of Libon, Knight of the Tabernacle, Knight of the Sacrificial Fire, Knight of the Serpent, Knight Trinitarian, Knight Evangelist, Knight of the White Eagle, Knight of Kadosh, Knight of the Black Eagle, Knight of the Royal Mysteries, Knight Grand Inspector of the First Series, Knight of the Red Eagle, Knight Master of Angles, Knight of the Holy City, Knight Adept of Truth, Knight Sublime Elect of Truth, Knight Philalethe, Knight Doctor of the Planispheres, Knight Savant Sage, Knight Hermetic Philosopher, Knight Adept Installator, Knight Adept Consecrator, Knight Adept Eulogist.

3.—Mystic Temple State Council, 45 Degrees.

Sec. 4. Knight Adept of Sirius, Knight Adept of Babylon, Knight Adept of the Rainbow, Knight Adept of the Seven Stars, Knight Commander of the Zodiac, Knight Barruke, Knight of the Luminous Triangle, Knight of the Zardust, Knight of the Luminous Ring, Knight Sublime Magi, Doctor of the Sacred Vedas, Prince Brahmin Sublime Scalde, Knight Scandinavian, Prince of the Sacred Name, Prince of the Golden Fleece, Prince of the Lyre, Prince of the Labyrinth, Prince of the Lybic Chain, Prince of Truth, Prince of the Covenant, Prince of the Sanctuary, Prince of the Temple of Truth, Commander of the Second Series, Orphic Sage, Sage of Eleu, Sage of the Three Fires, Sage of Mithra, Sage of Delphi, Sage of Samothrace, Sage of Eleusis, Sage of the Symbols, Sage of Wisdom, Sublime Sage of the Mysteries, Priest of the Sphynx, Priest of the Phœnix, Priest of the Pyramids, Priest of Helliopilis, Priest of Oru, Priest of Memphis, Pontiff of Serapis, Pontiff of Isis, Pontiff of the Kneph, Pontiff of the Mystic City, Perfect Pontiff, Past Master of the Great Work.

4.—Sovereign Sanctuary, 6 Degrees, Official and Meritorious.

Sec. 5. Patriarch Grand Commander, Patriarch Grand Generalissimo, Patriarch Grand Captain General, Patriarch Grand Inspector General, Patriarch Grand Orator and Prince, Sovereign Patriarch Grand Defender of Truth, Sovereign Sublime Magi 96°, which is the title of the Grand Master.

ARTICLE VI.

SEC. 1. The following extracts from the Ancient Minutes, Statutes and Edicts are hereby taken and adopted as a part of this Constitution, when not inconsistent with or repugnant to the former declarations of this constitution or the general law of Freemasonry, leaving the Grand Master, and future meetings of this body in this grand jurisdiction to interpret, explain, alter and amend, as time, circumstances and experience may in future dictate for the good order, working and harmonious action of this and subordinate bodies of this Rite, viz:

Extracts from the General Statutes and Ordinances of the Ancient Egyptian Masonic Rite of Memphis.

SEC. 2. Grand Councils of Past Masters of the Great Work of the Egyptian Masonic Rite of Memphis shall be under the immediate jurisdiction of the Sovereign Sanctuary, 90°.

SEC. 3. The principal meeting of a Grand Council, Masters of the Great Work, Senate of Hermetic Philosophers, and Chapter Rose-Croix, shall be held on or before the Sun's entrance into the first point of Aries, the 21st of March, when the election of officers shall be holden, and the festival of the Vernal Equinox celebrated,in honor of the revivification of Nature. A festival may be held on or before the Sun's entrance into the first point of Libra, about the 23d of September, to celebrate the Autumnal Equinox; also, on or before the Summer Solstice, about the 24th of June, and the Winter Solstice, about the 27th December.

SEC. 4. When at labor, the Temple of a Grand Council represents the place of meeting of the twelve

Deities of the Egyptian Mysteries, and is decorated
with the Banner of the Council, which is placed at
the noitheast of the altar. There must also be nine
Banners, each of which bears a sign of the Zodiac,
(the Winter signs, Scorpio, Sagitarius and Aquarius,
being omitted.) In the Vale of Amenthes is placed
the veiled Statue of Isis. In the Orient is displayed
the Symbol of Osiris and of Egyptian Theogony, the
Kneph, or Winged Egg of Earth.

SEC. 5. The insignia of a Past Master of the Great
Work, or any other Sanctuary officer or member, is a
collar, with gold fringe, sash, gauntlets, sword, red
belt, and white gloves. On the coilar are twelve
stars, in groups of three; on the point is embroidered
in gold the distinctive Symbol of Osiris, compasses
and square, with the number of degrees in scarlet.
The collar is made of orange silk, lined with cherry.

A Past Master of the Great Work may be
refused admittance into the Council or into any Senate or Chapter of the Egyptian Masonic Rite, if not
properly clothed.

OFFICERS.

SEC. 6. The Sublime Dai represents Osiris; his
jewel is a golden Delta, on which is engraved a Sun;
he wears a robe of celestial blue, showered with silver stars; the Sublime Dai possesses the 95°, and is,
during his term of office, by virtue of his position, an
actual member of the Sovereign Sanctuary 95°.

The First Mystagog represents Serapis; his jewel
is a rising Sun, engraved on a golden Delta; he wears
a scarlet robe; he is also, during his term of office,
an actual member of the Sovereign Sanctuary 95°.

The Second Mystagog represents Horus; his jewel
is a half Moon, on a golden Delta; he wears a scarlet
robe, and possesses, by virtue of his office, the 95°,

and is, during the term thereof, an actual member of the Sovereign Sanctuary.

The Orator represents Hermes Trismegistus; his jewel is a Scroll, engraved on a golden Delta; he wears a green robe; he is also, during his term of office, an actual member of the Sovereign Sanctuary 95°

The Treasurer wears a robe of dark blue; his jewel is a Chest, engraved on a golden Delta.

The Secretary represents Thoth; his jewel is the crossed Stylus, engraved on a golden Delta; he wears a gray robe.

The Archivist wears a white robe; his jewel is a Book, engraved on a golden Delta.

The Grand Expert represents Anubis; his jewel is a Sphinx, engraved on a golden Delta; he wears a yellow robe.

The Messenger of Science represents Harpocrates; his jewel is a shepherd's Crook, engraved on a golden Delta; he wears a black robe.

The Accompanier represents Charon; his jewel is an Oar, engraved on a golden Delta; he wears a black robe.

The Standard Bearer represents Sirius; his jewel is a Star on a Flag, engraved on a golden Delta; he wears a green robe.

The Sword Bearer represents Orion; his jewel is a Sword on a golden Delta; he wears a purple robe.

The Guardian of the Sanctuary represents Canopus; his jewel is a Dog's Head on a golden Delta; he wears a purple robe.

The Sentinel represents Hercules; his jewel is a Club, engraved on a golden Delta.

All Sir Knights applying for admission into a Grand Council must come well recommended from the Senate of which they are members.

No Illustrious Brother can be elected to preside as Sublime Dai unless he has regularly filled the office of First or Second Mystagog or Orator, or has previously presided one year as Grand Commander of a Senate of Hermetic Philosophers, or as Most Wise of a Chapter of Rose-Croix.

A Sublime Master of the Great Work, proven guilty of unmasonic conduct, and deprived of his membership in a Grand Council, cannot be received in any subordinate body of the Egyptian Masonic Rite, until again restored to his Masonic standing.

A Past Master of the Great Work has the right of appeal to the Sovereign Sanctuary 95°, (or Grand Master,) which is the Judicial Degree, and is the Grand Tribunal of the Rite.

On the death of a Past Master of the Great Work, each and every Past Master of the Great Work is solemnly bound to attend in full regalia, and assist in consigning the remains of the deceased to the bosom of our common mother earth. Provided that the sanction of the Grand Master, or the representative of the Grand Master, be granted to the Sublime Dai of the Grand Council of which the deceased was a member.

Toleration being inscribed on the banners of the Egyptian Masonic Rite, political or religious discussions are imperatively forbidden within our temples.

A Past Master of the Great Work must sign the By-Laws and Oath of Fealty, before he becomes an actual member of the Grand Council.

ARTICLE VII.

Chapters of Rose Croix of the Egyptian Masonic Rite of Memphis.

SEC. 1. Chapters of Rose Croix of the Egyptian Masonic Rite of Memphis shall be under the immediate jurisdiction of the Sovereign Grand Council General, Perfect Pontiff, Past Masters of the Great Work, 90°, of the State or Territory wherein located, under the auspices of the Sovereign Sanctuary.

SEC. 2. The Most Wise and Respectable Knight Senior and Junior Wardens elect shall receive the 95°, Orator and Prince, Grand Defender of Truth, by virtue of their office, which entitles them to membership in the Grand Council General during their term of office, after the expiration of which they shall be honorary members of the Grand Council General entitled to the rights and privileges as prescribed by the statutes. The Respectable Knight Orator shall receive the 90°, Perfect Pontiff, Past Master of the Great Work, by virtue of his office, and be entitled to all rights and privileges appertaining thereunto. The above mentioned degree, 95°, being official, can only be conferred by the Grand Officer, or installing officer of the body.

SEC. 3. No Chapter can be opened unless three of its officers and two of its members be present, or an officer of the Sovereign Sanctuary.

SEC. 4. A Knight of Rose Croix is bound by his honor to the service of his God, his country, and the Statutes of the Egyptian Masonic Rite; and he shall not fight another Knight Rose Croix on any pretext, but shall help, aid and assist him.

SEC. 5. No Chapter shall be closed without the box of fraternal assistance being first presented to the Sir Knights.

SEC. 6. In passing the ballot, if one black ball appear, it must be immediately declared closed at that conclave. It may be opened at the three following conclaves, when, if the black ball still appears, the Brother is rejected.

SEC. 7. If a Knight Rose Croix falls sick, all the rest must visit him, to see that he wants for nothing. If a Knight Rose Croix die, all the Knights must attend the funeral with the sash and jewel of this Degree; and if the deceased have no relatives they must cause his jewel to be buried with him. The name of a deceased Knight Rose Croix must not be stricken from the rolls, but a skull and cross-bones should be delineated beside it, to show that he no longer exists.

SEC. 8. Sir Knights Rose Croix wear black clothes, with white baldrick, guantlet gloves, sword, and red belt. On the front part must be painted or embroidered with a Cross, " IN HOC SIGNO VINCES." The Rose Croix jewel hangs on a ribbon, or is pinned on the left breast of the coat; it consists of a crowned Compass extended to ninety degrees. Between the branches of the Compass there must be on one side a Pelican, and on the other an eagle. Between these two emblems rises a Cross, on which is a Rose, with the letters Y. I. H. N. V. R. H. I. at bottom. The Official Jewel is a Serpent forming a Circle, within which is the interlaced Triangle, having in the centre the officer's distinctive mark. The seal of a Chapter of Rose Croix is a Serpent forming a circle, with the Rose on a cross in the centre, surmounted by a Delta, with the appropriate characters.

SEC. 9. No one can be admitted into a Chapter of Rose Croix unless he is a Master Mason in good standing, and be proposed by a member of the Rose

Croix. He shall sign the laws of the Chapter and the obligation of fealty to the Sovereign Sanctuary, which shall be kept in a book for that purpose in each and every Chapter.

Each Chapter shall at the end of each year pay the sum of two dollars for each candidate initiated, into the Sovereign Sanctuary.

The Sovereign Sanctuary is the Grand Body of the United States and British America, and sits when called by the Grand Master by twenty days summons.

Its regular meeting is on the first Tuesday on or before the 27th day of June in each year.

Special meetings may be called at any time by the Grand Master.

SEC. 10. The body is composed of its officers— Grand Master, Deputy Grand Master, Grand Representative and his Deputies, (one or more for each State,) Grand Senior Warden, Grand Junior Warden Grand Secretary, Grand Treasurer, Grand Prelate, Grand Orator, Grand Conductor, Grand Captain of the Guard, (who are also Grand Stewards,) Grand Guard of the Tower, Grand Sentinel, and members. Also, the three Pesiding Officers of the State Council in each State, all members of the 95°, and the Past Officers of the Sovereign Sanctuary and State Councils for each State.

All other bodies act under the supervision of the Sovereign Sanctuary, and any proceedings of inferior body can be appealed thereto.

The officers of the Sovereign Sanctuary are elected by ballot, and hold their offices as follows: Grand Master, for life; Deputy, four years; Grand Representative, two years; and each of the other officers for one year.

All Charters must issue from the Sovereign Sanctuary.

All charters, dispensations, and diplomas must be sealed with the Seal of the Sovereign Sanctuary and be signed by the Grand Secretary or Grand Master, or both, as the Grand Master shall direct.

In case of the death of the Grand Master, the Deputy Grand Master shall succeed to the office.

SEC. 11. The Grand Master, Deputy Grand Master, and Grand Representative, shall have the right to preside in all inferior bodies when they shall desire to do so, and shall instruct the inferior bodies in the work, when required, if they shall deem it necessary—the expenses of each to be borne by the Sovereign Sanctuary.

The fees for granting dispensations shall belong to the Grand Master; and all fees for making Masons and for the purpose of forming bodies or for other purposes of benefit to the Order, shall be charged in the discretion of the officer conferring the degrees ; but no person shall have the power or authority to confer degees but the Grand Master, Deputy Grand Master, Grand Representative, or his Deputies, by the Grand Master when commissioned, who shall, in each case, notify the Grand Secretary, and forward the oaths of fealty, which must in all cases be signed by the person taking the degrees, and forwarded or given to the Grand Secretary, who shall file and preserve the same in his office.

SEC. 12. No Chapter shall confer the Chapter degrees for a less sum than fifteen dollars—five dollars to accompany the petition.

SEC. 13. No Senate shall confer the Senate Degrees for a less sum than fifty dollars—ten dollars to accompany the petition.

SEC. 14. No Council shall confer the Council Degrees for a less sum than one hundred dollars— ten dollars to accompany the petition; and no note or other acknowledgement of indebetedness shall in any case be taken in lieu of money.

SEC. 15. The affiliation fee of the Sovereign Sanctuary shall be ten dollars; and for every person made in any Chapter, the sum of two dollars shall be paid the Sovereign Sanctuary.

All 90° members may become members of the Sovereign Sanctuary by affiliation, if elected by a vote of the same.

SEC. 16. Any member of the Egyptian Masonic Rite, in good standing, shall have the right to visit any of the bodies of this Rite of which he has taken the degrees, if he can prove himself qualified, or be properly vouched for, and in proper clothing; and when so admitted, he shall have the right to speak, vote, or exercise any other right or privilege that any other member of that particular body has, (except to vote on subjects or matters connected with or affecting the financial affairs or funds of that particular body,) on their office election.

SEC. 17. All other general Rules and Regulations of Free and Accepted Masons not inconsistent with the general statutes and constitutions of this Rite, are acknowledged as good Masonic Law by the Egyptian Masonic Rite of Memphis.

SEC. 18. The officers of the Grand Council shall consist of:

Sublime Dai, First Mystagog, Second Mystagog, Treasurer, Secretary, Orator, Grand Expert, Archivist, Messenger of Science, Accompanier, Standard Bearer, Sword Bearer, Guardian of Sanctuary, and Sentinel.

The first seven of whom shall be elected by ballot at the regular Convocation held nearest the Spring solstice (21st of March.) The remaining officers shall be appointed at the same Convocation by the Sublime Dai.

SEC. 19. The officers of a Senate consist of:

1. Sublime Grand Commander. 2. Most Learned Senior Knight Interpreter. 3. Most Learned Junior Knight Interpreter. 4. Illustrious Knight Recorder. 5. Ill. Knight of Finance. 6. Ill. Knight Archivist. 7. Ill. Knight Orator. 8. Ill. Knight Marshal. 9. Ill. Knight of Introduction. 10. Ill. Knight Accompanier. 11. Ill. Knight Captain of the Guard. 12. Ill. Knight Standard Bearer. 13. Ill. Knight Sword Bearer. 14. Ill. Knight Guardian of the Sanctuary. 15. Knight Sentinel.

All of whom (except those numbered 6, 9, 10, 11, 12, 13, 14 and 15,) shall be elected by ballot at the regular Convention held on the 21st of March, (now changed to December 31,) in each year, or at the regular Convention nearest to that date. The remaining officers shall at the same time be appointed by the Sublime Grand Commander.

ARTICLE VIII.

SEC. 1. The officers of the Chapter shall consist of :

1. Most Wise. 2. Respectable Knight Senior Warden. 3. Respectable Knight Junior Warden. 4. Sir Knight Orator. 5. Sir Knight Conductor. 6. Sir Knight Archivist. 7. Sir Knight Treasurer. 8. Sir Knight Captain of the Guard. 9. Sir Knight Guard of the Tower. 10. Sir Knight Prelate. 11. Sir Knight Organist. 12. Sir Knight Sentinel. And shall be elected at the annual election by ballot.

Each body shall make annual returns to the grand
body once in each year, stating the names of the
officers, and of the members initiated, and shall pay
the sum of fifty cents for each member, except those
who have been initiated during the previous fiscal
year and have paid the two dollars mentioned in
section 10; which report shall be made on or before
the 1st day of May in each year and signed by the
presiding officer and Secretary, and returned to the
Grand Master.

ARTICLE IX.

*Masonic Calendar of the Egyptian Masonic Rite of
Memphis.*

SEC. 1. March 1st answers to the 1st day of
the Egyptian month Thoth; April, Paophi; May,
Athir; June, Chocoac; July, Tibi; August, Mechi;
September, Shemenoth; October, Pharmathi; Novem-
ber, Pachon; December, Pagni; January, Epophi;
February, Mesori.

The following caption is to be used at the commencement of all edicts, proclamations, letters
patent, &c., &c., in all degrees of the Rite: "To the
glory of the Supreme Architect of the Universe. In
the name of the Sovereign Sanctuary of the Egyptian Masonic Rite of Memphis, in and for the Continent of America, sitting in the valley of America."

And must be dated as follows:

"Done this——day of the Egyptian month ———,
year of true light, 000,000,000, answering to the——
day of———, Era Vulgar, 18——."

ARTICLE X.

SEC. 1. All Charters shall be issued from the Sovereign Sanctuary or Grand Jurisdiction, and be signed

B

by the Grand Master, Deputy Grand Master, Grand
Representative, and Grand Orator, under the hand
and seal of the Grand Secretary, and be also sealed
with the private seal of each, when convenient to do
so, and when not sealed with the seal of the Grand
Representative, shall be signed and sealed by a Grand
Deputy Representative of the State, and may be issued to the Grand Master, signed in blank, to be by
him delivered to the Bodies when installed in ample form. Provided, however, that when there shall
be formed and installed in any State a Mystic Temple, they shall, when a Charter is issued for a Rose-
Croix Chapter or Senate, be by the Sublime Dai,
First and Second Mystagog, countersigned and certi
fied by the Secretary thereof; for which a fee of five
dollars shall be paid to each officer so countersigning,
which, with the exception of the five dollars paid the
Secretary, shall be paid over to the Treasurer of the
State Council, as other moneys are for general
purposes.

ARTICLE XI.

SEC. I. The fees for Charters shall be as follows :
For Rose-Croix Chapters twenty-five dollars ($25.)

For Senate of Hermetic Phillosophers fifty dollars
($50.)

For State Councils or Mystic Temple, one hundred
dollars ($100,) and the sum of twenty dollars each
for a dispensation under which to work before charter issues, and which sum shall be deducted from the
charter price when the charter shall thereafter issue.

SEC. 2. The officers of the Sovereign Sanctuary,
except the Grand Master and Deputy Grand Master,
may resign at any time, by tendering the same in
writing to the Grand Master; or he, the Grand Mas-

ter, may, for disobedience or other cause, suspend any or all officers, during the recess of the grand body, till its next regular meeting, when he shall report the same with his reasons in writing, briefly stating the causes, which the grand body may, in its discretion, affirm or reverse.

SEC. 3 The fees of the officers of the Sovereign Sanctuary, shall be as follows: To the Grand Master, the sum of five dollars each for all rituals supplied by him to the Grand or Subordinate bodies, with the fees for diplomas, charters and dispensations, and the making of Masons to form bodies or for the good of the order, and he shall also be entitled to reasonable traveling expenses while on the exclusive business of the Rite: Provided, however, that the Grand Master shall furnish all seals, rituals, charters, diplomas and printing, and the grand body shall not be chargeable with any of the foregoing expenses.

SEC. 4. The grand body shall furnish to each subordinate body, when installed, seven copies of rituals and one constitution and by-laws of this order, together with a charter and one diploma to each charter member thereof, at or immediately after installation, and which said rituals, by-laws, charter, seal, record and other property belonging to said body, shall be handed over to the succeeding officers at installation, to be by them again transmitted to their successors. The presiding officer of each and all the bodies of the Rite, shall have full power and control over the bodies in this Rite and their subordinate officers, subject only to the Grand Master, constitution, edicts, laws, rules of the Rite and order, and the decisions of the Grand Master, whose edict, rule, command and order, shall be final and conclusive, until reversed or annulled by a decision of the grand body at the next regular meeting.

ARTICLE XII.

SEC. 1. There shall be in this Rite two days of Masonic Festival observed, which may be in public or private, viz: The 24th day of June, commonly called St. John the Baptist's, and the 27th day of December, commonly called St. John the Evangelist's day, and one day which shall henceforth and forever be celebrated as a Masonic Holiday and Festival. viz: the birthday of this Rite in America, viz: the 17th day of June in each year, that being the day in the year A. D. 1867, that this body was formed in America, and the day on which these articles of organization and constitution were by us, in solemn conclave, signed and published to the world as the highest body of Masons on this continent or the habitable globe. Provided, however, that this constitution, (or such parts thereof as may be altered) may, by a notice in writing, read at a previous regular conclave and entered in the Journal of the Grand Secretary, taken up at the next regular meeting, and if passed by a two-thirds vote of all the members present, on the day of the election of its officers, be changed, amended or revised; but in no other way or manner whatsoever.

ARTICLE XIII.

SEC. 1. The Grand Master may, during the recess of the grand body, fill all vacancies that may occur in any body in the Rite.

SEC. 2. Dimits may be issued from the grand body as well as from subordinate bodies.

SEC. 3. Charters and Diplomas may also issue from

this grand body; provided, however, that after the
formation of a State grand body, dimits or diplomas to the State body, or the Senate, or Chapter,
may be issued by the State Council, under its seal.
But all diplomas shall bear on their face the seal of
this grand body, which shall be the Winged Egg of
Earth, known in the Egyptian language as the
Kneff, with the words "Great Seal of the Sovereign
Sanctuary, Valley of America," and such other de-
vices or emblems as the Grand Master shall direct,
whose duty it shall be to furnish and provide the
seal for this and all other grand bodies of the Rite, the
seal of this grand body and the official seals of the
Deputy Grand Representative and Grand Secretary
free of charge to this grand body.

SEC. 4. The Grand Master may, from time to
time, and it shall be his duty to issue edicts, orders,
rules and regulations for clothing, jewels and insignia of the Rite, and to prescribe the mode and
manner of working degrees, and the formation of
bodies; subject, however, to the constitution and
landmarks of the Order.

ARTICLE XIV.

SEC. 1. This Constitution, when by us duly signed
and promulgated shall be the law of this order,
together with such edicts and orders as may
from time to time, be issued by the Grand Master
and the general rules of the Ancient and Honorable
Society of Free and Accepted Masons throughout
the civilized cosmos; provided, however, that all the
bodies of this Rite shall have power to form such
by-laws, rules and regulations, as they may see fit
and proper, with the approval of the Grand Master,

not inconsistent with this constitution or the amendments or alterations hereafter attached.

Witness our hands, this 17th day of June A. D., 1867.

CHARTER MEMBERS.

B. F. Patrick, 95°, C. H. Brower, 95°, A. E. Clark, 90°, W. F. Wentworth, 90°, T. N. Holden, 90°, D. C. Hill, 90°, F. H. Nichols, 95°, D. R. Dyche, 95°, John Middleton, 90°, George H. Parker, 90°, W. T. Hancock, 90°, J. A. Allen, 96°, J. A. Van Buskirk, 90°, Ira S. Younglove, 95°, J. L. Marsh, 90°, A. W. Hitchcock, 90°, J. W. Clyde, 90°, Wm. Lewitt, 95°, M. N. Fuller, 90°, James Smith, 90°, E. B. Myers, 90°, J. H. Blake, 95°, S. E. Underhill, 95°, E. H. Keene, 90°, R. E. Storey, 95°, C. E. Leonard, 95°, C. E. Hyde, 90°, H. Starrett, 90°, L. K. Osborn, 95°, E. V. Roddin, 90°, G. L. Smith, 90°, H. R. Caberey, 90°, H. N. Hurlbut, 95°, T. T. Gurney, 95°, R. J. Morse, 90°, J. L. Day, 95°, L. W. Rouse, 90°, George McElwain, 95°, H. W. Bigelow, 95°, C. H. Cutler, 90°, C. C. Burt, 96°, L. A. Howland, 90°, D. A. Starritt, 90°, W. G. Swan, 90°.

After the routine business of this body, an adjournment was had till the 18th July, when the Convention and grand body adjourned sine die.

CALVIN C. BURT, 96°,
Grand Master.

SAMUEL E. UNDERHILL, 95°,
Grand Secretary.

EGYPTIAN MASONIC RITE OF MEMPHIS.

At a meeting of the Sovereign Sanctuary of the Valley of Chicago, held at their rooms, 92 Dearborn Street, on Thursday evening, February 6th, 1868, there were present:

M. W. Calvin C. Burt, 96°, Grand Master; R. W. J. Adams Allen, 96°, Deputy Grand Master; Ill. Bro. T. T. Gurney, 95°, Grand Prelate; Ill. Bro. D. R. Dyche, 95°, Grand Treasurer; Ill. Bro. Chas. E. Leonard, 95°, Grand Secretary, pro tem., and other Illustrious Brothers.

EXTRACT FROM THE MINUTES.

The names of the following Brothers, members of this Rite, were proposed for affiliation, and the ballot being spread, they were declared duly elected :

Ill. Bros. S. C. Coffinberry, 90°, 32° Scotch Rite, G. M., and P. G H. P. of Michigan, Constantine; G. B. Noble, 90°, K. T., P. E. Com. of Michigan, Detroit; T. H. Armstrong, 95°, K. T., P. E. Com., Detroit, Michigan; D. Burnham Tracy, 94°, 33° Scotch Rite, P. E. Com., Detroit, Michigan ; James Fenton, 90°, 32° Scotch Rite, Secretary Grand Lodge Michigan, Detroit; Edward Le Fever, 95°, P. H. P., Sub. Gr. Com. Cheops Senate, Rite of Memphis, Detroit, Michigan.; J. J. Bardwell, 95°, 32° Scotch Rite, P. H. P., M. W. Shemenoth Chap. Rite of Membhis, Detroit, Michigan; James W. Frisbie, 90°, K. T., 32° Scotch Rite, Detroit, Michigan; Ed. R. Landon, 90°, K. T., 32° Scotch Rite, Detroit, Michigan ; Frank Darrow, 90°, K. T., 32° Scotch Rite, P. G. M., P. G. Com. of Michigan, Pontiac; J. P. Fisk, 90°, K. T., 32° Scotch Rite, G. H. P. of Michigan, Detroit; A. G. Hibbard, 90°, K. T., 32 Scotch Rite, E. Com. Detroit Commandery, Detroit, Michigan ; Edward Lee, 90°, K. T., 33° Scotch Rite, P. G. M., P. G. Com. of Mississippi, Holly Springs; Lucius Fairchild, 90°, K. T., and Governor of Wisconsin ; John Spooner, 90°, Lieut. Governor of Wisconsin ; James K. Proudfit, 95°, K. T., Grand Generalissimo, and Adjutant Gen-

eral of Wisconsin; S. V. Shipman, 95°, K. T., P. E.
Com. Isis Senate, Rite of M., State Architect, Madison, Wis.; Chas. G. Heimstreet, 94°, K. T., M. W.
Chapter Rite of Memphis, Janesville, Wis.; O. C.
Palmer, 90°, K. T., Janesville, Wis.; Joel Squires,
94°, R. A., P. H. P., M. W. Hippocrates Chapter, Rite
of Memphis, Mineral Point, Wis.; Homer J. Persons,
95°, K. T., San Francisco, Cal.; B. H. Porter, 95°, R.
A., 32° Scotch Rite, P. H. P. New Jersey; Jerome
B. Gardner, 95°, K. T., H. P. Corinthian Chapter, No.
159, New York City; Chas. E. Noble, 90°, K. T.,
Agent M. C. R. R.; New York City; George S. Fancher, 95°, K. T., firm of A. T. Stewart & Co., New
York City; Seth Hart, M. D., 90°, R. A., New York
City; Henry B. Horton, 90°, K. T., Kt. Mar. Alexandria Senate, No, 2, Rite of Memphis, Chicago, Ill.;
Claud G. Avery, 95°, K. T., Sub. Gr. Com. of Osiris
Senate, No. 1, Rite of Memphis, Chicago, Ill.; Thos.
W. Blayney, 95°, R. A., Sen. Kt. Int. of Osiris Senate,
No. 1, Rite of Memphis, Chicago, Ill.; G. A. Richardson, 95°, Kt. Orator of Osiris Senate, No. 1, Rite of
Memphis, Chicago, Ill.; Chas. C. Brierly, 90°, K. T.,
Kt. Stand Bearer of Osiris Senate, No. 1, Rite of
Memphis, Chicago, Ill.; George W. Lyon, 90°, Kt.
Sword Bearer, Osiris Senate, No. 1, Rite of Memphis,
Chicago, Ill.; C. W. Nash, 90°, 33° Scotch Rite, Grand
Master, St. Paul, Minn.

In testimony whereof, we have made this Certificate, done in our Sanctuary, where abide Peace,
Tolerance, Truth, and the fullness of all that is good,
this sixth day of the Egyptian month Mesori,
answering to the sixth day of the month of February, A. L. 5868, Vulgar Era, 1868.

By order of the Grand Master.

Witness our hand and the seal of the Sovereign
Sanctuary, at the Valley of Chicago, this
[L. S.] sixth day of February, Vulgar, or Christian
Era, 1868.

SAM'L E. UNDERHILL, 95°,
Grand Secretary E∴ M∴ R∴ of M∴
By CHAS. E. LEONARD, 95°,
Grand Secretary, pro tem.

SECOND ANNUAL MEETING, 1868.

JUNE 23d, A. D. 1868.

The Sovereign Sanctuary for the Continent of America, was opened this day in ample form, by the M. W. Grand Master, C. C. Burt, 96°.

The report of the Grand Master was then referred to a committee of three, consisting of Ill. Bros. R. Cleveland, 95°, Claude G. Avery, 95°, Thomas W. Blayney, 95°.

The following resolution was then offered by Ill. Bro. C. E. Leonard :

Resolved, That the M. W. Grand Master make the nomination of officers for the ensuing year.

Which was seconded by Bro. R. Cleveland, and unanimously adopted.

The Grand Master then nominated the following officers, viz :

Jonathan Adams Allen, Deputy Grand Master.

H. J. Parsons, of San Francisco, Grand Representative.

George S. Fancher, of New York, Grand Orator.

S. V. Shipman, of Wisconsin, Grand Prelate.

James R. Proudfit, of Wisconsin, Grand Senior Warden.

B. H. Porter, of New York, Grand Junior Warden.

Thomas W. Blayney, of Chicago, Ill., Grand Secretary.

Claude G. Avery, of Chicago, Ill., Grand Treasurer.

Nelson Chittendon, of Wisconsin, Grand Conductor,

Edward Lee, of Mississippi, Grand Captain of the Guard.

Seth Hart, of New York, Grand Organist.

Nelson D. Plumb and Edward W. Roberts, of California, Grand Sr. and Jr. Masters of Ceremonies.

Charles C. C. Brierly, of Chicago, Ill., Grand Guard of the Tower.

William Lewitt, of Michigan, Grand Sentinel,

B*

The officers were installed by the Grand Master, and the grand body closed in peace and harmony to meet at such place as the Grand Master may determine.

THIRD ANNUAL MEETING.

JUNE 27th, 1871.

In pursuance of the following summons and notice from the Right Worshipful Grand Master, the Sovereign Sanctuary for the United States assembled this day, in the City of Jackson, State of Michigan:

ILLUSTRIOUS BROTHER AND DEAR SIR:

Whereas, At the general meeting of the Sovereign Sanctuary for the Continent of America, held in Chicago, on the 23d day of June, A. D. 1°68, a resolution was adopted to authorize the Grand Master to convene the Grand Body thereafter at such time and place as in his discretion and in force of circumstances should direct; and

Whereas, By an Edict of the Grand Master, the Annual Communication of the 24th of June, A. D. 1869, and the Annual Communication for the 28th of June, A. D. 1870, were adjourned to the 27th day of June, A D. 1871:

Now, Therefore. Considering the best intrests of the Craft, and that the grand body now require the annual meeting of said body to take place on the 27th day of June, A. D 1871, at the City of Jackson, and county of Jackson, and State of Michigan:

Therefore, Be it known that I, Calvin C. Burt, 96°, Grand Master, by virtue of the power and authority in me vested, do hereby order and direct, that the said Annual Meeting of the Sovereign Sanctuary for the Continent of America, be held at the City of Jackson aforesaid; and you are hereby summoned to be and appear, either in person or proxy, in said City of Jackson, the 27th day of June next, at 12 M., for the purpose of choosing officers for the ensuing term, and the transaction of such other business as may lawfully come before the said grand body. Hereof fail not under penalty of a violation of your obligation.

Done in our Sanctuary, where abides peace, tolerance, truth, and the fullness of all that is good, this sixth day of the Egyptian month, Athir answering to the sixth day of May, A. D. 5871, Vulgar Era, A. D. 1871.

Witness our hand and the seal of the Sovereign Sanctuary, [L. S.] at the Valley of Jackson, this sixth day of May, Vulgar, or Christian Era, A. D. 1871.

CALVIN C. BURT, 96°,
Grand Master.

The conclave having been called to order and opened in due and ancient form, the Worshipful Grand Master proceeded to state his reasons for not holding conclaves in the years 1869 and 1870, and that he had issued his edicts accordingly. The Sovereign Sanctuary unanimously approved and affirmed the course taken by him in that regard.

The minutes of the last conclave were then read by the Grand Secretary for the information of the Sir Knights present.

Sir Knights Thos. W. Blayney and J. M. Brown were chosen a Committee upon Credentials.

The conclave then adjourned till 3 o'clock, and upon reassembling; the Committee reported upon the several appointments of proxies made by absent members, all of which were approved and affirmed by the Sovereign Sanctuary.

Letters of apology for absence were then read from Sir Knights C. Avery, R. Cleveland, C. E. Leonard, N. C. Chittenden, Edward Lee, Seth Hart, and several others, and were ordered to be laid on the table.

The election of officers being next in order, it was moved by Ill. Sir Knight Shoemaker, seconded by Ill. Sir Knight Mitchell, and unanimously

Resolved, That the Worshipful Grand Master be requested to nominate to the Sovereign Sanctuary for election such persons for officers as in his judgment were best fitted for the several positions to be filled.

The Grand Master accordingly nominated for Deputy Grand Master, the Hon. Michael Shoemaker, of Michigan.

A ballot was taken, and Col. Shoemaker was declared elected.

The following Sir Knights were then nominated for the several offices set forth, balloted for and declared unanimously elected :

For Grand Representative, J. Mabbett Brown, of Michigan.
For Grand Secretary, Thomas W. Blayney, of Illinois.
For Grand Orator, J. C. Wood, of Michigan.
For Grand Prelate, J. C. Dyer, of Michigan.
For Grand Senior Warden, Benjamin Porter, of Michigan.
For Grand Junior Warden, George S. Fancher, of New York.
For Grand Treasurer, G. A. Baldwin, of Michigan.
For Grand Senior Master of Ceremonies, B. F. Prentiss, of Michigan.
For Grand Junior Master of Ceremonies, W. W. Childs, of Michigan.
For Grand Organist, Seth Hart, of New York.
For Grand Conductor, Nelson Chittenden, of Wisconsin.
For Grand Captain of the Guard, Governor Lucius Fairchild, of Wisconsin.
For Guard of the Tower, Hugh Richards, of Michigan.
For Grand Sentinal, Thomas J. Conely, of Michigan.
For Grand Marshal, Fidus Livermore, of Michigan.

And were duly installed by the Grand Master, M. W. Bro. Calvin C. Burt, 96°.

The Worshipful Grand Master then delivered his address, replete with valuable information as to the great antiquity of the Rite and the symbolic character of the ritual, as well as suggestive of several matters which he was of opinion the Sovereign Sanctuary might take action on, which would tend to the benefit of the institution.

Committees were appointed to take action on his suggestions and the conclave took a recess until Wednesday, the 28th day of June, at 7 P. M. to hear the reports of the Committees.

JUNE 28th, 1871.

The grand body was opened in ample form by M. W. Bro. Calvin C. Burt, 96°, Grand Master. There were present R. W. Bro. M. Shoemaker, 96°, Grand Senior and Junior Wardens, Secretary and other brethren.

On motion of Bro. M. Shoemaker, 96°, adjourned until June 29th.

JUNE 29th 1871.

The Committee on Amended Constitution reported the following, which was taken up section by section, and adopted, and spread upon the Record.

CALVIN C. BURT, 96°,

[L. S.]   *Grand Master ad Vitem.*

THOS. W. BLAYNEY, 95°,
            Grand Secretary.

The Amended Constitution of the Rite of Memphis, rules, regulations, and by-laws of the Sovereign Sanctuary, for the habitable and civilized world, Masonic Brotherhood and Fraternity, viz: We the officers and members of said Body, in solemn conclave assembled, the 27th day of the Egyptian month

Chocas, in the year Anni Lucia 5871, answering to
the Vulgar or Christian Era, June, 1871, according to
the recommendation of the M. W. Grand Master in
his last address, due notice having been given, we do
hereby amend the constitution and by-laws of the
Rite and the Sovereign Sanctuary of the Egyptian
Masonic Rite of Memphis, as follows, viz :

ARTICLE I.

SEC. 1. The name and style of this Masonic
body shall continue to be known and called the
Sovereign Sanctuary for the Continent of America,
and since the cessation to work these degrees in
France, its jurisdiction, embracing the whole civilized
world where Masonry is known and tolerated,
supreme in itself, paying allegiance to none, but fra-
ternizing with all that is good, and they who recognize one God, Almighty Creator of all, the immortality of the soul of man, and the general law of Masonic jurisprudence throughout the habitable globe.
Peace, tolerance, truth, and brotherly love. Know
we that

SEC. 2. This body shall continue to be composed of its members, the Grand Officers of the
95°, as follows : the present Grand Master ad vitem
96°, or for his natural life; Deputy Grand Master,
96°, for four years.

The office of Grand Representative, having been
abolished at the Quadriennial Communication of
June, 1878, and the following to stand in its place,
viz : The Grand Master shall appoint one or more
Deputy Grand Represesentatives in every State or
Territory, who shall hold their office during his
pleasure, and who shall report to him all proceedings,
and they, when commissioned by him, (the Grand

Master,) shall have power to make Masons for the purpose of forming bodies in the Rite, and may with his consent and approval, endorsed on the commission or appointment, then appoint deputies to assist in forming bodies, and they shall be entitled to the 95°, and receive the same when they are appointed by the Grand Master, and shall be compensated by the Deputy Grand Representative, and continue during his pleasure; provided, however, that they shall be residents of the same State or Territory where the Deputy Grand Representative resides, unless the Grand Master shall, by dispensation, otherwise direct residents of another Territory; provided, also, that the Deputy Grand Representatives and their Deputies shall keep a full record of each and all their proceedings for their use and for the inspection of the Grand Master; Deputy Representative, 95°, during the pleasure of the Grand Master; Grand Orator 95° ; Grand Prelate, 95° ; Grand Marshal, 95° ; Grand Senior Warden, 95° ; Grand Junior Warden, 95°; Grand Secretary, 95° ; Grand Treasurer, 95° ; Grand Conductor, 95° ; Grand Senior Master of Ceremonies, 95° ; Grand Junior Master of Ceremonies, 95°; Grand Guard of the Tower, 95°; Grand Sentinel, 95°; for the term of four years from election, and until their successors are installed in office. Also all past Grand Officers in good Masonic standing, who shall not be otherwise objectionable to the Grand Master or to the officers of the State Council ; the three first officers of each Chapter and each Senate, till a State Council is formed in a State ; the Deputy Grand Representative and their Deputies then in office, being in possesssion of the 95 °, without which no brother shall be admitted to the councils or deliberations of the Sovereign Sanctuary or

Grand Body. The Grand Master, Deputy Grand Master, and Deputy Grand Representative shall have the right to make Masons at sight for the purpose of forming bodies, or install when duly commissioned by the Grand Master for that purpose, except the Grand Master, who shall never be deprived of this right to make Masons at sight, and if he choose, may, by special dispensation or edict, deputize any person having the 95° to do such business for him; but all fees receivable therefrom at such price as he (the Grand Master) may fix, shall belong to and be perquisites of the Grand Master, whose opinion and authority shall, in all cases, be absolute, but may be reversed by the grand body, when duly appealed from, at the next regular meeting of the Sovereign Sanctuary. The Grand Master, Deputy Grand Master, or in the case of the death of the Grand Master, two other officers and two members, at a regular or a special meeting called by the Grand Master, shall constitute a quorum, in the presence of the Grand Master, to open the grand body, at its stated conclave, or called meetings, which may be called by the Grand Master or Deputy, (in case of the death of the Grand Master,) at any time by summons or publication, so that due and timely notice, according to Masonic usage, may be given.

SEC. 3. The regular meetings of the grand body, Sovereign Sanctuary, shall be held quadriennially, or once in four years, at such time and place as the Grand Master shall designate and order, the next meeting to be held on or near the third Monday in June, A. D. 5874, and quadriennially thereafter. In all cases notice by summons shall be given (if possible) at least twenty days before the time of meeting of said body, viz: in case of regular quad-

riennial meeting; but called meetings shall be legal
a nd valid when ordered by the Grand Master, upon
such notice as the Grand Master shall di rect. Notice
and summons may be given by enclosing a written
or printed notice in an envelope directed to the postoffice address, or last place of residence of the
brother summoned, at least twenty days before the
time of such meeting, and prepaying the postage
thereon. And notice to any of the bodies of this
Rite may be given by such notice being directed to
the Secretary or presiding officer of such body,
placed in the postoffice, prepaid as aforesaid, twenty
days before the time of meeting as aforesaid.

SEC. 4. Officers and brethren, except the presiding officer, may appear by proxy, which may be returned with and attached to the summons or notice
(if it is in writing or signed by the person) and directed to the brother who is to act as proxy, or to
the Grand Master.

SEC. 5. The Grand Master shall preside at all
meetings of this body; except in case of his death,
at a regular meeting, the Deputy shall preside. In
case he do not preside, then the Senior Warden; or
in case of his death. absence or inability, then the
Junior Warden. In all cases the person who, by the
constitution, shall preside, shall, for that time, possess
the same power as the Grand Master, and be obeyed
in a like manner as the Grand Master should be
were he in person present,except that any other person
except the Grand or Deputy Grand Master acting
temporarily as Grand Master, shall not, except in the
grand body while in session, and while so acting, be
empowered to do any act whatever, by reason of his
having acted in the capacity of Grand Master during
a session of the Sovereign Sanctuary, and then only
as presiding officer.

SEC. 6. The annual election of officers required to be chosen by ballot shall be held as follows, (except State Grand Councils,) viz : Senates of Hermetic Philosophers and Rose-Croix Chapters, shall be held at the nearest regular meetings preceding the 31st day of December of each year, and the officers installed during said month, unless, for cause shown, the Grand Master shall by dispensation otherwise direct.

SEC. 7. At all meetings of the Sovereign Sanctuary and other bodies of this Rite, three officers and two members shall constitute a quorum to open the grand body or Chapter, Senate or Council, except at election meetings, and in other bodies than the Sovereign Sanctuary, special communications. In the first case at least five persons shall be present, unless the Grand or Deputy Grand Master otherwise direct while presiding.

SEC. 8. No brother shall be eligible to the office of Sublime Dai, Sublime Grand Commander, Most Wise of any of the bodies of this Rite, unless he shall have first served as Warden of that body or of the body in which he seeks to be elected, for a full term, unless it be for the purpose of forming a new body, or by dispensation in writing, or the Grand Master shall otherwise direct.

SEC. 9. The seven first officers in a Senate or Rose-Croix Chapter shall be elected by ballot, at the regular meeting of each body in each year. The other and remaining officers of each body may be appointed by the regular presiding officer, unless the members, by a majority of votes, shall otherwise determine, which the presiding officer of each body on the night of the election shall, on the request of any member of the body, put to vote by ballot or otherwise as he may see fit or order. All officers who are regularly elected and installed shall hold their offices until the next regular meeting, and until their successors are qualified, unless they shall die, be removed or become otherwise disqualified; in which case they may be filled by the presiding officer, or by a special election, called by him on due notice. No person but the Grand Master or some person especially by him in writing deputed, shall have the right to make Masons at sight. The fees therefor shall belong to and be the exclusive money of the Grand Master.

SEC. 10. And no person shall be made or the degrees communicated to him for a less sum than ten dollars, unless by express permission of the Grand Master; and no such person shall be so made or degrees communicated to him unless he first sign the oath of fealty, which shall be filed in the office of the Grand Master. No petition for the formation of a Chapter shall be acted upon by the Grand Master unless the fee of five dollars for each person so made, and not less than twenty persons shall constitute a petition, unless the Grand Master shall otherwise order in writing, on or accompanying the petition, signed by each of them as petitioners; and no person so signing a petition, unless he is a member of the Rite in good standing, shall be received, unless such fee be first paid.

SEC. 11. No person shall be received into any organized Chapter in this Rite, unless by a petition, signed by him, presented to the Chapter at a regular communication, and accompanied by a petition fee of at least five dollars, which petition shall be voted upon before it is received by said Chapter; and if a majority of votes are against it, this petition shall be laid on the table and the money refunded; which transaction shall be recorded in the minutes of the

Chapter. If a majority vote to receive the petition, it shall be referred to a committee of at least three brothers in good standing, who shall make diligent inquiry as to the standing and Masonic character of the applicant, and report thereon at the next regular communication of the body. If favorable, he shall be balloted for in due and ancient form. If elected, he shall, upon payment of not less than ten dollars in addition to the petition fee, in money, be initiated; and the Most Wise shall require the voucher or receipt of the treasurer or secretary, to be exhibited to him, that he has received the money for the initiation fee before they shall be begun or conferred, or the "neophyte" admitted, to his first degrees. In case the neophyte is rejected, his fees shall be immediately returned to him, and his name iu full shall be written in the black book on the black roll of the Sanctuary, together with the date of his rejection. Such person so refused admission, shall not be again balloted for in less than one year from the date of his rejection, unless for good cause shown the Grand Master, by dispensation, at a request of the members of the Chapter, shall otherwise order.

SEC. 12. Dimit petitions for membership, if any, shall be in writing, signed by the person applying, and shall be voted upon in such way and manner as the body by its by-laws provides, except in case of initiation, which shall be by secret ballot, and in no case until he has paid his fees into the treasury, who shall give vouchers for the same, to be exhibited before he be received into the body, and which shall not be less than for the Chapter, fifteen dollars; Senate,$50; Council,$100; Sovereign Sanctuary,$10; unless the Grand Master shall, by dispensation, otherwise order. Five dollars must in each and every case accompany the petition or application; provided, that under circumstances for the good of the order, the Grand Master may, by dispensation, allow a body, for one year, to initiate for a less sum, but not otherwise; but any Chapter, Senate or Council, has the right to *increase* its fees, by a resolution printed in its by-laws, to such higher sums as they or a majority of its members may direct; provided, however, that no Chapter or body of this Rite shall change its by-laws more than once a year. One copy of all by-laws of Rose-Croix Chapters or Senates shall be delivered to the Grand Master, and one copy be filed with the Grand Secretary of the Sovereign Sanctuary, as soon as the same are promulgated; provided, however, that no by-laws of any Chapter, Senate or Council, shall contravene any of the provisions of this constitution, or the laws and edicts of the order. But any such by-laws shall be null and void, and subject the body that shall continue their existence to discipline by the Sovereign Sanctuary.

Sec. 13. The bodies of this Rite shall pay to the grand body, the Sovereign Sanctuary, annual dues as follows: The Rose Croix Chapter shall pay at the expiration of every first Monday in December, the sum of two dollars for every person initiated into such Chapter before the election of officers for the coming year, which shall accompany the annual return to the Grand Master, which shall be made before the third Monday in the month of January following election, and before the officers are installed, and shall contain the names of the officers for the coming year, also the name, residence, and number of brethren who are members of the body, including the names of those who have died, removed, or have been expelled during the past year, which shall be signed by the Secretary, and certified to by the presiding officer of the body, and sent by express to the residence of the Grand Master as aforesaid.

SEC. 14. Every Senate shall make like returns to the Grand Master, as by Section 13 of this Constitution, the Rose Croix Chapter is required to do, until the formation of a State Grand Council according to law (except that the Senate is not required to pay the two dollars fee for its membership,) after which time the returns of the Rose Croix Chapter to the Grand Master shall be only the fee of two dollars for each old member—the other returns as to members, deaths, etc., and shall be made by the Rose Croix Chapter to the State Council within whose jurisdiction said Chapter shall be, but the fee of two dollars shall be always paid to the grand body or Grand Master for such body.

ARTICLE II.

SEC. 1. The third body of this Rite, viz, the State Council, when duly organized and its officers installed, shall have the control and supervision of all Chapters and Senates within its jurisdiction in the first customs, which shall be co-extensive with the State for which it is chartered. It shall be composed of its officers as provided in section——of this Constitution, and such members as may from time to time be, by vote, admitted into its counsels. No person who has not received the 90 degrees, can become a member of this body, viz, Grand Council, which shall hold its sessions at such time as by law is provided therefor, which shall be at least once in each year. It shall have appellate and exclusive (in the first instance) jurisdiction of all the Chapters and Senates in the State, subject to the appellate jurisdiction of the Sovereign Sanctuary. It shall make, once in every year, returns, and deliver a copy of its by-laws to the grand body or Master at his residence, viz; the number of members, the names of its officers and its members, together with full returns from all Senates and Rose Croix Chapters within its jurisdiction, stating the names of bodies, their officers, and shall give certificates to all such as are by law entitled to represent the several bodies of the Rose Croix Chapter and Senate in the Sovereign Sanctuary for the current year, forwarding a list thereof to the Grand Secretary at the end of every four years, one month before, and in time for the quadriennial meetings of the grand body, and a copy to the Grand Master at least twenty days before the time of its meetings. For a failure so to do, the body will be subject to lose its right of representation, and forfeit its charter. Each Rose Croix Chapter, Senate or Council, which shall fail or who shall neglect to pay over its dues to the Sovereign Sanctuary, to the Grand Master, or to make its returns or fail to comply with each, any or all of the aforesaid rules, shall be subject to suspension, expulsion, and forfeit its charter, and the Grand Master is empowered to suspend or punish each and every body or person who shall fail or neglect to make a full compliance therewith.

Sec. 2. The State Council, when organized and installed, shall hold its meetings annually, the first of which shall be on or before the first Tuesday in January of each year, at such place as may be designated within the State, or may, by a vote of the body, be called, and each Rose-Croix Chapter shall be entitled to representation, viz: the Most Wise, Senior and Junior Wardens. Each Senate shall have the representation of the Sublime Grand Commander, Senior and Junior Wardens of each Senate ; provided, however, that one person may represent the body and have three votes, in case the Chapter or Senate which he represents shall so direct in writing. The State Council shall make rules, by-laws and regulations for its manner of conducting its business, not inconsistent or in contravention of this Constitution, subject to the approval of the Grand Master, who shall have power to correct and dictate the form and manner of its work. The Grand Master and his Deputy, and the Deputy Grand Representatives, shall visit the Grand Council from time to time, examine its work, and make such suggestions as they may deem for the good of the order. But the full charge of each Chapter and Senate in a State shall be vested in the State Coouncil, when fully formed and chartered. They may determine questions of Masonic law and jurisprudence, in the first instance, subject to the opinion of the Grand Master, from whose opinion appeal may be had to the grand body, when convened. The officers shall be elected by ballot as in the other bodies, and may be installed and install their successors in office, for all time to come. Special meetings may be called by the Sublime Dai, upon the usual Masonic notice.

Sec. 3. But at all regular election meetings each Chapter, Senate and Council in the jurisdiction, shall be summoned by a written notice, duly served at least ten days before the time of meeting, and also notice given to the Grand Master, that he may be present, if he shall see fit, which notice shall be at least ten days before the time of meeting.

Sec. 4. The following fees shall be paid for is-suing charters by this grand body, and dispensation by

the Grand Master to work the degrees till a charter is
issued, viz: Chapter of Rose-Croix, seventy-five
dollars; dispensation for the forming of a Chapter,
twenty dollars; Senate of Hermetic Philosophers, one hundred dollars; dispensation to form a
Senate, thirty dollars; State Council, one hundred
and fifty dollars; dispensation to form a State Council, fifty dollars, which shall be deducted from the
charter fee when that is issued.

SEC. 5. The officers elected at a Council shall
each hold their offices and continue the same for the
term of one year from the date thereof, viz: To the
27th day of January, A. D. 1874, and those elected
hereafter shall hold their several offices for the term
of four years, or until their successors are elected and
duly qualified, unless they shall die, resign, or become otherwise disqualified, or shall, by the Grand
or Deputy Grand Master, acting as Grand Master,
be suspended or expelled, which suspension shall not
hold longer than till the next regular meeting of the
grand body, when such order of the Grand Master
shall by him be submitted to the grand body for
decision.

ARTICLE III.

SEC. 1. The Grand Master shall have the power,
and it shall be his duty, to suspend any brother or
officer for gross unmasonic conduct during the recess
of the grand body and until the next regular meeting thereof, which suspension shall be in writing,
and contain a statement of the cause or reasons
therefor, a copy of which shall be served on him
personally, if possible or convenient; if not, by put-
ting the same in the post-office, as is provided for in
case of summons; a copy shall also be filed with the

c

Grand Secretary, or at the regular meetings, and contained in the Grand Master's report.

SEC. 2. All trials shall, in the first instance, be in the Rose-Croix Chapter, by a commission or committee of not less than three nor more than seven, issued by the Most Wise of the Chapter to which the person accused belongs, or nearest to his place of residence, in case he reside in the State where there is a Chapter working. If he does not reside in said State, then in any Chapter where he may be nearest found, or the complaining brother resides; provided, however, that brother is a member of the 90°, may, if he demands it, be tried by a commission of 95° members issued out of the State Council. When the accused is a 95° member he may require to be tried by a commission issued out of the Sovereign Sanctuary, by making application in writing to the Sublime Dai of that State Council, enclosing a copy of the notice and charges, with a request for a commission to issue from such Senate, which shall, when issued, contain the same charges, and suspend the action by the commission issued by the Rose Croix Chapter. If convicted, shall pay the reasonable costs and charges, and be by the Sublime Dai sentenced, reprimanded, or suspended, but shall not be expelled unless by a vote of two-thirds of the members present. In case he is discharged, the complainant shall pay the reasonable costs of the proceedings, to be determined by the Sublime Dai. All charges and complaints must be in writing, filed in the body from which the commission is issued, and a copy of the same served on the person charged at least thirty days before the time of meeting for the trial; and all returns must state the day and manner of service, and the trial shall be conducted in a private manner, and the evidence taken shall not be by any brother or member disclosed to any person not a Mason during the progress of the trial, and not afterwards, except for good cause or the purpose of Masonic warning. All presiding officers may for gross unmasonic conduct committed in the Chapter, Senate, Council or Sanctuary, in presence of such officers, suspend the offender for the term of one year, or till an appeal can be had by the body over which such officers preside; and in all cases the party may appeal from such decisions to the highest body of the Rite, if he is in possession of the 95°, and in other cases, to the State Council, if one is formed for the State where he is tried—until such formation, he may appeal to the grand body, and in case the trial shall result in favor of the accused, the Grand Secretary shall issue to such brother, on demand, a certificate under the seal of their body, which shall state such trial and acquittal; but in case of conviction in a Chapter or Senate, the secretary or presiding officer shall immediately notify the Grand Secretary of the State Council, and he shall notify the Secretary of the grand body, and in case a conviction is had in the grand body, he shall notify the Grand Secretary of the State Council, if any is formed; if not, the Secretary of the body to which the offending brother had belonged. All appeals shall be transmitted to the appellate body, within six months, or deemed abandoned; and all appeals received thirty days before the communication of the body to which they are appealed, shall be determined at that meeting, unless for good cause shown, they shall be continued to the next term. Provided, however, that in all cases where there is no State Council, the commission may issue from the Sovereign

Sanctuary, signed by the Grand Secretary and the Grand Master, or both of them. And provided further, that all 90° and upward members may, if they so desire, be tried by commission issued out of State Council, when there is one in working order; or, if not, then the Sovereign Sanctuary, as is provided for in Section 21, Article 1. And provided that for cause shown and by dispensation issued, the Grand Master may order any offending brother tried by commission, to be issued out of the Sovereign Sanctuary, as is also provided for in Section 21. And any and all commissions shall have power, and it shall be their duty, to report their opinion and pronounce judgment thereon, subject to approval and reversal by the body from which it was issued, at the next regular meeting thereof.

SEC. 3. An expulsion from any of the bodies of this Rite for any crime shall work an expulsion from all; and an expulsion from any other Masonic body, for a crime committed after the party was made a Mason, shall, on motion, be made an expulsion from all the bodies of the Rite, except from office in the Sovereign Sanctuary; but it may, by motion, on due notice, be made an expulsion from the body by a two-thirds vote of the members present at a regular or called meeting, of which the offender has had due notice, and a copy of the charges served on him, and he given an opportunity to be heard in his defense.

SEC. 4. When any brother has been by any one of the bodies of this Rite duly expelled, and the time for appeal having expired, he may, by motion, be expelled from all the rights and benefits of the Rite of Memphis on this continent, of which immediate notice shall be given him by the secretary having the record.

SEC. 5. The Grand Master shall have full power, and it shall be his duty to see that these and all other rules and edicts shall be enforced, and he shall have power from time to time to make and promulgate such other rules, edicts, regulations and commands as may, in his judgment, be for the benefit, good order and good government of the bodies of the Rite; and may, from time to time, enforce, and by dispensation release from the present effect of any rule, law or edict, till the next meeting of this grand body, when, in his judgment, the good of the craft shall be benefited thereby; he shall have full power to appoint officers, fill vacancies, confer degrees, make Masons at sight, do all other acts and perform all other service, make, order and command by rule, order, edict, or by-law, all such acts, things and prerogatives as Grand Masters in the past have done, may now do, and shall have been or are severally empowered to do.

SEC. 6. The Grand Master shall have the care, custody and possession of all property and effects that does now or may hereafter belong to the grand body; and all Chapters, Senates and Councils, when they shall, from any cause, cease to work, shall immediately deliver over to the grand body, on demand, all rituals, records, property of every kind which they shall have at the time the same may, from any cause, cease to work. Any Chapter, Senate or Council that shall contumaciously refuse to obey the rules, regulations and laws of the order, or the edict of the Grand Master, shall forfeit all right under any charter, or by dispensation to them granted, and the same together with all the Chapter or Senate property, charters, rituals and furniture, or any thing else proper and necessary for the working of the degrees, or doing business of the order; and all such things shall become the exclusive and entire property of the grand body, and upon demand, shall be delivered over to the Grand Master for the use of the grand body.

SEC. 7. The duty of the several officers in the Rite, are the same as in other Masonic bodies; and the right to preside shall remain in the presiding officer when present, and in case of his absence, the next in rank; but any officer shall, when acting in the place of his superior officer, be obeyed and sanctioned the same as the proper officer, and with like effect.

SEC. 8. It shall be the duty of the Conductor of the Chapter and the Senate to serve all notices, unless for good cause shown, the presiding officer shall direct otherwise; and in the State Council, it shall be the duty of the Conductor to serve, in like manner. all notices and summons; but in the Sovereign Sanctuary, it shall be the duty of the Marshal to serve all such papers and perform all other of the lawful commands of the Grand Master or the grand body.

SEC. 9. Services performed by any officer of the Rite, otherwise than those performed in the regular work of the bodies, should be paid a just compensation; for, as the laborer is worthy of his hire, so should we, as Masons, reward each other. The Grand Master is authorized by edict or rule to fix the price of payment of all persons who aid and assist him in the performance of labor in forming bodies or furnishing supplies of any kind for the good of the order, or the propagation of the good of this order; and for that purpose, he may draw his order on the Treasurer, who shall pay the same. All Senate Conductors, Wardens, Marshals, Guards, and all other officers who shall perform manual labor or service, other than the regular workings of the degrees, may, by a rule or by-law of the Chapter, Senate or Council, be paid such sum for the stated compensation as shall, by a vote of the body, be ordered.

SEC. 10. The Deputy Grand Representative shall be paid for the organization of his deputies, all necessary and proper traveling fees and postage, out of fees by him received, or the Treasurer of the grand body; but all others, except the officers of the grand body, shall be paid out of the respective body to which they belong and do service for.

SEC. 11. The order for forming bodies shall be as follows: In any State or Territory there must be at least eight working Rose-Croix Chapters, before a Senate can be organized.

SEC. 12. There shall be at least four Senates in a State or Territory before a State Council can be formed, and there can be but one State body in any one State or Territory.

SEC. 13. No Chapter or Senate shall ordinarily be formed of less than twenty members, who shall sign the oath of fealty, and a petition therefor, which shall be issued by the Grand Master, and when signed, shall be returned to him, together with the initiation fee of each member, which shall not be less than five dollars for each member, and the balance of the money for degrees, rituals and dispensations, shall be paid before the degrees are gven or the body organized; provided, however, the Grand. Master may, by dispensation issued, form bodies of less than twenty (20) members.

SEC. 14. This constitution shall not be amended ex\ecpt at a regular quadriennial meeting, in which notice shall have been given at a former meeting of the body in writing, and which shall be filed by the Secretary in a book kept by him for that purpose; provided, however, that new rules, edicts and regulations may be made, from time to time, by the Grand Master or the grand body for the explanation of this constitution, and the better and more efficient enforcement and construction of the same.

SEC. 15. Persons elected to any office in the Rite may be refused installation, or being put into office, who are at the time indebted for dues to the grand body in any sum, or for money in this society, or any of the subordinate bodies of this Rite, or for money collected and withheld therefrom, after demand for the same has been m de and refused or neglected to be paid over for the space of five days.

SEC. 16. Any member of•this Rite, on payment of dues, may obtain from the secretary of the body of which he is a member, a dimit from such body, and it shall not be necessary for a vote by the Chapter or body before granting such dimit; and thereafter the said member, while so dimited, shall not be liable to pay dues to any of the bodies of this Rite, except the Sovereign Sanctuary, to which he shall pay, if an unaffiliated member thereof, the sum of one dollar per year, so long as he continue to be an unaffiliated Mason in good standing, and reside within its jurisdiction; and provided, further, that no dimit shall be given from the Sovereign Sanctuary to any person whatever.

SEC. 17. Any member of the Rite holding an office therein, shall have the power to resign when he shall so desire, upon giving due notice to the secretary of the body, except the Grand and Deputy

Grand Masters, who are instructed and obliged not to resign during their term of office.

SEC. 18. This constitution shall take immediate effect, and all former constitutions, laws, rules and edicts, not inconsistent herewith, are hereby continued. But all constitutions, laws, rules and edicts, to which this is amendatory, that are not conformatory hereto, or that are in conflict herewith, are hereby repealed. But such repeal shall not effect any act done or right acquired under or by virtue of such former constitution or law.

Signed by the committee of revision as follows :

M. SHOEMAKER, 96°,

JAMES C. WOOD, 95°,

FIDUS LIVERMORE, 95°,

Revising Committee.

Dated June 28th, A. D. 1871.

Approved and passed in due form at a regular meeting of the Sovereign Sanctuary.

THOMAS W. BLANEY, 95°,

Grand Secretary.

OFFICE OF THE GRAND SECRETARY, }
CHICAGO, AUGUST 5h, 1872. }

I hereby certify the foregoing to be a true copy taken from the minutes and records of this grand body.

[L. S.] THOMAS W. BLANEY, 95°,

Grand Seceetary.

Compared and approved by me.

[L. S.] CALVIN C. BURT, 96°,

Grand Master ad vitem.

C*

FOURTH MEETING, 1874, DETROIT MICH.

Illustrious Brother and Dear Sir:

WHEREAS, At the Annual Meeting of the Sovereign Sanctuary for the Continent of America, held in Jackson, on the 27th day of June, A. D 1871, a resolution was adopted to authorize the Grand Master to convene the grand body hereafter at such place as, in his discretion and in force of circumstances, should direct ; and

WHEREAS By an amendment of Article 4, Section 10, of the Constitution of this Order, passed at the Annual Meeting of the Sovereign Sanctuary, June, 1871, it was directed that the meetings of this Body should be thereafter held quadriennially, the first of which should be held on the third Monday in June. 1874;

THEREFORE, Be it known that I, Calvin C. Burt, 96°, Grand Master, by virtue of the power and authority in me vested, do hereby order and direct that the said quadriennial meeting of the Sovereign Sanctuary for the Continent of America, be held at the city of Detroit, in the county of Wayne and State of Michigan, and you are hereby summoned to be and appear (either in person or by proxy) at Castle Hall, in the city of Detroit, on Monday, the 15th day of June next, at 12 M , for the purpose of choosing officers for the ensuing term, and the transaction of such other business as may lawfully come before the said grand body. Hereof fail not, under a penalty of a violation of your obligation.

Done in our Sanctuary, where abide peace, tolerance, truth and the fullness of all that is good, this sixth day of the Egyptian month Athir answering to the sixth day of May, A. L 5874, Vulgar Era, 1874.

Witness our hand and the seal of the Sovereign Sanctuary, [L. S.] at the Valley of Jackson, this sixth day of May, Vulgar, or Christian Era, A. D 1874.

CALVIN C. BURT, 96°,

Grand Master E.∴ M.∴ of R . M.∴

THOMAS W. BLAYNEY, 95°,

Grand Secretary.

STATE OF MICHIGAN, CITY OF DETROIT, CASTLE }
HALL, June 15, A. L. 5874, A. D. 1874. }

At High 12 the Sovereign Sanctuary for the Continent of America, was by M. W. Bro. Calvin C.

Burt. 96°, opened in ample form, with a constitutional number of brethren present who had been convened by virtue of the foregoing summons, and the following summary of proceedings agreed upon for publication, viz:

A committee on credentials was by him appointed, such consisting of Brothers J. L. Holmes, 95°, H. J. Blanchard, 95°, J. L. Mitchell, 95°, and labor was suspended till 2 p. m., at which hour the grand body resumed its labors. The Grand Master delivered his quadriennial address, and read his report of official decisions, proceedings and edicts, and dispensations granted, and a full report of the financial condition of the Order, which was placed on file, together with the new constitution, which was there for the first time, read for information.

On motion of Bro. Prentiss, ordered that 5,000 copies of the same be printed under the direction of the Grand Master, and a sufficient sum drawn from the Treasurer to pay therefor.

Electing officers was then declared in order, Brothers Benjamin Porter, 95°, and T. V. Davey, 95°, acting as tellers. The ballot was spread and the folfowing officers were duly elected for the next four years, or until June, A. L. 5878, viz:

Grand Master, Calvin C. Burt, 96°, Michigan; Deputy Grand Master, Abram T. Metcalf, 96°, Michigan; Grand Representative, John L. Mitchell, 95°, Michigan; Grand Orator, Reuben Cleavland, 95°, Illinois; Grand Prelate, George S. Fancher, 95°, New York; Grand Senior Warden, Benjamin Porter, 95°, Michigan; Grand Junior Warden, Harry G. Blanchard, 95. Michigan; Grand Secretary, Fred C. Losey 95°, Kentucky; Grand Deputy Secretary, Thomas W. Blaney, 95°, Illinois; Grand Treasurer, James L.

Holmes, 95°, Michigan ; Grand Conductor, J. Mabbett
Brown, 95°, Illinois ; Grand Senior M. of C., Brouse
T. Prentiss, 95°, Michigan ; Grand Junior M. of C.,
Oscar M. Barrett 95°, Illinois ; Grand Captain of
Guard, Lucius Fairchild, 95°, Wisconsin ; Grand
Marshal, James A. Dyer, 95°, Michigan ; Grand
Guard of Tower, Edward Lee, 95°, Mississippi ;
Grand Sentinel, Edward W. Roberts, 95°, California ;

Who after being duly installed by the Grand
Master, took their stations, and business of a private
character was then taken up and disposed of.

Bro. B. T. Prentiss, 95°, offered the usual resolution that the next regular meeting of the grand body
meet at such place as may be designated by the
Grand Master, and for the best interest of all the
grand officers, and the fraternity at large, which
was unanimously adopted, and the Grand Master requested to give at least twenty days notice of the
time and place of said Grand Meeting.

Appealed cases were then disposed of, and other
routine private business.

The Grand Master was requested to take charge of
all property belonging to the grand body, and cause
the same, together with all jewels, rituals, books,
papers and clothing belonging to the grand body,
and have the same fully insured, in his own name,
for the benefit of the grand body, and draw his
order on the Treasurer for the amount ; also that the
Great Seal destroyed by the Chicago fire be replaced
at the expense of this grand body, and that the
Secretary furnish the Grand Master with a brief
sketch of their proceedings, (or such as may be made
public,) and that 5,000 copies be printed for general
circulation, under the supervision and direction of
the Grand Master,

Whereupon, the grand body closed in love, peace and harmony, *sine die*.

In testimony whereof, we have made this certificate; done in our Sanctuary, where abide peace, tolerance, truth, and the fullness of all that is good, this day of the Egyptian month Pachon, answering to the sixth day of the month of November, A. L., 5877, Vulgar Era 1877.

By the Grand Master,

CALVIN C. BURT, 96°.

Witness our hand and the seal of the Sovereign [L. S.] Sanctuary, at the valley of Chicago, this day of November, Vulgar, or Christian Era, 1877.

FRED C. LOSEY, 95°, Louisville, Ky.

Grand Secretary, E∴ M∴ R∴ of M∴

By THOMAS W. BLANEY, 95°, Chicago, Ill.

Grand Secretary, pro tem.

[From the close of this grand meeting till the Convention of 1878 the proceedings of which follow the report, thirty-two Chapters were formed in the State of Michigan, besides a large number in other States.]—AUTHOR.

FIFTH MEETING, JUNE 24, 1878, QUINCY,

On the 6th day of May, A. L. 5878, the following summons was issued to the officers and members of the Rite, Sharon Chapter No.——, having proposed to take care of the members and represent the first eighteen degrees of the Rite, and exemplify them before the grand body:

Illustrious Brother and Dear Sir:

WHEREAS, At the Annual Meeting of the Sovereign Sanctuary for the Continent of America, held in Jackson, on the 27th day of June A. D. 1871, a resolution was adopted to authorize the Grand Master to convene the grand body hereafter at such place as, in his discretion and in force of circumstances, should direct; and

WHEREAS, By an amendment of Article 4, Section 10, of the Constitution of this Order, passed at the Annual Meeting of the Sovereign Sanctuary, June, 1871, it was directed that the meetings of this Body should be thereafter held quadriennially, on or near the third Monday in June, in each year at such place as the Grand Master should deem for the best interest of the craft, and direct;

THEREFORE, Be it known, that I, Calvin C. Burt, 96°, Grand Master, by virtue of the power and authority in me vested, do hereby order and direct that the said quadriennial meeting of the Sovereign Sanctuary for the Continent of America, be held at the city of Quincy, in the county of Branch, and State of Michigan and you are hereby summoned to be and appear (either in person or by proxy,) at Masonic Hall, in the city of Quincy, on Monday, the 24th day of June next, at 12 M., for the purpose of choosing officers for the ensuing term, and the transaction of such other business as may lawfully come before the said grand body. Hereof fail not, under penalty of a violation of your obligation

Done in our Sanctuary, where abide Peace, Tolerance, Truth, and the fullness of all that is good, this sixth day of the Egyptian month Athir, answering to the sixth day of the month of May A. L. 5878, Vulgar Era, 1878.

Witness our hand and the Seal of the Sovereign Sanctuary, at [L. s] the Valley of Jackson, this Sixth day of May, Vulgar, or Christian Era, 1878

CALVIN C. BURT, 96°.
Grand Master E∴ M∴ of R∴ M∴.

Attest : THOMAS W. BLAYNEY, 95°.
Grand Secretary.

QUADRIENNIAL MEETING OF 1878.

MASONIC HALL, QUINCY, MICH.,
JUNE 24, 1878.

The Sovereign Sanctuary for the civilized Cosmos, assembled at Quincy, at high 12, on the 24th day of June, 1878. pursuant to the order of the M. W. Grand Master, Calvin C. Burt, 96°, by summons of more than twenty days notice, as is provided for by Article 1, Sec. 3, of our Constitution,

The Sovereign Sanctuary was then opened in ample form, by M. W. Grand Master Calvin C. Burt, 96°, there being a constitutional number of officers and brethren present, viz: M. W. Grand Master, Calvin C. Burt, 96°, R. W. C. W. Straight, 95°, Grand Representative, ad interim, to fill the place of Past R. W. Grand Representative, John L. Mitchell, 95°, suspended. R. W. Bro. C. V. R. Pond, 95°, R. W. Bro. F. E. Marsh, 95°, R. W. Bro. H. D. Pessell 95°, Representatives of Sharon Rose-Croix Chapter, No. 36, Quincy, Mich.; R. W. Bro. B. F. Dawson, 95°, R. W. Bro. H. Freygang, 95°, R. W. Bro. Lewis D. Jones, 95°, Representatives of Angola Chapter No. 41, Angola, Ind.

Prayer was offered by R. W. Bro. C. V. R. Pond, 95°, acting, Grand Prelate, after which Bro. Pond offered the following resolution, viz:

Resolved, That all 90° members of the E M. R of M. in attendance, and in good standing, be admitted to and made members of the Sovereign Sanctuary by affiliation.

The resolution was adopted and they were so admitted: R. W. Brothers Dan W. Sawyer, H. D. Young, H. Lounsburg, W. J. Wilbur, R. W. Berry, C. S. Skinner, J. W. Mason, J. C. Bennett, of Quincy, J. F. Hicks, of Tecumseh, John Peters and Alonzo Powers, of Angola Chapter No. 1, Angola, Ind., A. Wilson, D. W. Young, G. W. Delts and Wm. Lennox, of Quincy, David Woodward, of Clinton, Mich., H. H. Hunt, E. S. Throop, L. Higgins, N. C. Skinner, Rev. R. D. Clark.

F. H. Skinner, of Quincy, was invested with 95°, and admitted.

A motion was then made to affiliate the above named brothers, which motion prevailed,

The M. W. Grand Master then appointed as a Committee on Credentials, R. W. Bros. Pond, Marsh and Pessell.

The M. W. Grand Master then declared labor suspended until three o'clock P. M.

3 O'CLOCK P. M., JUNE 24TH, 1878.

Labor was resumed by order of the M. W. Grand Master, Calvin C. Burt, 96°, and the aforesaid brothers being present. The Committee on Credentials then submitted their report, which, on motion, was received, viz:

To the Sovereign Sanctuary of the E. M. R. of M., sitting in the valley of Quincy, June 24th, 1878:

Your Committee on Credentials beg leave to report as follows: We find the following in person in due form, vouched for by the M. W. Grand Master, Calvin C. Burt, 96°. H. G. Blanchard, 95°, M. W., Detroit, Mich., 3 votes; B. T. Prentiss, 95°, M. W., Detroit, Mich., 3 votes; B. H. Porter, 96°, M. W., Sterling, Ill., 3 votes; G. S. Fancher, 95°, Grand Prelate Sovereign Sanctuary, New York City, 1 vote; W. W. Likins, 95°, M. W., Placerville, Cal., 3 votes; Charles S. Hemstead, 95°, M. W., Janesville, Wis., 3 votes; J. C. Wood, 95°, P. G. Prelate of Sovereign Sanctuary, Jackson, Mich., 3 votes; P. R. Dow, 95°, S. W., Janesville, Wis., 3 votes; W. H. Gains, 95°, M. W., Painesville, Ohio, 3 votes; J. M. Brown, 95°, P. G.R., Chicago, Ill., 1 vote; Reuben Cleveland, 95°, S. G. Commandery M. W., Chicago, Ill., 6 votes; G. W. Esterly, 95°, M. W., Whitewater, Wis., 3 votes; C. Lee, 95°, D. G. R., Holly Springs, Miss., 1 vote and some sixty other 95° members,

Letters are, in the estimation of this Committee, sufficient to warrant the reporting of the proxies as entitled to 6 votes.

Your Committee also report the following representative delegates entitled to seats : C. V. R. Pond, 95°, M. W., of Sharon Chapter, No. 36, Quincy, Mich. ; F. E. Marsh, 95°, S. W., of Sharon Chapter, No. 36, Quincy, Mich. ; H. D. Pessell, 95°, J. W., of Sharon Chapter, No. 36, Quincy, Mich.; B. F. Dawson, 95°, M. W., Angola Chapter, No. 1, Angola, Ind. ; H. Freygang, 95°, S. W., Angola Chapter, No. 1, Angola, Ind. ; L. D. Jones, 95°, J. W., Angola Chapter, No. 1, Angola, Ind., and entitled to 1 vote each.

The report was adopted.

A resolution was offered by the R. W. Grand Secretary, Dan W. Sawyer, as follows :

Whereas, The times are hard and money scarce, and we desire good men more than money, and Chapters are formed slowly, and with great labor ; therefore

Resolved, That in the opinion of this grand body, the charge of $200 to the bodies organizing Chapters for rituals and charters should not be enforced, and notice is hereby given of our intention to change the law on that subject and for the purpose of forming more Chapters, before the adjourned meeting or the next regular meeting of this grand body, such charge shall be remitted to the Grand Master. This resolution to take effect from the date of the last meeting of this grand body, June 27, 1874.

The above resolution, after due consideration and discussion, was adopted ; after which the Quadriennial Address of the M. W. Grand Master was delivered, preceded by a grand and glorious general history of the E.·. M.·. R.·. of M.·., and on conclusion, the Grand Master appointed as a committee on division and reference of the address, with power to appoint sub-committees, Rt. W. Brothers Pond, Straight and Pessell.

A motion in writing by Rt. W. Bro. Hicks, that the M. W. Grand Master appoint a committee to investigate the charges, &c., against certain members named, prevailed, and the M. W. Grand Master appointed as such committee, R. W. Bros. R. W. Berry, B. F. Dawson and H. D. Pessell.

The committee on sub-division of the M. W. Grand Master's address, reported as follows:

Committee on Legislation:

R. W. Brothers Dawson, Pessell and Straight.

Committee on Constitution;

R. W. Brothers Jones, Lownsberry and Wilson.

Committee on Grievances:

R. W. Brothers Freygang, Marsh and C. D. Skinner.

The M. W. Grand Master then called the Sovereign Sanctuary from labor, to refreshment, until 9 o'clock A. M. Tuesday, June 25th, 1878.

Rt. W. Bro. DAN W. SAWYER, 95°,
Grand Secretary.

MASONIC HALL, QUINCY, MICH.,
June 24, 1878.

The Sovereign Sanctuary of the civilized Cosmos assembled at Quincy, at 9 o'clock A. M., June 25th, 1878, pursuant to suspension of labor, the M. W. Grand Master, Calvin C. Burt, 96°, in the chair, together with all the before-mentioned officers and members.

The Sanctuary was opened, called to labor in ample form by the M. W. Grand Master Calvin C. Burt, 96°, and was then suspended from labor in the 95°, for the purpose of witnessing the opening of a Chapter in due form, and the exemplification of the work of 18°, by Sharon Rose-Croix Chapter, No.

36. Pursuant to notice, Sharon Rose-Croix Chapter, No. 36, E∴ M∴ R∴ of M∴ sitting in the valley of Quincy, Mich., was opened in Ancient and Primitive form, on the 18°, in the presence of the grand body.

There were present besides the officers and members of the Sovereign Sanctuary, the Chapter officers, to-wit: The Most Wise, Resp. Knight C. V. R. Pond; Senior Warden, Resp. Knight F. E. Marsh; Junior Warden, Resp. Knight H. D. Pessell; Orator, Resp. Knight R. W. Berry; Archivist, Resp. Knight Dan W. Sawyer; as Conductor, Resp. Knight W. J. Wilbur; Treasurer, Resp. Knight H. Lownsberry; ¯Capt. of Guard, Resp. Knight C. D. Skinner; Guard of Tower, Resp. Knight J. N. Salisbury; as Sentinel Sir Knight J. W. Mason; and Resp. Knights D. W. Young, A. Wilson and J. C. Bennett, of Sharon No. 36, Quincy. Visiting Resp. Knights B. F. Dawson, H. Freygang, L. D. Jones, John Peters, and Alonzo Powers, of Angola, Indiana, and J. F. Hicks, of Tecumseh, Michigan.

The Most Wise, R. Kt. C. V. R. Pond declared. Sharon Chapter open. The reading of the Graven Tablets was dispensed with. The M. W. then declared the Chapter labor of the 18° suspended, and opened it on the 4° or Discreet Master for labor.

Brother Powers, of Angola, Ind., consented to serve as the Neophite for the purpose of exemplifying the work; which being done, the Chapter was declared closed on the 4° and opened on the 5°, when the 5° was duly communicated. The Chapter was then called from labor on the 5° and duly opened on the 6°. The 6° was then conferred upon Brother Powers in ancient form. The Chapter was then declared closed till the further order of the Grand Master, and they retired.

The Sovereign Sanctuary resumed labor by order of the M. W. Grand Master, Calvin C. Burt, 96°, on the 95°.

On motion of Brother C. W. Straight, it was resolved that the quadriennial election of officers of this grand body take place in this hall at 4 P. M., to-day.

A motion was made to appoint a committee of three to propose the names of persons for officers, to be elected at this sitting of the Sovereign Sanctuary, to the offices of the Sovereign Sanctuary for the coming four years which prevailed, and Brothers Pond, Strait and Hicks, were appointed such committee where labor was suspended by the M. W. Grand Master, until 2½ o'clock P. M.

Rt. W. Bro. DAN W. SAWYER,

Acting Grand Secretary.

2½ O'CLOCK P. M.

Labor was resumed by order of the M. W. Grand Master, Calvin C. Burt, 96°, aforesaid officers and brethren being present.

The Committee on Constitution reported on the proposed amendment to Art. 1, Sec. 2, of the present Constitution, on notice given at the meeting of 1874, as follows :

That the office of Grand Representative be and the said office is hereby abolished, and in place thereof, there shall be, by the M. W. Grand Master, appointed one or more Deputy Grand Representatives, brothers who, when commissioned by and under his hand and seal, shall have power to confer degrees and make Masons for the purpose of forming Chapters, Senates and Councils, within the State or Territory for which they may be appointed, to continue during his will and pleasure, that the Grand

Representatives shall, on demand, deliver over to the
present acting Deputy Grand Representative, R. W.
Bro. C. W. Strait, 18°, the seal, books, papers and all
properties pertaining to his office of Grand Representative.

Resolved, That this amendment to the Constitution take immediate effect.

L. D. JONES,
H. LOWNSBERRY,
W. J. WILBUR.

(Signed,)

RESOLUTIONS ADOPTED.

The Committee on Jurisdiction reported as follows :

The geographical jurisdiction of a Rose-Croix
Chapter shall extend to a line at equal distance from
the next nearest Chapter. A Chapter may be formed
at any place where the constitutional number may
request it, or Grand Master direct. There shall be at
least five or more Chapters in a State before a Senate
can be formed.

The constitutional number required to form a
Chapter shall be twenty (20) or more Master Masons
in good standing.

The constitutional number required to form a Senate shall be twenty (20) or more Rose Croix Masons,
in good standing, provided the Grand Master may
issue a dispensation or charter for a body to a less
number for a Chapter, Senate or Council, at his
pleasure.

There shall be formed in each State, not less than
fifty (50) Rose-Croix Chapters before a Council can
be formed, unless by dispensation the Grand Master
otherwise direct.

The Grand Master may issue charters to Chapters or
Senates or Councils, for such number as he shall see

fit, during the adjournment of this Sovereign Sanctuary, and the grand officers shall sign charters in blank for that purpose, when he shall. request it, either at the session or during its vacation.

B. F. DAWSON, ⎫
C. W. STRAIGHT, ⎬ *Committee.*
H. D. BESSELL, ⎭

Report adopted by sections.

The hour for the quadriennial election of officers having arrived, the Committee submitted the following list of officers, who were each unanimously elected to the offices, as follows :

First ballot for Deputy Grand Master. Whole number cast was one hundred and seventy, of which Bro. William Brown, ot Battle Creek, Mich., received ninety, and Bro. H. D. Bessell, of Quincy, Mich,, received one, twenty-eight scattering.

First ballot for Grand Senior Warden. Whole number of votes cast one hundred and seventy, Bro. B. F. Dawson, of Angola, Ind., having received them all, was declared unanimously elected.

First ballot for Grand Junior Warden. Whole number cast one hundred and seventy, and Bro. David Woodward, of Clinton, having received them all, was declared unanimously elected.

First ballot for Grand Orator. Whole number cast one hundred and seventy, and Bro. J. M. Brown, of Chicago, having received them all, was declared unanimously elected.

First ballot for Grand Prelate. Whole number cast one hundred and seventy, and Bro. George S. Francher, of New York, having received them all, was declared unanimously elected.

First ballot for Grand Secretary. Whole number cast was one hundred and eighteen, and Bro. F. E.

Marsh, M. D., of Quincy, Mich., having received them all, was declared unanimously elected.

First ballot for Grand Treasurer. Whole number cast one hundred and eighteen, and Bro. H. D. Bessell, of Quincy, Mich., having received them all, was declared unanimously elected.

First ballot for Grand Conductor. Whole number cast was one hundred and fourteen, Bro. H. Freygang received one hundred and thirteen and Bro. C. V. R. Pond, received one, and on motion, Bro. H. Freygang, of Angola, Ind., was declared unanimously elected.

First ballot for Grand Captain of the Guard. Whole number cast was one hundred and ten, and Bro. James C. Wood, of Jackson, Mich., having received them all, was declared unanimously elected.

First ballot for Grand Guard of the Tower. Whole number cast was ninety-eight, and Bro. Charles S. Hemstead, having received them all, was declared unanimously elected.

First ballot for Grand Sentinel. Whole number cast was one hundred and nineteen, and Bro. W. W. Lickens, of Placerville, California, having received them all, was declared unanimously elected.

The officers present were then duly installed and took their stations.

The M. W. Grand Master then declared the labor of the Sovereign Sanctuary suspended, until 9 o'clock A. M., Wednesday, June 26th, 1878.

DAN W. SAWYER,

Grand Secretary.

In the presence of the grand body, in the Sanctuary rooms, were then convened Sharon Chapter, No. 36. Bro. C. V. R. Pond, then took the Chair and opened the Chapter in ancient and primitive form, for the purpose of exemplifying the work of the Chapter degrees.

The Chapter was called from labor on the 18° and opened in due form on the 13° or Royal Arch degree. The officers being in their proper chairs, and there being present also Bros. H. H. Hunt, H. D. Young, J. C. Bennett, F. H. Skinner, N. C. Skinner, William Lennox, A. Wilson, and D. W. Young, of Sharon, No. 36. Visiting brothers in attendance were R. W. Brothers, B. F. Dawson, H. Freygang, L. D. Jones and John Peters, of Angola, Ind., J. F. Hicks, of Tecumseh, Mich., and David Woodward, of Clinton, Mich.

The reading of the Graven Tablets was dispensed with. Bro. Lewis Higgins, a Master in Geometry, together with Bros. B. D. Clark, and Rt. W. Bro. John Peters, who were in waiting, after being duly prepared were received into the Chapter, and exalted as Knights of the Royal Arch in ancient form.

Bro. Higgins retired and was prepared to receive the 14°, or Knight of the Secret Vault, which, being completed, he retired and was prepared to receive the 15° or Knight of the Flaming Sword. That being finished, he was ready to receive the 16° or Knight of Jerusalem. Which being done, Sir Knight Higgins retired and was prepared to receive the 17° or Knight of the Orient. Sir Knight Higgins thereupon retired to be prepared for receiving the 18° or Knight of the Rose Croix, all of which were conferred in ancient and primitive form.

The Graven Tablets of the evening were read for approval. The " poor box" was passed for the benefit of the good of the order, and no further business appearing in the Chapter degrees, it was called from labor until Tuesday evening, July 2d, 1878, at 7½ o'clock, P. M.

Rt. W. Bro. DAN W. SAWYER, *Archivist,*
Sharon Chapter, No. 36.

WEDNESDAY, A. M., JUNE 26, 1878.

The Sovereign Sanctuary was declared open, and labor resumed by the M. W. Grand Master Calvin C. Burt, 96°, the aforesaid officers and brethren being present. The subject of uniforms for Knights of the Rose-Croix was called up and properly discussed, and a motion that a Committee of three be appointed for the purpose of determining what other if any regalia shall constitute the regalia or clothing of a Rose Croix-Chapter, members or officers, and also to confer with some responsible manufacturers to ascertain at what price it can be procured, and who can be relied upon to make proper work and that said committee report at the next meeting of this Sovereign Sanctuary, the result of their investigation. Motion prevailed.

A motion to adopt a resolution of R. W. Bro. C. V. R. Pond, that the committee on charges against Bros. Porter, Mitchell and Finch, be granted further time and be permitted to report at an adjourned session of the Sovereign Sanctuary, and that two more brothers be added to said Committee on Grievances, as follows: Bros. James C. Wood, of Michigan, and H. Freygang, of Indiana, was adopted.

Motion by Bro. C. W. Straight, that a committee of three be appointed to examine the Constitution and the proceedings of the Sovereign Sanctuary, held at Detroit, Michigan, in 1874, to ascertain if there be anything therein making it necessary to meet in Jackson, or anything pertaining thereto, was adopted.

D

The committee so appointed, were R. W. Brothers Pond, Pessell and Hicks.

The Committee appointed on uniforms, &c., were R. W. Brothers Freygang, Pond and Woodward.

The committee to examine Constitution, &c., reported as follows:

Your Committee, to whom was referred the subject of the legality of the call of the Grand Master for this quadriennial meeting of the Sovereign Sanctuary, at Quincy, Mich., June 24th, 1878, would respecfully report, that they find in the book of records, printed proceedings of a meeting held in Detroit, June, 1874, in which appears a resolution, offered by Brother B. T. Prentiss, conferring full power upon the Grand Master, to call the grand body where he shall see fit.

(Signed,)
C. V. R. POND,
J. F. HICKS, } *Committee.*
H. D. PESSELL.

The report was accepted, and committee discharged.

The following resolution was offered by Brother Dawson, of Indiana:

Resolved, That the thanks of this Sovereign Sanctuary be given to the M. W. Grand Master, Calvin C. Burt, 96°, and to R. W. Brothers Dan W. Sawyer, Grand Secretary, for diligent labor and work, and the members of Sharon Rose Croix Chapter, No. 36, for the kindness and the trouble they have taken to make our stay pleasant and agreeable while here.

The resolution was unanimously adopted.

The following notice of amendment to Constitution to be proposed hereafter, was offered by R. W. Brother C. V. R. Pond, 95°.

Resolved, That the Constitution be so amended as to make the office of Grand Master of the Sovereign Sanctuary an elective office, after the death of the present Grand Master, Calvin C. Burt, 96°. This amendment to be acted upon and to go into effect when it can do so constitutionally.

Also another motion by Grand Rep. Bro. C. W. Straight.

Resolved, That Section 3 of the Constitution of this grand body be amended by striking out the word "quadriennially" and substituting the word "annually."

The M. W. Grand Master, after prayer by the acting Grand Prelate, Bro. C. V. R. Pond, declared labor suspended, to be resumed again at Jackson, Mich., Tuesday, November 12th, 1878, at 10 o'clock A. M., whereupon the grand body closed in peace and harmony.

CALVIN C. BURT, 96°,
Grand Master ad vitem.

DAN W. SAWYER,
    Deputy Grand Secretary.

On the 12th day of November, A. D. 1878, pursuant to the action of the grand body, and a notice from the Grand Master, labor was resumed; there being present M. W. Grand Master C. C. Burt, 96°; R. W. William Brown, 95°, Deputy Grand Master; R. W. Benjamin F. Dawson, 95°, Grand Senior Warden; R. W. David Woodward, 95°, Grand Junior Warden; R. W. James C. Wood, 95°, Grand Captain of the Guard; R. W. Bro. C. W. Straight, 95°, Deputy Grand Representative for Southern Michigan; R. W. Bro. F. B. Smith, 95°, Grand Deputy Representative for Northern Michigan; R. W. L. D. Jones, 95°, Deputy Grand Representative for Indiana; R. W. Bro. B. F. Dawson, 90°, Most Wise of Angola Chapter, No. 1, of Angola, Ind., and R. W. Bro. L. D. Jones, 95°, Senior Warden of Angola Chapter, No. 1, of Angola, Ind.; R. W. Bro. N. B. Smith, 95°, Most Wise of Owasso Chapter, No. 47, of Michigan; R. W. Bro. William Brown, Most Wise, of Athir Chapter, No. 27, of Battle Creek, and the proxies of twenty-seven Chapters of Rose-Croix, and other 95°, Masons; also the following representatives in

Sovereign Sanctuary, in person or proxy, viz: No. 5,
Shemenoth Chapter, Chicago; No. 3, Karnack,
Beloit, Wisconsin; No. 4, Oriental, Janesville, Wis-
consin; No. 6, Shemenoth, Detroit, Michigan; No. 8,
Pyramid, Madison, Wisconsin; No. 1, Osiris Senate,
Illinois; No. 64, Athir Chapter, Battle Creek, Michi-
gan; No. 3, Isis Senate, Madison, Wisconsin; No.
32, Osiris Chapter, East Saginaw, Michigan; No. 21,
Lake Chapter, Painesville, Ohio; No. 13, Delta
Chapter, Detroit, Michigan; No. 36, Sharon, Quincy,
Michigan; No. 4, Theber Senate, Janesville, Wiscon-
sin; No. 1, Hippocrates, Mineral Point, Wisconsin;
Howell, Chapter, U. D. Michigan; Manchester, Chap-
ter, U. D. Michigan; Ionia Chapter, U. D. Michigan;
Lyons Chapter, U. D. Michigan; Tecumseh Chapter,
U. D. Michigan; Lansing Chapter, U. D. Michigan:
Lowell Chapter, U. D. Michigan; White Water, U. D.
Wisconsin; Ann Arbor Chapter, U. D. Michigan;
Grand Ledge Chapter, U. D. Michigan; Homer Chap-
ter, U. D. Michigan; Adrian Chapter, U. D. Mich-
igan; Phœnix Chapter, U. D. Painesville, Ohio,

The following Senates and Chapters were represented in the Sovereign Sanctuary, after roll call,
viz:

Senates—Mitzian, Michigan; Hermes, Michigan;
Theber, Michigan; Cheope, Michigan; Osinia, Illi-
nois; Emanuel, Chicago; Isis, Wisconsin; Plato,
Michigan,

Chapters—Shemenoth, Illinois; Alexandria, Illinois; Hippocrates, Wisconsin; Romae, Wisconsin;
Oriental, Wisconsin; Shemenoth, Michigan, Covenant, Michigan; Pyramid, Wisconsin; Velta, Mich-
igan; Oriental, Michigan; Phœnix, Michigan; Central, Michigan; Athir, Michigan.

The Sovereign Sanctuary was opened in ample form.

On motion of C. W. Straight, ordered that all visiting brethren of the 90° be admitted as members of the grand body, and that the fee therefor be remitted.

Labor was then suspended in the grand body till 2 o'clock P. M.

At 2 o'clock P. M., Nov. 12th, labor was then resumed, there being present: M. W. Grand Master Calvin C. Burt, 96°; R. W. Bro. Wm. Brown, 95°; R. W. Bro. B. F. Dawson, 95°, Grand Senior Warden; R. W. Bro. David Woodward, 95°, Grand Junior Warden; R. W. Bro. James C. Wood, 95°, Grand Captain of the Guard; R. W. Bro. F. B. Smith, Most Wise of Owasso Chapter, No. 47, together with other members and visiting brethren, being a constitutional number of brethren and officers.

Brothers Seymour D. Gilbert, 90°; Sanford Hunt, 90°; Matt D. Blosser, 90°; Arthur Case, 90°; David Shepard, 90°; M. W. Riker, 90°; Isaac F. Crissman, 90°, were duly admitted as members of the grand body, and received each the 95°.

On motion of Bro. C. W. Straight, 95°, it was ordered that each delegate and representative attending the session, be furnished with a certificate by the grand body, through the Grand Secretary, of such attendance, and the grand body recommended that each Rose-Croix Chapter, pay the reasonable expenses of such attendance.

M. W. Grand Master then called attention of the grand body to the following communication, which was read and submitted and placed on file; whereupon R. W. Bro. C. W. Straight, reported as follows: That he had called upon Bro. John L. Mitchell, 95°, late Grand Representative, and demanded of said Mitchell the seal, records, &c., which said John L. Mitchell refused to deliver up or to return to the grand body.

On motion of Bro. C. W. Straight, 95°, Bro. Sandford Hunt, 95°, was elected Deputy Grand Secretary.

The body being officially notified that Bro. M. W. Liking, 95°, of California, was an expelled Mason, the office to which he was elected (Grand Sentinel,) was then declared vacant, and the Grand Secretary requested to notify Bro. Liking accordingly, and Bro. Reuben Cleveland, 95°, of Chicago, Ill., was appointed Grand Sentinel, and Bro. Fidus Livermore, 95°, Grand Marshal.

Labor was then suspended till Wednesday, November 13th, at 10 A. M. On Wednesday, November 13th, 1878, 10 o'clock A. M., the Sovereign Sanctuary was opened in ample form, M. W. Bro. C. C. Burt, 96°, and the officers and members of yesterday being present. Labor was then resumed, R. W. Bro. William Brown, 96°, acting as M. W. Grand Master. The Most Worshipful Grand Master, C. C. Burt, 96°, then called for the report of a former committee on uniform and masonic clothing. There being only one member of said committee, R. W. Bro. D. Woodward, 95°, present, it was ordered that the whole subject of uniforms be left with the Grand Master to issue such edict as in his opinion would be most convenient and useful, and at the same time harmonize the equipment of officers so that the same uniform could be worn on all occasions in meetings of the Chapter, Senate, Council, and Sovereign Sanctuary, except when the official positions of officers in the Council are especially designated by the Ritual.

The Grand Master then reported the formation of forty Rose-Croix Chapters since the last meeting of this body in June, of this year, and that there was installed and ready for installation in Michigan, fifty-eight Rose-Croix Chapters, and about 2,374 90° Masons within the State of Michigan.

The Grand Master also reported the following edict as to the clothing and emblems of the Rite, viz : That the letters on the segment or circle of the Rose-Croix jewel, be as follows : H. I. V. N. Y. R. H. I., with name and date, on the obverse side engraved, also cross with I. N. R. I., a six-pointed star or interlaced triangle be worn on cap or baldrick, and any of the jewels of the Rite at discretion; that the ring for 90 and upward members be worn on third finger of the left hand, with three or more Deltas, All-Seeing Eye, Tripletaw, or T. on H., and number of degree taken, with full name inside and degree, and by edict ordered the same to be entered in the Journal, as the law on this subject.

The Committee appointed to inquire into and report upon the action of John L Mitchell, 95°, and others, in reference to the organization of a clandestine Sovereign Sanctuary of E. M. Rite of Memphis, at the City of Jackson, Michigan, on the 24th day of June, A D. 1878, have had the same under consideration, and submit the following report and accompanying resolutions:

The committee find first that Grand Master Calvin C. Burt, 96°, by virtue of the Constitution of the Order, called a Quadriennial meeting of the Order to meet at Quincy, Michigan, June 24th, 1878.

2d—That the said John L. Mitchell and three or four other members of the Sovereign Sanctuary, after the meeting of the said Sovereign Sanctuary had been called at Quincy by the Grand Master, insisted that the said Quadriennial meeting should be held at Jackson instead of Quincy.

3d—That because the said Grand Master would not change the call for the meeting, the said Mitchell, former Grand Representative, called a meeting to organize a Sovereign Sanctuary of the E. M. Rite of Memphis, to be held at Jackson, June 24th, A. D. 1878.

4th—That the said Mitchell had no power or authority in the Constitution to make such a call, or pretended organization.

5th—That said Mitchell, and others, after being duly notified of the call at Quincy, did meet at Jackson, on said 24th day of June, and pretended to elect officers of the said pretended Sovereign Sanctuary, and did this without the knowledge or consent of many of those who were pretended to be elected to said offices.

6th—That some of said officers, so pretended to be elected, were not qualified to hold them under the Constitution, not having taken the necessary degrees.

7th—That a number of those so pretended to be elected repudiate their election and refuse to act with the said Mitchell. regarding the whole proceeding as clandestine.

8th—That officers were elected at the regular meeting of the Sovereign Sanctuary and have been duly installed.

9th—That according to the Constitution and the oath of every member of the Order, the pretended organization of a Sovereign Sanctuary at Jackson, June 24th, 1878, is clearly clandestine.

10th—That at the meeting of the Sovereign Sanctuary at Quincy, a committee was appointed to call upon the said Mitchell and demand of him the seal of the Grand Representative ; that said committee did call upon said Mitchell and demand said seal, and said Mitchell did refuse to deliver the same to said committee.

BENJAMIN F. DAWSON,
WILLIAM BROWN,   Committee.
B. F SMITH,

Resolved, First, That the Sovereign Sanctuary pretended to be organized at Jackson, June 24, 1878, by the said John L. Mitchell and others, is a clandestine body.

Resolved Second, That said Mitchell, by his refusal to deliver up to the Sovereign Sanctuary the seal of the office of Grand Representative, which he formerly held, and his proclaiming and insisting that the said pretended organization at Jackson, June 24, 1878, is the valid and regular organization of said Order, has violated the Constitution of the Order and the obligations he took when he entered the Order.

Resolved, Third, That the meeting at Quincy, June, 1878, was a legal and valid meeting, and that the action of the M. W.

Grand Master, Calvin C. Burt, 96°, in suspending the said John L. Mitchell and others from the rights and privileges of this Sovereign Sanctuary, is fully endorsed.

All of which is respectfully submitted.

BENJAMIN F. DAWSON, ⎫
WILLIAM BROWN, ⎬ *Committee.*
B. F. SMITH ⎭

On motion, the report was received and adopted, and committee discharged.

A true copy of the report and resolutions adopted at the meeting of the Sovereign Sanctuary, Nov. 13th, A. D. 1878.

SANFORD HUNT, 95°,
Deputy Grand Secretary.

On Motion of Bro. Straight, Bro. Sandford Hunt, who had kept the minutes of the body, was elected Deputy Grand Secretary.

On like motion of Bro. Straight, the Secretary was directed to give to each of the Representatives of Chapters a certificate of attendance and mileage, with the request that such Chapter sending the Representative pay the same.

On motion of Bro. L. D. Jones, 95°, ordered that the proceedings, or so much thereof as are of a public nature, be published in pamphlet form by the Grand Master, at the expense of this grand body.

On like motion of Bro. B. F. Dawson, 95°, ordered that this Body call off to resume labor on the 24th day of June, next, if the Grand Master so elect, and at such place as he shall deem for the best interests of the Order, and shall summon the craft thereto when so called, this quadriennial communication stands over until said 24th day of June, at 12 o'clock meridian.

Attest: CALVIN C. BURT, 96°,
By SANFORD HUNT, 95°, *Grand Master,*
Deputy Grand Secretary.

Nov. 14, 1878.,
ᴅ*

Done in our Sanctuary, where abide Peace, Tolerance, Truth, and the fullness of all that is good, this 14th day of the Egyptian month Pachon, answering to the 14th day of the month of November, A. L. 5878, Vulgar Era, 1878.

Witness our hand and the Seal of the Sovereign Sanctuary, at the Valley of Jackson, this
[L. S.] Fourteenth day of November, Vulgar, or Christian Era, 1878.

CALVIN S. BURT, 96°,
Grand Master, E. M. R. of M. Ad vitem.
SANDFORD HUNT, 95°,
Deputy Grand Secretary.

The history of the Egyptian Masonic Rite of Memphis having grown out of the Old Rite, called the Ancient and Primitive Rite of Memphis, I give first the abridged history of that rite viz., as follows, and which will be followed up with the history of the E. M. R. of Memphis to the present time, and the following copies of charters and correspondence show how the Rite was instituted and propagated up to the break in the Rite, the expulsion of Seymour and the forming of a Sovereign Sanctuary in Chicago.—AUTHOR.

HISTORY

OF THE

EGYPTIAN MASONIC RITE OF MEMPHIS,

BEFORE CALLED

ANCIENT AND PRIMITIVE RITE,

From its first organization in America down to the reduction of
Degrees to 33 and the 96 Rite denounced by Seymour
and the 33° adopted and the 96° founded in
Chicago, 1867.

Jacques Etienne Marconis de Négre, in person,
established the first organization of the Ancient and
Primitive Rite New in York City, November 9, 1856,
under the name and title of " A Supreme Council,
Sublime Masters of the Great Work, Ninetieth De-
gree," and appointed the following as the first officers :
Ill. Bro. John Mitchell, 95th Degree, Sublime Dai ;
Ill. Bro. Samuel D. Wilson, 95th Degree, First
Mystagogue; Ill. Bro. Wm. F. Dubois, 93d Degree,
Second Mystagogue ; Ill. Bro. J. Franklin Wells,
94th Degree, Orator; Ill. Bro. John Hanna, 94th
Degree, Secretary ; Ill. Bro. John M. Atwood, 95th
Degree, Treasurer.; Ill. Bro. David McLelland, 95th
Degree, Archivist ; Ill. Bro. George T. Dollinger, 94th
Degree, Grand Expert; Ill. Bro. Theophilus Pratt,
95th Degree, M. of C.; Ill. Bro. Anthony Allaire,
94th Degree, Messenger of Science; Ill. Bro. Josiah
S. Grindle, 94th Degree, Guardian of the Sanctuary.

The following is a copy of the provisionary charter
or warrant, entitling the Council to work the degrees
to the Ninetieth Degree, inclusive ;

COPY OF THE ORIGINAL CHARTER, NINETIETH DEGREE.

A LA GLOIRE, DU SUBLIME ARCHITECTE DES MONDES,

Au Nom Du Grand Hiérophante,

SALUT SUR TOUS LES POINTS DU TRIANGLE.

RESPECT A L'ORDRE.

The Grand Hierophant, Sublime Master of the Light Sacred
Depositary of the Traditions, Supreme Chief of the Order,
Grand Elect of the Sacred Curtain, Sublime Commander of
the Three Legions of the Knights of the Order, Member of the
Alidee, decorated with the Grand Star of Sirius of Eleuisis,
President of the Temple of Mysteries 97th and last degree,
Honorary Grand Master of the Philosophical Persian Rite, one
of the Grand Commanders and Inspectors of the Rite of
Misraim Honorary Member of the Supreme Grand Council,
and Sovereign Grand Consistory of the Ancient and Accepted
Scotch Rite, Grand Dignitary of the Supreme Chapter of the
Royal Arch, etc., etc., and the members composing the Celestial
Empire of the Masonic Order of Memphis,

Declare regularly constituted the Supreme Council of the
Sublime Master of the Great Work, sitting in the Valley of
New York and let all know that this Council is authorized, 1st,
to take the title of Supreme Council of the Masters of the
Great Work 2d, to labor the 90th degree of our Antique and
Venerated Rite. 3d, to fix the price of the monthly receptions,
affiliations and cotisations. 4th, to confer the aforesaid degree
to each Mason who shall possess the qualities required from our
Masonic laws. Let all know equally that this Supreme Council is exempt from all contribution against the Celestial Empire,
and that the number of its members is unlimited The Sublime Dai is appointed for seven years, that he must comply
with and obey the General Statutes and Rules, and let them be
respected; that he must execute the labors as they are indicated
in the rituals, and to establish conferences in order to make
enjoy all the active members of the masonic and scientific instruction of the 90th degree. The Sublime Dai is bound to
deny the entrance of the Temple to any Brother not clothed
with the Masonic costume of his degree; to any Brother who
should not present himself in a decent and convenient condition; to any not active Brother who should not be bearer of a
title in due form.

The Very Illustrious and Very Enlightened Brother, John Mitchell being one of the principal founders of the aforesaid Council the Grand Hierophant declares, after the advice of the Patriarchs, Chie's of the Order, that he shall keep the Presidency during seven consecutive years, and that he could be re-elected.

In consequence of this we invite all the Masons who shall see the present writings to acknowledge to the aforesaid Council the rights and prerogatives which are granted to it by our General Statutes, desiring it may enjoy of the plentitude of its attributions. Given and approved in our Sanctuary where reposes the Venerated Arch, a place enlightened with a divine ray, where reigns peace, science, virtue, concord, union and the plentitude of all good.

VALLEY OF PARIS, the 7th day of the 5th month of the real light, 000,000,000, 1856, (Er. Vul.)

Enregistered on the Great Glod Book by us Grand Chancellor of the Order.

The G. Hierophant S. M. of the L. S D. of the Traditions, Sup. Chief of the Order. [L. S.]

DELAPLANA, 95° [L. S.]   J. ET MARCONIS DE NEGRE, 97°

G Arch Keeper of the Seals, (fol 354, No. 469.)

BARON OTHON DE BRAUNECKER, 95°. [L. S.]

M. LETRILLARD, 95°.   A. VEYRATY. 95°,
LARMARTIN, 95°,   MORISSAND, 95°,
COCHOY, 95°,   GARAY, 95°,
ROUX, 95°,   LIOULT, 95°,
S. ROLLIN, 95°,   MOREAU, 95°,
AUDIBERT, 95°,   H. VOISEMBERT, 95°,
DELIGNE, 95°,   PRE VILLARET, 95°,
H. DAUGY, 95°,   RUAUX, 95°,
SALARIER, 95°,   DAUMAS, 95°,
MORIZOT, 95°,   J. B HANSO DE VILLA, 95°
CORBISIER, 95°,   BURNET, 95°,
MERLANCHON, 95°.

Enregistered by us, G. Secretary, (fol. 347, No. 463,)

B. NETTER, 95°.   [L. S.]

March 1, 1857, Ill. and En. Bro.Marconis de Négre organized a "Sovereign Grand Council General,

Ninety-fourth degree, with Ill. Bro. David McLellan, Ninety-fifth degree, as Sovereign Grand Master." The following is a copy of the charter given into his hands:

COPY OF CHARTER OF THE NINETY-FOURTH DEGREE.

A LA GLOIRE DU SUBLIME ARCHITECTE DES MONDES,

Au Nom Du Grand Hierophante,

Sous les Auspices du G.·. Empire de l'Ordre Mac.·. de Memphis.

A TOUS LES MACONS REPANDUS SUR LES DEUX HEMISPHERES.

Salut, Amitie, Fraternite,

A TOUTES LES LOGES A TOUS LES CHAPITRES, AREOPAGES,

Senats et Conseils travaillant notre Rit Antique et Primitif.

Union, Prosperite, Courage, Force, Tolerance.

Nous G. Hierophante Sub. Maitre de la L. Chef. Sup. de l'Ordre et membres composant le Sanctuaire des Patriarches Grand Conservateurs de l'Ordre. Declarons Constituer par les presentes un Conseil Sup. du 94ᵉ Degre. Ce Souverain Grand Conseil General est autorise a travailler du 1ᵉ au 94ᵉ Degre de l'Ordre a la Vallee de New York sous la Presideuce de Notre T. . Ill. . et T.·. Cel·. F.·. David McLellan l'Un des Pat G. Conservateur de l'Ordre membre honoraire du G Empire, Prince de M., decore de la G. Etoile, de Sirius, de l'Alidee, de la toison d'or 95.·. D·. En consequence le Souverain Grand Conseil General, est autorise a fonder des Loges, Chapitres, Areopages, Senats et Conseils jusqu'au 90ᵉ Degre, en ce Conformant a l'article 29 titre 3 des Statuts genereaux de notre Rite antique et venere.

Nous invitons prions et ordonnons a toutes nos Loges, Chapitres, Areopages, Senats et Conseils, que ces presentes verront, de reconnaitre le sus dit Conseil en cette qualite, et d'accueiller favorablement tous les actes emanes de son sein, a moins qu'ils ne soient contraires, a nos lois sacrees, desirant que nos Atteliers, accordent un acceuil beinveillant a tous les ff.·. qui se presenteront de leur part, avec un titre en bonne et due forme et qu'ils recoivent les honneurs dus a leurs qualites Maconniques nous entendons qu'il en soit de meme de ceux crees par le sus dit conseil

Le rite Maconnique de Memphis, ayant inscrit la tolerance en tete de ses lois sacree, il ordonne a tous ses enfants de fraterniser avec les macous de tous les rits maconniques connus, et de es admettre dans leurs travaux, en consequence ce conseil ne pourra sous aucun pretexte enfreindre cette loi.

Le Souverain Grand Council General est autorise a faire un reglement particulier pour son administration interieur, et a fixer le prix des initiations, augmentation de salaire, des Diplomes, Brefs et Patentes.

Considerant qu'en Vertu d'une decision speciale du G Hierophante Chef Sup. de l'Ordre declarant qu'il ya urgence, ce conseil supreme est et sera considere comme etant conseil representatif de l'Ordre pour les Etats Unis d'Amerique.

Fait dans notre Sanctuaire ou repose l'arche Veneree des traditions, lieu eclaire d'un rayon divin ou regnent la paix, la concorde, l'union la science, et la plenitude de tous les biens.

Vallee de Paris, le 7ᵉ J.·. du 10ᵉ m.·. de l'an de la V.·. L.·. 000,000,000, 1857. (E. V.)

MARCONIS DE NEGRE, 97.·.
G.·. H.·. Chef.·. Sup.·.   [L. S.]

Enreg.·. sur notre Grand Livre d'Or, fol. 215, No. 329, le 17ᵉ J.·. du 10 ·. mois teveth de l'an de la V.·. L.·. 000,000,000, DELAPLANE, 95.·.   [L. S.]

B. NETTER, 95.·.
Gd.·. P.·. S.·.

LAMBERT, 95.·.
Gd ·. Ch.· D.·. L.·.

AUDIBERT, 95.·.
S.·. G.·. C..·

TH. LEVY, 95.·.
G.·. Et ·. D. . L ·.

CORDEY, 95.·.
P.·. Gr.·. C.·.

Enreg.·. Par nous G.·. Chancelier de l'Ordre fol. 7, No. 35, J. ROUWEL, 95 ·   [L. S.]

AD. DE POURDERLET, 95.·

Vu Par nous Grand Tresorier General de l'Ordre, fol. 87, No. 120.
E. SAMPSON, JR., 95.·.
G.·. T.·. G.·. D.·. L.·.   [L. S.]

H. F. LEVY, 95.·.
G.·. S.·. G.·. L.·.

Declarons Par les Presentes constitues egalement le College Lythurgique et le Supreme Conseil de Radiation.

MARCONIS DE NEGRE, 97 ·.
C.· LABROT, 95.·.   G.·. H.·. CHEF.·. SUP.·.

Ill. and En. Bro. de Negre, having seen these
bodies of the Rite well established, announced his
intended departure for his native land, and, at a
meeting of the Council held· March 25th, 1857, the
following resolutions were adopted, suitably engrossed, and presented to him :

Whereas, Our Most Ill. and En. Grand Hierophant is about to
return to his home in France, and in the consideration of the
distinguished favors he has with such liberal hands been pleased
to shower upon us ; it is

Resolved, That the sincere thanks of the officers and members
of this S. Council, Ninetieth Degree, be, and are hereby
tendered him, with the hope that he will believe us anxiously
solicitous of his safety and well being in his journey, wishing
that the Supreme Architect of the Universe may take him
under His especial care and long preserve him a monument of
every Masonic virtue.

Resolved, That a copy of the above be presented to Ill. Bro.
Marconis de Negre.

The first election of the Sup. Council, Ninetieth
Degree, was held May 2, 1857, when the following
officers were elected and appointed : Ill. Bro. John
Mitchell, Sub. Dai; Ill. Bro. Josiah S. Grindle, First
Mystagogue; Ill. Bro. Albert P. Moriarty, Second
Mystagogue ; Ill. Bro. Thomas S. Vaughn, Orator ;
Ill. Bro. M. L. Mann, Secretary; Ill. Bro. John M.
Atwood, Treasurer; Ill. Bro. Chas. C. J. Beck, Grand
Expert; Ill. Bro. Henry Gimber, Mess. of Science ;
Ill. Bro. P. J. Kiernan, Accompanier; Ill. Bro. J. B.
Hawkins, Guardian of the Sanctuary; Ill. Bro.
Hugh Flack, Sentinel.

May 16, 1857, the first translation of the Ritual
of the Rite was placed in the hands of the Sov.
Grand Master.

From this date during the years 1857 and 1858,
the Rite steadily increased in numbers and prosperity, many of the names most prominent in Free-

masonry were added to the Roll, and the Ancient and Primitive Rite stood first among all the Masonic organizations. This vast membership and unequaled progress, created the demand for the establishing of other bodies of the Rite, and November 29, 1859, the Sov. Grand Council was duly convened by Ill. Bro. David McLellan, Sov. Grand Master. A petition was received from a constitutional number of brethren and the first charter in America was granted for a Senate of " Knights Grand Commanders of the Temple," 35th degree, of which the following is a

COPY.

To the Glory of the Sublime Architect of the Universe:

IN THE NAME OF THE GRAND HIEROPHANT, UNDER THE AUSPICES OF THE GRAND EMPIRE OF THE MASONIC ORDER OF MEMPHIS.

Salutation. Friendship. Fraternity.

To all Lodges, Chapters, Areopages, Senates and Councils, working our Ancient and Primitive Rite.

UNION, PROSPERITY, COURAGE, STRENGTH AND TOLERANCE.

We, the Sov. Grand Master, Patriarch, member of the Mystic Temple, Representative of the Grand Hierophant, Decorated with the Grand Star of Sirius, the Cross of the Alidee, and the Golden Fleece, Grand Commander of the three Legions of the Knights of Masonry, &c., &c., and the President of the Liturgical College and Sov. Grand Tribunal of the Order,

By virtue of the supreme power with which we are invested, do constitute, and declare by this patent to be constituted, in the Valley of New York, a Senate of "Knights Grand Commanders of the Temple," 35th degree of the O.·.

And we further declare and proclaim our Very Ill. and Enlightened Bro. H. J. Seymour, Prince of Memphis, 94°, decorated with the Alidee and the Grand Star of Sirius, to be the "Prince Grand Commander," (President,) and the Ill and En. Bros. Sublime Masters of the Great Work whose names are herein written, to be officers of the said Senate, to wit: Peter W. Neefus, John Sheville, Albert P. Moriarty, O. H. Hart, W. J. Kay, Abraham

G. Levy, Albert Webb, J. W. Orr, Charles W. Merritt, William V. Brown, John Hanna, Thomas Orihuela, Charles J. Dodge, J. R. Carreras, Wm. V. Webster, John Wallace, Robert Latta, Hugh Gardener, Charles McDonald, P. A. Rink, Peter V. Yerance, Garrett Yerauce and Clement M. Hancox.

We, the Sov. Grand M., however, reserving to ourselves our prerogative to appoint the Archivist of the said Senate, and we further authorize and empower our Very Ill. and En. Brother, the Prince Grand Commander, and our Ill. and En. Brethren whose names are above written, to open and hold said Senate under the exclusive jurisdiction of the Sov. Grand Council General, and to confer the degrees hereaf'er specified, according to our Ancient and Primitive Rite, namely, from the 26th to the 35th, exclusively, and from the 4th to the 25th, inclusive, from the date of this patent, until the Sov. Grand Council General shall have constituted in the Valley of New York such Chapters, Areopages, Senates or Councils whose province it shall be to confer the degrees from the 4th to the 25th, inclusive. And we do further authorize and empower our Very Ill. and En. Brother, the Prince Grand Commander, and the officers of said Senate, to hear all cases and matters relative to the brethren within the jurisdiction of the said Senate, to install their successors in office after being elected and chosen ; to invest them with all the powers and dignities of their respective offices; and to deliver to them this patent ; and such successors shall, in like manner, install their successors and deliver the patent as above directed. All this shall they do, and all th s shall be, and hereby is, granted to them duiing the continuance of the said Senate.

Provided, always, that the above named Ill. and En. Brethren and their successors, do pay and cause to be paid all respect and obedience to the Sov. Grand Council General, its constitution, general rules and regulations, and also the general statutes of the Order, otherwise and upon the failure to conform to this provision, this patent of constitutions shall be void and of no force or virtue.

Done in our Sanctuary, where reigns Peace, Virtue Knowledge, and the fullness of all that is good. Witness our hand and seal. (Signed)

David McLellan, Sov. Gd. Master, P. G. C. of the O. 96th degree.

Valley of New York, the Twenty-eighth of the Eleventh Month of the Year of True Light 000,000,000, 1859 (E. V.)

(Signed) Samuel D. Wilson, P. Sov. Gd. Pont., 95th degree,

Registered in the Great Book of Gold, No. 93, 35. In conformity to the Statute.

(Signed) John Mitchell, Pr. Sov. G. I., of the Grand Tribunal, 95th degree.

The first meeting of this Senate was held May 11th, 1860.

July 13, 1860, the Sov. Grand Master conferred the 94th degree upon the following brothers belonging to the Sup. Council of the Ancient and Accepted Scottish Rite for the U. S. of America, to wit :

Edmund P. Hays, 33d degree, M. P. Sov. Grand Com.; Hopkins Thompson, 33d degree, 1st Lieut. Gr. Com.; Robert E. Roberts, 33d degree, Gr. Treasurer; George Osborn, 33d degree, Gr. Sec. Genl. H. E.; Wm. Jarvis, 33d degree, Captain of the Guard; Benjamin C. Leveridge, 33d degree, Gr. Orator and K. of S.; Charles W. Atwood, 33d degree.

And upon petition they were balloted for and elected as affiliated members of the Senate and Council.

Dec. 14, 1860, the Sov. Grand Master granted the Senate a dispensation to confer the degrees of the Rite from the 35th to and inclusive of the 42d.

Jan. 25, 1861, a charter was granted to organize a Senate in New Jersey, under the name and title of Excelsior Senate, No. 1, of New Jersey, located in Hoboken. The following were the first officers :

Ill. Bro. F. McDonough, Sub. Gr. Commander; Ill. Bro. James M. Riper, Sen. Kt. Interpreter; Ill. Bro. G. L. Hull, Jun. Kt. Interpreter; Ill. Bro. J. Harvey Lyons, Orator; Ill. Bro. Hazen Kimball, Recorder; Ill. Bro. J. H. Wilson, Treasurer; Ill. Bro. R. Thomas, Marshal; Ill. Bro. S. Bayles, Kt. of Introduction; Ill. Bro. Samuel Lemons, Jr., Accompanier; Ill. Bro. G. Sinclair, Guardian of the Sanctuary; Ill. Bro. T. W. Harndon, Sentinel.

April, 1861, the Sov. Grand Master, David McLellan, Major of the 79th Regiment of the National Guard, State of New York, being ordered to the seat of war, addressed the subjoined letter to Bro. Seymour:

26 SPRUCE STREET, N. Y., April 27, 1861.

Ill and En. Bro. H. J. Seymour:

Your note is received. Having volunteered to go with my regiment to the City of Washington, and my term of office—five years—having expired by limitation, I herewith forward to you the charter of the Sovereign Grand Council General, 94th degree, together with the original charter of the Grand Council, 90th degree, given to me by Ill. Bro. John Mitchell, and I wish it to be distinctly understood that the position of Sov. Grand Master which I now resign be occupied by you, and that all brothers of our beloved Rite recognize and obey you as the Sov. Grand Master of the Rite in America.

I am, respectfully and fraternally yours,

DAVID McLELLAN, 96th degree.

Upon the expiration of the term of office of Grand Master McLellan, he relinquished active supervision over the Rite, and, as seen in the foregoing letter, the executive powers devolved upon Ill. Bro. H. J. Seymour.

Ill. Bro. Mitchell having also resigned all jurisdiction of the Sup. Council, proceeded to the seat of war, where he lost his life while gallantly heading his company at the battle of Williamsburg, Va., May 5, 1862.

In June, 1862, Boston Senate, Forty-second Degree, was organized, with Ill. Brothers J. D. Jennings, Ninety-fourth Degree; A. K. P. Welch, Samuel C. Lawrence and others, as the first officers.

The Grand Council deeming it of interest to ascertain its status in Europe, delegated Ill. Bro. Seymour, and a voyage to the old world was resolved upon.

Accordingly he sailed for Europe, and in Glasgow he found the Rite in a prosperous condition, under

the administration of Ill. Bro. Donald Campbell.
Arriving in Paris, he was cordially received by the
Grand Hierophant, and found the Rite there working
under the auspices of the Grand Orient of France.

He was made the recipient of the high honorary
degrees, and obtained Letters Patent for the formation of "The Sovereign Sanctuary, A. and P. Rite,"
in and for the continent of America.

The following is a true copy of

THE CHARTER OF THE SOV. SANCTUARY.

A LA GLOIRE DU SUBLIME ARCHITECTE DES MONDES.

Au Nom Du Grand Hierophante.

Nous Grand Hierophante Sublime Maitre de la Lumiere depositaire Sacre des traditions, Chef Sup.˙. de l'ordre, ayant la
plus graude confiance dans la Sagesse et la science Maconnique
de notre tres Illustre et Tres Eclaire f.˙. H. J. Seymour:

Declarons en vertu de l'article 26 de nos Statuts generaux
nommer et elever par ces presents notre Tres Ill. . f.˙. H. J. Seymour Sublime mage 96 degre de l'Ordre decore de la grande
Etoile de Sirius, de l'Alidee, de la Chaine Lybique et du Ramean
d'or d'Elensis, Souv · Grand Maitre de l'Ordre, Maconnique de
Memphis en Amerique.

En Consequence, nous l'autorisons a fonder a la Vallee de
New York, une puissance maconnique de notre rite Antique et
Venere, compose, savoir, 1ᵉ d'un Sanctnaire de Memphis gouv-
ernment General de l'Ordre 95ᵉ, 2ᵉ d'un Temple Mystique administration 90ᵉ . d.˙. d. . L.˙.—3ᵉ d'un Souv.˙. grand conseil
general des grands Insp.˙. Reg.˙. 90ᵉ d.˙. et a fonder des Ateliers
Chapitres, Areopages, Senats, Consistoires et Conseils, travaillant du Premier au Quatre vingt quatorzieme degre de l'Ordre
pour la propagation des Lumieres et le bien de l'humanite. En
Consequence nous accordons a notre T.˙. Ill. . et T.˙. Ecl.˙ f.˙
H J. Seymour, la Suprematie du Sanctuaire de l'Ordre maconnique de Memphis en Amerique avec tous les droits et prerogatives attaches a cette haute dignite.

Fait et approuve par notre conseil Sup.˙. Vallee de Paris le
21ᵉ, jour du 6me mois de l'an de la V.˙. L.˙. 000,000,000, 1862:
(E. V.)

Le Grand Hierophaute Sublime Maitre de la Lumiere
Depositaire Sacre des Traditions,
Chef. Sup. de l'Ordre Maconnique
de Memphis.   [L. s]

J. ET MARCONIS DE NEGRE, 97.∴

Vu par nous Grand Chancelier Administra-
[L. s.]   teur General de l'Ordre No. 1375.

M. D. DURAND, 97.∴   P. PERNAUD, 95.∴

L'Orat.∴ de la D.∴ ▢ des Sectateurs de
Menes.

CH. FONDEURY, 95.∴   [L. s.

P. Le Secret.∴. General de l'Ordre Mac.∴
de Memphis.   [L. s.]

P. FABRE, 95.∴

[*Vised and Sealed by the following Officers of the Grand Orient of France.*]

⋯⋯⋯⋯⋯   Scelle et Enregistre Sous le No.
: Seal of :   28,911 du Gd Livre des Sceaux
: Secretary :
: Gen. G. O. :   du Grand Orient de France.
: of France. :
⋯⋯⋯⋯⋯   LE CHEF DU SECRETARIAT,

THEVENOT.

Vu et Fraternellemeut accueilli au Grand Orient de
France, O.∴ de Paris, ce 3 Septem-
bre, 1862, E ∴ V.∴   Le Grand   [L. s.]
Maitre adjoint de l'Ordre Maconni
que en France.

HEUILANT.

Vu et approuve
le Marechal de France, Grand Maitre
de l'Ordre Maconnique.   [L. s.]

MAGNAN.

TRANSLATION.

TO THE GLORY OF THE SUBLIME ARCHITECT OF THE WORLD.

In the name of the Grand Hierophant.

We, Grand Hierophant, Sublime Master of Light, Depositary of the Sacred Traditions, approving the past acts, having
confidence in the wisdom and masonic knowledge of our Illustrious and Enlightened Brother Harry J. Seymour, do by these
presents and in virtue of the 26th Article of the General Statutes of the Order, create, constitute, appoint our aforesaid Illustrious Enlightened Brother H. J. Seymour, Sublime Magi, 96th

degree, decorated with the Grand Star of Lucius, Cross of Alidee, the Lybique Chain, and the Golden Branch of Eleuses, Sovereign Grand Master of the Masonic Order of Memphis for America.

And we, Grand Hierophant, and we, members of the Sanctuary of Memphis, sitting in the Valley of Paris, do by this Patent authorize and empower our Illustrious Enlightened Brother Harry J. Seymour, 96th degree, to create, found and organize a Sovereign Sanctuary 95th degree in the Valley of New York, for the general government of the order in America, also a Mystique Temple and Sovereign Grand Council General 94th degree, for the regulation of the order, and also to create, found and establish Lodges, Chapters, Consistories, Senates, Areopages, Councils and Sov. Grand Councils Gen., working from the 1st to the 96th degree of the order, for the propagation of our Ancient and Primitive Rite, for all time.

Accordingly, by these presents, we declare, proclaim and certify our Very Illustrious and Very Enlightened dear Brother Harry J. Seymour, Supreme Chief *ad vitem* of the Masonic Order of Memphis for America, with all the rights and prerogatives attached to this high family.

Done and approved by our Council sitting in the Valley of Paris, this 21st day of the 6th month, in the year of true light, 000,000,000, A. D. 1862.

P. Le Secret. ·. General de l'Ordre Mac. ·.

    de Memphis.

[L. S.]   P. FABRE.

                L'Orat. ·. de la D. ·. ▭ des Sectateurs
                de Menes.

                           CH. FONDEURY, 96. ·.   [L. S.]

Scelle et Enregistre Sous le No.
    28,911 du Gd. Livre des Sceaux
    du Grand Orient de France.

    LE CHEF DU SECRETARIAT,

[L S]   THEVENOT.

                Vu et Fraternellement accusilli au Grand Orient de
                France, O. ·. de Paris, ce 3 Septem-
                bre, 1862, E. ·. V. ·.   Le Grand   [L. S]
                Maitre adjoint de l'Ordre Maconni-
                que en France.

        Vu par nous Grand Chancelier Administra-
[L. S.]   teur General de l'Ordre, No. 1,375.

                           M. D. DURAND, 97. ·.

[L. S.]   J. ET MARCONIS, 97. ·.

To the Glory of the Sublime Architect of the Universe.

MASONIC RITE OF MEMPHIS.

Peace. Tolerance. Truth.

SOVEREIGN SANCTUARY OF AMERICA OF THE MASONIC
RITE OF MEMPHIS.

OFFICE OF THE T. . I. · GRAND MASTER GENERAL,
VALLEY OF NEW YORK, [E. V.] Jan. 1865.

To all Masons to whom these presents may come, Greeting :

Know ye, that we, the Thrice Illustrious Grand Master General of the Ancient and Primitive Rite of Memphis in and for the Continent of America, by virtue of the high power in me vested by the Grand Orient of France, have and do by these presents, and do hereby declare and appoint our Very Illustrious Brother Calvin C Burt, for and during his natural life Deputy Grand Master General of the Ancient Primitive Rite of Memphis for the Continent of America, irrevocable, with full power to make Masons at sight, form Chapters, Senates, Councils, and do all other acts as fully and as valid as I myself can or could do. And, for the purpose of identity, have caused him to sign his name in full on the margin hereof.

Approved and given under my hand and seal, this 28th day of
[L. S.] February, E. V. 1865.

HARRY J. SEYMOUR, 96°,
T.·. Ill.·. G.·. M·. General.

The first meeting of the Sov. Sanc. was held Nov. 7, 1862, at which were present the following officers :
Ill. Bro. H. J. Seymour, Grand Master General; Ill. Bro. A. G. Levy, Grand Administrator; Ill. Bro.· Charles C. J. Beck, Grand Chancellor; Ill. Bro. Thos. Picton, Grand Secretary; Ill. Bro. P. W. Neefus, Grand Treasurer; Ill. Bro. H. F. L. Bunting, Grand Master of Ceremonies; Ill. Bro. J. F. Wells, Grand Keeper of the Temple; Ill. Bro. Nehemiah Peck, Grand Representative.

It was duly opened by the presentation of the Ill. Grand Master General's warrant of authority. Reso-

E

lutions were received from Councils and Senates, acknowledging its jurisdiction, and Ill. Bro. Seymour as the Most Ill. Grand Master General.

The following edict was issued on completion of permanent organization :

To the glory of the Supreme Architect of the World. In the name of the Sovereign Sanctuary of Ancient and Primitive Freemasonry, according to the Rite of Memphis, in and for the Continent of America. Salutation on all points- of the Triangle. Respect to the Order.

To all to whom these presents shall come, Greeting :

BE IT KNOWN, That the Grand Hierophant and Sublime Magi of the Rite of Memphis, in solemn conclave, assembled in their Sanctuary, No. 16 Rue Cadet, in the Valley of Paris, on the twenty-first day of the sixth month of the year one thousand eight hundred and sixty-two, did confer upon the undersigned, H. J. Seymour, the 96th Grade of the Ancient and Primitive Rite; and did, in approval of his Masonic services in propagating the Rite in America, grant the aforesaid a charter or warrant, constituting him Sovereign Grand Master General of the Rite of Memphis, *ad vitem*, in and for the Continent of America; vesting him with full powers to create and organize a Sovereign Sanctuary of Patriarchs, 95th degree, for the general government of the Rite in America: also, the power to organize Mystic Temples (Grand Councils General,) and to appoint their officers; also, to organize and grant warrants for the formation of Sublime Councils, Senates, Chapters, and other bodies of the Rite; also, the full power to confer from the fourth degree to the ninety fifth degree, inclusive, upon any person he shall deem worthy of that honor.

THEREFORE, I, the Sovereign Grand Master, do proclaim, in pursuance of the power in me vested, the following Patriarchs of the Rite to comprise the officers of the Sovereign Sanctuary of Ancient and Primitive Freemasonry in and for the Continent of America; and I require all Masons of our beloved Rite to recognize them in their high qualities as such, and to respect them accordingly, viz:

Ill. Bro. John J. Crane, M. D., 95th degree, Grand Administrator General; Ill. Charles C. J. Beck, 95th degree, Grand Chancellor General; Ill Bro. Robert D. Holmes, 95th degree, Grand Expert General; Ill. Bro. Thomas Picton, 95th degree, Grand

Secretary General; Ill. Bro. Peter W. Neefus, 95th degree, Grand
Treasurer General; Ill Bro. Abram G. Levy, M D., 95th de
gree, Grand Inspector General; Ill. Bro George F. Woodward,
M. D., 95th degree, Grand Examiner General; Ill. Bro. Bradley
Parker, M. D. 95th degree, Grand K. General of the G. Book;
Ill Bro. H. F L. Bunting, 95th degree, Grand Master General
of Ceremonies; Ill. Bro J. B Y. Sommers, 95th degree, Grand
Keeper General of the Sanctuary.

All of which is now officially promulgated and ordered to be
publicly announced in all Mystic Temples, Councils, Senates,
Chapters and other Bodies working our Ancient and Primitive
Rite.

Done in a Sacred Sanctuary, where repose Peace, Virtue, and
the fullness of all that is good; this, the Fourth day of the
Egyptian month Athir, in the year of True Light, 000,000,000
(answering to the Fourth day of June, one thousand eight hundred and sixty-three, vulgar era.)

In testimony of all which, I have hereunto affixed my signature
[L s] and seal.

H. J. SEYMOUR, 96th Degree,
Sovereign Grand Master.

Letters of acceptance from the first appointed officers of the Sovereign Sanctuary, were received and
placed on file.

A petition having been presented for a charter for
a Mystic Temple in the New England States, it was
duly granted, and the following is a true copy :

COPY OF CHARTER FOR NEW ENGLAND

MYSTIC TEMPLE, 94th DEGREE, PRINCES OF MEMPHIS.

To the GLORY of the SUPREME ARCHITECT of the
UNIVERSE.

"Do unto others whatsoever ye would that others should do unto you."

In the name of the Sovereign Grand Master, (Chief Supreme.)

Under the auspices of the Sov. Sanctuary, Sov. Patriarchs of the
Masonic Order of Memphis.

Salutation. Friendship. Fraternity.

TO ALL THE LODGES, CHAPTERS, ARE PAGES, SENATES AND
COUNCILS, WORKING OUR ANCIENT AND
PRIMITIVE RITE.

Union, Prosperity, Courage, Strength and Tolerance.

We, the Sovereign Grand Master (Chief Supreme,) and we the

Sov. Patriarchs, composing the Sov. Sanctuary of the Masonic Order of Memphis, by virtue of the Supreme Power with which we are invested by the Celestial Empire of Memphis, sitting in the Valley of Paris, under the cognizance of the Grand Orient of France: Do declare and proclaim that we have cre ited and constituted, and by these presents, do create and constitute a MYSTIC TEMPLE, Sovereign Princes of Memphis, 94th degree (Nov. Gd. Council General,) for the Valley of New England, comprising the States of Maine, New Hampshire, Vermont, Massachusetts, Rhode Island and Connecticut, with full powers to issue Dispensations and Charters for the formation of subordinate bodies, to work the degrees of the Ancient and Primitive Rite of the Masonic Order of Memphis, to the 90th degree, Sublime Masters of the Great Work, inclusive; subject, however, to the approval of the Sovereign Sanctuary sitting in the Valley of New York.

And we do further proclaim that our Very Ill. and En Brother Albion K. P. Welch, 95th degree, to be Gd. Mas. of Light; Very Ill. and En. Brother Samuel C. Lawrence, 94th degree, Gd Orator; Daniel W. Lawrence, 94th degree, Gd. Annalist (Sec'ty. ;) Benjamin F. Nourse,94th degree, Gd. Treasurer; Caleb C. Allen, 94th degree, Administrator (Examiner ;) Charles C. Southard, 94th degree, Keeper of Rites; James C. Bullen, 95th degree, Ceryce; John Davis Jennings, 95th degree, Representative.

And, we do further authorize and empower the aforesaid Mystic Temple (Sovereign Grand Council General,) to hear all causes and matters relative to the order within the above mentioned jurisdiction. and to install their successors into office, after having been duly elected and chosen, and to invest them with all the powers and dignities of their respective offices and to deliver to them these authorizations; and such successors shall in like manner install their successors, henceforth and forever.

Provided always, that the above named Ill. and En. Brethren and their successors, do pay and cause to be paid all due respect and obedience to the Sovereign Sanctuary, its constitution, rules and regulations, and also to the general statutes of the order. Otherwise, and upon the failure to conform to these provisions, this Patent of Constitution shall be void and of no force or virtue.

Done in our Sanctuary, wherein reigns Pe ce, Virtue, Knowledge, and the fullness of all that is good.

Valley of New York, the thirtieth day of the month Mec'ir, (June,) in the year of True Light 000,000,C00 (E. V.) 1863.

Signed,

> H. J. SEYMOUR, 96th degree,
> Sov. Gr. Mss. of Light,
> Chief Supreme of C. E.   [L. S.]

THOS. PICTON, Sov. Pat. 95th degree,
Secty. Genl. Celestial Empire.

JNO. J. CRANE, M. D., 95th degree,
Grand Administrator.

[L. S.]

J. B. YATES SUMMERS, 95th degree,
Grand K. of S.

CHAS. C. J. BECK, 95th degree,
Gd. Chancellor Celestial Empire.

ROBERT D. HOLMES, 95th degree,
Grand Expert.

[L. S.]

PETER W. NEEFUS, 95th degree,
Grand Treasurer.

HENRY F. L. BUNTING, 95th degree,
Grand Master of Ceremonies.

[L. S.]

GEO. F. WOODWARD, 95th degree,
Grand Examiner.

ABRAM G. LEVY, 95th degree,
Gd Inspector Genl. Celestial Empire

August 1863, a dispensation was granted for Sesostris Senate, No. 2. of New York, located in Brooklyn, to Ill. Bros. John B. Harris, R. W. Dockson, John
Ellard, T. E. Purdy, first officers.

March, 1864, Ill Bro. J. Q. A. Fellows, of New Orleans, La., was appointed Grand Master of Light,
Mystic Temple, Ninety-fourth degree, in and for the
State of Louisiana, and made an honorary member of
the Sov. Sanc.

June 11, 1864, the following appointments were
made by the Sov. Grand Master:

Ill. and En. Bro. Charles E. Gillett, Ninety-fourth
degree, Grand Representative in and for the State of
Michigan.

Ill. and En. Bro. Stephen H. Johnson, Ninety-fifth
degree, (Senior Grand Warden of the Grand ⌑, State

of New York,) Dep. Representative for the district in and about Schenectady, N. Y.

Ill. and En. Bro. Orrin Welch, Ninety-fifth degree, (R. E. Grand Com. of Kt. Templars, State of New York,) Dep. Representative for the district in and about Syracuse, N. Y.

Ill. and En. Bro. John L. Lewis, Ninety-fifth degree, (Past Grand Master of the Grand □, State of New York,) Dep. Representative for the district in and about Penn Yan, N. Y.

Ill. and En. Bro. Clinton F. Paige, Ninety-fifth degree, (Grand Master of the Grand □, State of New York,) Dep. Representative for the district in and about Binghamton, N. Y.

July 31, 1864, Zoroaster Senate, No. 3, of New York, was organized at New York, and the following duly installed as the first officers:

Ill. Bro. Andrew M. Underhill, Sub. Gr. Commander; Ill. Bro. Alvin Graff, Sen. Kt. Interpreter; Ill. Bro. Edward Bouton, Jun. Kt. Interpreter; Ill. Bro. D. Snedeker, Orator; Ill. Bro. J. H. LeBar, Recorder; Ill. Bro. David Graham, Marshal; Ill. Bro. J. H. Gardener, Kt. of Finance; Ill. Bro. Sewall Fisk, Sentinel.

Hermes Senate, No. 1, of District of Columbia, at Washington, was instituted September 5, 1864. Officers:

Ill. Bro. Rev. Robert M'Murdy, Sub. Gr. Commander; Ill. Bro. John F. Sharretts, Sen. Kt. Interpreter; Ill. Bro. Z. D. Gillman, Jun. Kt. Interpreter; Ill. Bro. Hon. Alexander W. Randall, Orator; Ill. Bro. Hon. Green Adams, Archivist; Ill. Bro. W. P. Dole, Recorder.

Sesostris Senate, No. 2, of New York, was dedicated, and its officers duly installed, December 21, 1864,

An official communication from the Grand Orient of France, dated Paris, May 1, 1865, No. 314, Vol. 30 of correspondence, was received by the Sovereign Sanctuary, notifying that body of the appointment by his Excellency, the Marshal Magnan, Grand Master of France, of M. W. Brother Robert D. Holmes as Grand Representative of the Grand Orient of France, near the Sov. Sanctuary : also a letter of thanks and acceptance of Grand Representative of Sov. Sanctuary, near the Grand Orient of France, from Ill. Bro. Heuilant, Thirty-third Degree.

Copy of appointment of M. W. Robert D. Holmes, as Grand Representative :

Grand Orient of France, Supreme Council for France and the French possessions:

PARIS, May 1, 1865.

Ill. Bro. ROBERT D. HOLMES:

I have the pleasure to inform you, that in compliance with the wish of the Grand Officers of the Rite of Memphis, our Grand Master, Marshal Magnan, has appointed you Representative of the Grand Orient of France, near the Grand Sanctuary of Memphis, sitting in the Valley of New York.

I feel assured that this appointment, upon which I congratulate you, will be fruitful in happy results to our Order, and for Masonry in general.

Accept, illustrious sir and brother, the assurance of our distinguished consideration and brotherly love.

CUSSSOLS,
Deputy Grand Master.

Copy of acceptance of Ill. Bro. Heuilant, Thirty-third Degree, Gd. Rep. to G. O. of France :

GRAND ORIENT OF FRANCE, Paris, April 27, 1865

Ill. Grand Master and Brethren:

I have received, with great satisfaction, the diploma sent me and have placed it in my library, where my eyes will naturally rest upon it whenever I sit down to write.

I had decided to retire from my official station, and only accepted the post of Deputy Grand Master when the difficult situation of Masonry in France seemed to call on every Mason for help, but I will act as your representative with all the zeal and devotion at my command

Accept the assurance of my Masonic sentiments and sincere wishes for the prosperity of our noble institution

HEUILANT,

Grand Officer, Chancellor of the Legion of Honor.

The first Chapter of Rose-Croix, Gramercy, No. 1, of New York, was instituted at New York, June, 1865. Officers:

Ill. Bro. W. P. Patten, Most Wise; Ill. Bro. J. O. Halsey, Senior Warden; Ill. Bro. H. M. Clark, Junior Warden; Ill. Bro. J. H. Forshay, Orator; Sir Kt. F. C. Van Orden, Captain of the Guard.

George Washington Rose-Croix Chapter, No. 2, of New York, was organized the same month at New York. Officers:

Ill. Bro. Andrew M. Copeland, Most Wise; Ill. Bro. W. T. Lloyd, Senior Warden; Ill. Bro. J. Lovelock, Junior Warden.

The Senate of Knights Commanders of the Temple, was reorganized as Samothrace Senate, No. 1, of New York, June 7, 1865. Officers:

Ill. Bro. Abram G. Levy, Sub. Gr. Commander; Ill. Bro. W. P. Patten, Sen. Kt. Interpreter; Ill. Bro. John Hanna, Jun. Kt. Interpreter; Ill. Bro. Thomas Bennett, Orator.

Seymour Senate, No. 2, of District Columbia, was instituted at Washington, August 7, 1865. Officers:

Ill. Bro. J. H. Rathbone, Sub. Gr. Commander; Ill. Bro. R. T. Campbell, Sen. Kt. Interpreter; Ill. Bro. E. W. Francis, Jun. Kt. Interpreter; Ill. Bro. John R. Thompson, Orator.

The Sovereign Grand Master General visited the Sixteenth Triennial Convocation of the Grand Encampment of Knights Templars of the United States, held at Columbus, Ohio, on the 5th, 6th, and 7th days of September, 1865; and there conferred the Degrees of the A. and P. Rite upon a number of prominent members of the Fraternity in that State.

Socrates Senate, No. 4, of New York, was instituted at Newburg, in the fall of 1865. Officers:

Ill. Bro. P. S. Haines, Sub. Gr. Commander; Ill. Bro. G. F. Wiltsie, Sen. Kt. Interpreter; Ill. Bro. David A. Scott, Jun. Kt. Interpreter; Ill. Bro. J. C. Chapman, Orator; Ill. Bro. John Dale, Recorder; Ill. Bro. Thomas P. Ramsdell, Kt. of Finance; Ill. Bro. S. Stanton, Marshal; Ill. Bro. John W. Forsyth, Kt. of Introduction; Ill. Bro. C. M. Leonard, Accompanier; Ill. Bro. Thomas W. Purdy, Captain of the Guard; Ill. Bro. J. H. H. Chapman, Guardian of the Sanctuary; Ill. Bro. Andrew Lawson, Sentinel.

Highland Rose-Croix Chapter, No. 8, of New York, was also organized at Newburg at the same time. Officers:

Ill. Bro. G. Fred Wiltsie, Most Wise; Ill. Bro. David A. Scott, Senior Warden; Ill. Bro. Samuel Stanton, Junior Warden; Ill. Bro. Joseph H. H. Chapman, Orator; Sir Kt. Thomas W. Purdy, Conductor; Sir Kt. John Dale, Archivist; Sir Kt. Thomas P. Ramsdell, Treasurer; Sir Kt. John W. Forsyth, Captain of the Guard; Sir Kt. Chauncey M. Leonard, Guard of the Tower; Sir Kt. Andrew Lawson, Sentinel.

At a meeting of the Sovereign Sanctuary, August 26, 1865, Ill. Brothers Guiseppe Garibaldi, Thirty-third Degree, Past Grand Master of the G. O. of Italy, and Francesco de Lucca, Thirty-third Degree, Grand Master of the Italian Freemasonry, were elected honorary members of the Sovereign Sanctuary; Ill. Bro. Ludovico Frapolli, Thirty-third Degree, was ap-

E*

pointed as the Grand Representative of the Sovereign Sanctuary, near the Grand Orient of Italy.

An official letter from Ill. Bro. G. Garibaldi, dated "Orient of Caprera, September 26, 1866," was received, acknowledging the reception of the appointment of Deputy Representative for Italy, and acceptance of the same.

Dispatches from the Grand Orient of Italy, dated "Turin, October 1, 1865," were received, in which the Grand Master, Francesco de Lucca and Ill. Bro. Frapolli, accepted the appointments given them by the Sovereign Sanctuary, and informed our Grand Body that Ill. Bro. John J. Crane, Thirty-third Degree, and the Ill. Grand Mas. Gen. H. J. Seymour, had been nominated and elected members of the Grand Orient of Italy.

Columbian Rose-Croix Chapter, No. 3, of New York, was organized at New York, June, 1866. Officers:

Ill. Bro. James Morrow, Most Wise; Ill. Bro. A. B. Barnes, Senior Warden; Ill. Bro. Jesse T. Dingee, Junior Warden; Ill. Bro. John Shannon, Orator; Sir Kt. George W. Sloan, Conductor; Sir Kt. William H. Jones, Archivist; Sir Kt. W. H. Bromley, Treasurer; Sir Kt. Charles S. Abbott, Captain of the Guard; Sir Kt. J. H. Mendenhall, Guard of the Tower; Sir Kt. Edwin Reynolds, Prelate; Sir Kt. A. F. Carpenter, Organist; Sir Kt. James McCaughie, Sentinel; Sir Kts. C. S. Abbott, P. McKay, Robert Birnie, Trustees.

Architect Rose-Croix Chapter, No. 4, of New York, was organized at Yorkville, August, 1866. Officers:

Ill. Bro. James Gorton, Most Wise; Ill. Bro. W. H. Marshall, Senior Warden; Ill. Bro. Richard Banfield, Junior Warden; Ill. Bro. Moses Bernhard, Orator;

Sir Kt. Richard Schofield, Conductor. Sir Kt. William A. Conklin, Archivist; Sir Kt. J. T. Van Winkle, Treasurer; Sir Kt. J. A. Pendleton, Captain of the Guard; Sir Kt. Herman Elstroth, Guard of the Tower; Sir Kt. W. H. Merriam, Sentinel.

Primitive Rose-Croix Chapter, No. 5, of New York, was organized at New York, September 7, 1866. Officers:

Ill. Bro. Benjamin S. Hill, Most Wise; Ill. Bro. Charles Latour, Senior Warden; Ill. Bro. Geo. Russ, Junior Warden; Ill. Bro. Robert Boyd Hardy, Orator; Sir Kt. John S. Loughery, Conductor; Sir Kt. H. Clay Lanius, Archivist; Sir Kt. William Scott, Treasurer; Sir Kt. H. R. Chapman, Captain of the Guard; Sir Kt. Adam White, Guard of the Tower; Sir Kt. Robert John Somerville, Prelate; Sir Kt. Richard Horner, Organist; Sir Kt. Andrew Ferguson, Sentinel; Sir Kts. J. Macdonald, William Fullager, John T. Davis, Trustees.

Passaic Rose-Croix Chapter, No. 1, of New Jersey, was organized at Newark, September 24, 1866. Officers:

Ill. Bro. James B. Taylor, Most Wise; Ill. Bro. William D. Rutan, Senior Warden; Ill. Bro. David Ayres, Junior Warden; Ill. Bro. Jacob W. Crane, Orator; Sir Kt. Eliphalite Smith, Jr., Archivist; Sir Kt. William Prinver, Treasurer; Sir Kt. Edw. Pressinger, Captain of the Guard; Sir Kt. Francis Bell, Guard of the Tower; Sir Kt. David A. Johnson, Prelate; Sir Kt. William O'Brien, Sentinel.

Olive Branch Rose-Croix Chapter, No. 6, of New York, was organized at Brooklyn, October 17, 1866. Officers:

Ill. Bro. Charles Latour, Most Wise; Ill. Bro. Henry E. Day, Senior Warden; Ill. Bro. J. Windle Fowler,

Junior Warden; Ill. Bro. A. G. Bishop, Orator; Sir
Kt. William J. Read, Conductor; Sir Kt. J. W. Buck-
bee, Archivist; Sir Kt. H. L. Foote, Treasurer; Sir
Kt. Hiram Bloomer, Jr., Captain of the Guard; Sir
Kt. Lawrence Tower, Guard of the Tower; Sir Kt.
W. F. Gilbert, Organist; Sir Kt. J. W. Hastings, Sen-
tinel; Sir Kts. William McBride, William E. Sprague,
J. W. Burnham, Trustees.

Oriental Rose Croix Chapter, No. 1, of the District
of Columbia, was organized at Washington, November, 1866. Officers:

Ill. Bro. J. B. Will, Most Wise; Ill. Bro. John
Lockie, Senior Warden; Ill. Bro. A. G. Dietrick, Jun
ior Warden.

Ancient Rose-Croix Chapter, No. 2, of the District
of Columbia, was organized at Washington, November, 1866. Officers:

Ill. Bro. John R. Thompson, Most Wise; Ill. Bro.
George W. Francis, Senior Warden; Ill. Bro. Stephen
A. Doyle, Junior Warden; Ill. Bro. Robert A. Cham-
pion, Orator; Sir Kt. M. H. Dillon, Conductor; Sir Kt.
H. O. Hood, Archivist; Sir Kt. C. F. Jarvis, Treas-
urer; Sir Kt. M. B. Gordon, Captain of the Guard;
Sir Kt. Albert Partridge, Guard of the Tower; Sir
Kt. T. Creaser, Sentinel.

Hercules Sublime Council, No. 1, of the District of
Columbia, was organized at Washington, the same
month.

January 4th, 1867, a charter was granted for a
Mystic Temple, 32d degree, Princes of Memphis, for
the State of Louisiana, and the following were appointed the first officers:

Ill. Bro. J. Q. A. Fellows, Grand Master of Light;
Ill. Bro. Edward Barnett, Grand Orator; Ill. Bro.
William R. Whittaker, Grand Annalist; Ill. Bro.

Thomas O. May, Grand Treasurer; Ill. Bro. J. P.
Buckner, Grand Ceryce; Ill. Bro. Robert Watson,
Grand Keeper of Rites; Ill. Bro. E. T. Parker, Grand
Examiner; Ill. Bro. Harry T. Hayes, Grand Master
of Ceremonies; Ill. Bro. Thomas Cripps, Grand Con-
ductor; Ill Bro. J. B. Walton, Grand Guard of the
Council; Ill. Bro. Alfred Shaw, Grand Representative.

At the same time, January, 1867, charters were
issued for Mizraim Chapter, No. 1, of Louisiana, and
No. 15 of the Sovereign Sanctuary; Heliopolis Senate,
No. 1, of Louisiana, and No. 10 of the Sovereign
Sanctuary; and Delta Sublime Council, Thirtieth
Degree, No. 1 of Louisiana, and No. 2 of the Sover-
eign Sanctuary, all at New Orleans.

OFFICERS OF MIZRAIM CHAPTER.

Ill. Bro. Hugh Breen, Most Wise; Ill. Bro. W. C.
Driver, Senior Warden; Ill. Bro. J. W. Davis, Junior
Warden; Ill. Bro. John Anderson, Orator; Sir Kt.
A. W. Benedict, Conductor; Sir Kt. J. W. Pearce,
Archivist; Sir Kt. D. C. Johnson, Treasurer; Sir Kt.
J. D. Scott, Captain of the Guard; Sir Kt. Andrew
Heero, Guard of the Tower; Sir Kt. T. Carroll, Pre-
late; Sir Kt. Thomas Cripps, Organist; Sir Kt. T. D.
Clarke, Sentinel.

OFFICERS OF HELIOPOLIS SENATE.

Ill. Bro. W. L. Stanford, Sub. G. Com.; Ill. Bro. J.
Anderson, Senior Knight Interpreter; Ill. Bro. W. C.
Driver, Junior Knight Interpreter; Ill. Bro. C. L.
Walker, Orator; Ill. Bro. B. R. Lawrence, Recorder;
Ill. Bro. D. C. Johnson, Knight of Finance; Ill. Bro.
C. H. Reed, Archivist; Ill. Bro. J. D. Scott, Marshal;
Ill. Bro. J. H. Behan, Knight of Introduction; Ill.
Bro. J. W. Davis, Accompanier; Ill. Bro. T. Carroll,
Captain of the Guard; Ill. Bro. A. Heero, Standard

Bearer; Ill. Bro. J. W. Pearce, Sword Bearer; Ill. Bro. T. D. Clarke, Guardian of the Sanctuary; Ill. Bro. T. Cripps, Organist; Ill. Bro. H. Breen, Sentinel.

OFFICERS OF DELTA SUBLIME COUNCIL.

Ill. Bro. J. W. Davis, Sublime Dai; Ill. Bro. H. Breen, First Mystagogue; Ill. Bro. W. C. Driver, Second Mystagogue; Ill. Bro. J. Anderson, Orator; Ill. Bro. J. W. Pearce, Secretary; Ill. Bro. D. C. Johnson, Treasurer; Ill. Bro. A. Heero, Grand Expert; Ill. Bro. A. W. Benedict, Archivist; Ill. Bro. J. D. Scott, Messenger of Science; Ill. Bro. B. R. Lawrence, Accompanier; Ill. Bro. W. L. Stanford, Standard Bearer; Ill. Bro. T. D. Clarke, Sword Bearer; Ill. Bro. T. Carroll, Guardian of the Sanctuary; Ill. Bro. T. Cripps, Organist; Ill. Bro. C. H. Reed, Sentinel.

The M. Ill. G. Master visited Peoria, Illinois, and on the 9th of February, 1867, instituted Pyramid Rose Croix Chapter, No. 1, of Illinois. Officers:

Ill. Bro. Justin E. Dow, Most Wise; Ill. Bro. Thos. D. Gautt, Senior Warden; Ill. Bro. C. A. Rich, Junior Warden; Ill. Bro. William Rounseville, Orator; Sir Kt. Charles Spalding, Conductor; Sir Kt. W. Copeland, Archivist; Sir Kt. M. E. Erler, Treasurer; Sir Kt. J. Higbie, Captain of the Guard; Sir Kt. F. M. Barrett, Guard of the Tower; Sir Kt. Samuel Tart, Prelate; Sir Kt. F. M. Reinhart, Organist; Sir Kt. T. H. Randolph, Sentinel.

Isis Senate of H. P., 20th degree, No. 1, of Illinois, was instituted at the same time and place, and the following officers installed:

Ill. Bro. Wm. Rounseville, Sub. Grand Commander; Ill. Bro. C. Spalding, Senior Knight Interpreter; Ill. Bro. Samuel Tart, Junior Knight Interpreter; Ill. Bro. W. Y. Francis, Orator; Ill. Bro. W. Copeland,

Recorder; Ill. Bro. M. E. Erler, Knight of Finance; Ill. Bro. F. M. Barrett, Archivist; Ill. Bro. J. E. Dow, Marshal; Ill. Bro. F. M. Reinhart, Knight of Introduction; Ill. Bro. D. Spencer, Accompanier; Ill. Bro. John Higbie, Captain of the Guard; Ill. Bro. H. E. Seley, Standard Bearer; Ill. Bro. T. D. Gautt, Sword Bearer; Ill. Bro. T. H. Randolph, Sentinel.

Cheops Rose-Croix Chapter, No. 2, of Illinois, was instituted at Peoria, February 24, 1867. Officers:

Ill. Bro. Louis Furst, Most Wise; Ill. Bro. J. P. Singer, Senior Warden; Ill. Bro. J. Lorenz, Junior Warden; Ill. Bro. Marx Moses, Orator.

Diogenes Senate, No. 2, of Illinois, was organized at the same time and place. Officers:

Ill. Bro. J. N. Neglas, M. D., Sub. Grand Commander; Ill. Bro. Aug. Rcen, Senior Knight Interpreter; Ill. Bro. Henry Ullman, Junior Knight Interpreter; Ill. Bro. G. Stiehl, Sentinel.

NOTE.—Cheops Chapter and Diogenes Senate, work in the German language.

Covenant Rose-Croix Chapter, No. 5, of Illinois, was organized April 24, 1867, by the Gd. Mas. Gen., assisted by Ill. Bro. William Rounseville, Thirty-third Degree, at Eureka. Officers:

Ill. Bro. David P. N. Sanderson, Most Wise; Ill. Bro. J. A. Davis, Senior Warden; Ill. Bro. L. T. Blair, Junior Warden; Ill. Bro. E. P. Hall, Orator; Sir Kt. Thomas Bullock, Jr., Conductor; Sir Kt. James W. Finley, Archivist; Sir Kt. Peter Bennage, Treasurer; Sir Kt. Thomas H. Gray, Captain of the Guard; Sir Kt. Alonzo Hale, Guard of the Tower; Sir Kt. Sylvester Wright, Prelate; Sir Kt. W. G. Vandyke, Sentinel.

Emanuel Rose-Croix Chapter, No. 3, of Illinois, and No. 17 of the Sanctuary, was instituted, and the following officers for the ensuing year were installed and inducted into office in A. and P. form, at Pekin, during the same month:

Ill. Bro. Dr. Samuel Wagenseller, Most Wise; Ill. Bro. N. W. Green, Senior Warden; Ill. Bro. Henry Wilkey, Junior Warden; Ill. Bro. John S. Milam, Orator; Sir Kt. John Cohonour, Conductor; Sir Kt. W. W. Clemens, Archivist; Sir Kt: Peter Weyrich, Treasurer; Sir Kt. F. S. Hubbler, Captain of the Guard; Sir Kt. W. H. Siebert, Guard of the Tower; Sir Kt. John B. Orr, Sentinel.

Jubulum Rose-Croix Chapter, No. 4, of Illinois, at Moawequa, Zodiac Rose-Croix Chapter, No. 6, of Illinois, at Chillicothe, and Bezaleel Rose-Croix Chapter, No. 7, of Illinois, at Lacon, were organized during the same Spring.

Eleuisis Rose-Croix Chapter, No. 1, of Iowa, was organized April 30, 1867, at Burlington. Officers:

Ill. Bro. Mortimer E. Gillette, Most Wise; Ill. Bro. William E. Woodward, Senior Warden; Ill. Bro. Warner Miller, Junior Warden; Ill. Bro. Samuel W. Snow, Orator; Sir Kt. Logan Steece, Conductor; Sir Kt. E. C. Parsons, Archivist; Sir Kt. Geo. A. McArthur, Treasurer; Sir Kt. Samuel J. Lane, Captain of the Guard.

Karnak Senate of H. P., No. 1, of Iowa, was organized at Burlington, April 30, 1867. Officers:

Ill. Bro. William E. Woodward, Sub. Grand Commander; Ill. Bro. R. M. Raab,Sen. Knight Interpreter; Ill. Bro. Samuel J. Lane, Junior Knight Interpreter; Ill. Bro. William Bolton, Orator; Ill. Bro. H. R. Rhein, Recorder; Ill. Bro. Samuel Lehman, Knight of Finance; Ill. Bro. Solomon Kohn, Archivist; Ill. Bro. M. E. Gillette, Marshal; Ill. Bro. E. C. Parsons, Knight of Introduction; Ill. Bro. S. W. Snow, Accompanier;

Ill. Bro. Frank X. Kuechen, Captain of the Guard; Ill. Bro. G. A. McArthur, Standard Bearer; Ill. Bro. Christian Miller, Sword Bearer; Ill. Bro. J. M. Broad, Sentinel.

Pythagoras Senate of H. P., No. 3, of Illinois, was organized at Eureka, May 9, 1867. Officers:

Ill. Bro. David P. N. Sanderson, Sub. Grand Commander; Ill. Bro. Sylvester Wright, Senior Knight Interpreter; Ill. Bro. B. D. Meek, Junior Knight Interpreter; Ill. Bro. James N. Finley, Recorder; Ill. Bro. J. A. Davis, Knight of Finance; Ill. Bro. Henry Damerill, Archivist; Ill. Bro. E. P. Hall, Orator; Ill. Bro. Thomas Bullock, Jr., Marshal; Ill. Bro. Sampson Shockley, Knight of Introduction; Ill. Bro. J. J. Rassmussen, Accompanier; Ill. Bro. L. T. Blair, Captain of the Guard; Ill. Bro. Thomas H. Gray, Standard Bearer; Ill. Bro. Ezra P. Meek, Sword Bearer; Ill. Bro. Alonzo Hale, Guardian of the Sanctuary; Ill. Bro. John G. Wood; Sentinel.

E. A. Guilbert, P. G. Master Grand Lodge of Iowa; R. W. Simeon D. Welling; R. W. Geo. B. Van Saun; R. W. F. H. Griggs; R. W. James L. Enos; R. W. J. Chapman, and R. W. T. Schriener, received the degrees at the Annual Grand Lodge Communication at Burlington, Iowa, 1867.

Sirius Sublime Council, 30th Degree, No. 1, of Illinois, was organized at Peoria, on Wednesday, June 12, 1867. Officers:

Ill. Bro. J. N. Neglas, Sublime Dai; Ill. Bro. H. E. Seley, First Mystagogue; Ill. Bro. D. T. N. Sanderson, Second Mystagogue; Ill. Bro. William McLean, Orator; Ill. Bro. M. E. Erler, Treasurer; Ill. Bro. Charles Spalding, Secretary; Ill. Bro. George Broad, Grand Expert; Ill. Bro. John G. Treager, Standard Bearer; Ill. Bro. William Oberhouser, Sword Bearer;

Ill. Bro. D. W. Meek, Messenger of Science; Ill. Bro. Charles A. Rich, Archivist; Ill. Bro. C. W. Carroll, Accompanier; Ill. Bro. J. M. Eiser, Guardian of the Sanctuary; Ill. Bro. F. M. Barrett, Sentinel.

Here the Edict reducing Degrees to Thirty-three was made known.

Marconis de Négre having surrendered the title of Grand Hierophant, and vested the control of the Ancient and Primitive Rite in the Grand Orient of France; December the 20th, 1685, the Sovereign Sanctuary adopted and issued the following in 1867:

About this time Seymour, the Grand Master, came to Illinois for the purpose of informing the Memphis Masons in that State, and the Author, who was a Grand Magi and Deputy Grand Master in the original Memphis Rite of 96° There was at that time completed, or nearly so, by the Author, two Councils 90°, two Senates 48°, and ten Rose-Croix Chapters 18°, and about one hundred 90° unaffiliated Masons. The Edict or pretended reduction was as follows:

EDICT.

To the Glory of the Supreme Architect of the Universe. In the name of the Sovereign Sanctuary of Ancient and Primitve Freemasonry according to the Rite of Memphis, in and for the Continent of America, sitting in the Valley of New York. Salutation on all points of the Triangle. Respect to the Order:

To all Masons to whom these presents shall come, Greeting:

Whereas, The Grand Orient of France, and the Grand Bodies of the Masonic Rite of Memphis, have mutually agreed that there shall be but Thirty-three Degrees; the 31st, 32d, and 33d of which shall be conferred only by authorization of the Supreme Body; and

Whereas, Said agreement was solemnly ratified by the late Ill. Brother, the Marshal Magnan, 33d degree, Grand Master of Masons for France and the French possessions, and the Ill. Bro. Marconis de Négre, and the officers of the Grand Orient and Rite of Memphis; and

Whereas, The Officers and Members of the Ancient and Primitive Rite of Memphis, deem it for the best interests of the Rite and Masonry generally, that the degrees be condensed; thereby concentrating the sublime Morals, Symbols, Allegories, Antique Legends and Philosophical Dissertations, into Thirty three degrees, the better to maintain its unity, exercise benevolence, propagate knowledge, and avoid the differences which unhappily exist in other Masonic Rites:

Therefore, We, the Grand Master General, by and with the advice and consent of the Grand Officers of the Ancient and Primitive Rite *do hereby agree* that the Ancient and Primitive Rite of Memphis shall consist of Thirty-three Degrees, divided as hereinafter designated:

Section I —Chapter of Rose Croix.

4th Degree, Discreet Master; 5th Degree, Sublime Master; 6th Degree, Sacred Arch: 7th Degree, Secret Vault; 8th Degree, Knight of the Sword; 9th Degree, Knight of Jerusalem; 10th Degree, Knight of the Orient; 11th Degree, Rose-Croix.

Section II.—Senate of Hermetic Philosophers.

12th Degree, Knight of the Red Eagle; 13th Degree, Knight of the Temple; 14th Degree, Knight of the Tabernacle; 15th Degree, Knight of the Serpent; 16th Degree, Knight Kadosh; 17th Degree, Knight of the Royal Mystery; 18th Degree, Grand Inspector; 19th Degree, Sage of Truth; 20th Degree, Hermetic Philosopher.

Section III.—Sublime Council.

21st Degree, Public, Grand Installator; 22d Degree, Public, Grand Consecrator; 23d Degree, Public, Grand Eulogist; 24th Degree, Patriarch of Truth; 25th Degree, Patriarch of the Planispheres; 26th Degree, Patriarch of the Sacred Vedas; 27th Degree Patriarch of Isis; 28th Degree, Patriarch of Memphis; 29th Degree, Patriarch of the Mystic City; 30th Degree Master of the G∴ W∴ P∴ P∴

Section IV.—Official.

31st Degree, Grand Defender of the Rite; 32d Degree, Sublime Prince of Memphis; 33d Degree, Sov. Grand Conservator of the Rite.

And, furthermore, it is decreed, that the Ancient and Primitive Rite do now and forever waive and renounce all claim over the first three or Symbolic Degrees, and that no person shall be received unless he be a Master Mason in good standing.

(Signed,)

H. J. Seymour, 33°, *M Ill. Sov. Grand Master General.*
John J. Crane. M. D . 33°, *Grand Administrator General.*
John W. Simons, 33°, *Grand Chancellor General.*
Robert D. Holmes, 33°, *Grand Expert General.*
James B. Taylor, 33°, *Grand Secretary General.*
Peter W. Neefus, 33°, *Grand Treasurer General.*
Bradley Parker, M.D , 33°, *Gr. Keeper. Gen of the Golden Book.*
Henry F. L Bunting, 83°, *Grand Master of Cer. General.*
John J. Thompson, 33°, *Grand Guardian of the Sanctuary.*
A. M. Underhill, 33°.
John Hanna 33°.
P. S. Haines, 33°.

The New York Masons generally refused to consent to the reduction, and the chief officers of the Sanctuary came out in a card and refused to have any further Masonic intercourse in the Rite, dissolved the body that had existed for some time, and published the following in the public prints of New York and elsewhere, viz:

CARD.

NEW YORK, Nov. 30, 1867.

The undersigned members of the Ancient and Accepted Rite of Freemasonry, and attached to the Supreme Council of the Northern Jurisdiction by active and honorary membership, claiming their allegiance to that body as superior to any other system of ineffable Masonry, have dissolved their connection with Harry J. Seymour and the A and P. Rite of Memphis; and hereby declare unauthorized the further use of our names in connection therewith.

JOHN W. SIMONS, 33°
CLINTON F. PAIGE, 33°
ORRIN WELCH. 33°
JOHN L. LEWIS, 33°

Although the foregoing edict of the Grand Orient of France purports to have been issued two years before, so secret had been the proceedings, that none save Seymour was aware of its action and the reduction.

But the publication of this card from four of the leading Masons in the United States, was the last straw that broke the camel's back, and everything was in a state of turmoil, and confusion reigned supreme; the temple was destroyed, and Seymour and the few that followed him, renounced the 96th Degree Rite of Memphis, and the Memphis Masons of Illinois founded the present institution, which has elected and installed officers ever since, and is to-day the only true or legal head of Egyptian or Memphis Masonry in America.

[See first part of this book for the Convention in Chicago, June 17, 1867.—AUTHOR.]

ABRIDGED HISTORY

OF THE

EGYPTIAN MASONIC RITE OF MEMPHIS.

Before collecting the various evidences of antiquity
of this venerable order, whose records were and had
been musty with age long before even the Pyramids
were begun or finished, which would give a date of
at least 2500 years before the Christian Era date began, I quote from a work recently written in New
York, called the General History and Encyclopedia
of Freemasonry, edited and published by Mr. Robert
Macoy, an authentic modern writer, who has with
considerable labor and ability condensed the history
of the Masonic Rite, and on page 124, under the
head of the Egyptian Masonic Rite says, "according
to Heroditus, the secret institution of Isis, with its
wonderful mysteries and imposing ceremonies, made
its appearance simultaneously with the organization
of Egyptian society and the birth of Egyptian
civilization."*

At first, says Mr. Macoy, who copies from others,
the initiation was probably a simple mystic drama,
representing the progress of man from a barbarous
to a civilized state, and his advancement and strug-
gles through gloom and terror towards a supreme
perfection, whether in time or in eternity. This is

---

*This being about 250,000 years before the Christian era, for
Egypt had been twice in Barbarism and is now in a semi barbarous state, when the Bible history began its date.

seen in the hieroglyphical representation of the judgment of *Amenti*. It was a picture of an ordeal or scrutiny to which the candidate was subjected preparatory to initiation. The ceremonies of initiation itself was a progress through gloom and terror, and all possible mental terrors, toscenes of indescribable beauty and glory.

The principal seat of the mysteries was at Memphis, (commonly called Memphi.) They were of two kinds, the greater and the lesser; the former taught by the Priests of Isis and Serapis, the latter by those of Osiris. The candidate was required to furnish proof of a pure life as an evidence that he was fitted for enrollment, (in our parlance that he was worthy.) When these conditions were fulfilled, he was required to spend a week in solitude and meditation, abstain from all unchaste acts and confine himself to a light diet, and to purify his blood by frequent ablutions and severe mortifications of the flesh. Being thus prepared, the candidate was ordered to enter the pyramid during the night, when he had to descend on his hands and knees through a narrow passage without steps, until he reached a cave-like opening, through which he had to crawl to another subterranean cave, on the wall of which he found inserted the following words : "*The mortal who shall travel over this road alone without hesitancy or looking behind*, shall be punished by fire, by water and by air, and if he can surmount the fear of death he shall emerge from the bosom of the earth, he shall revisit the light and claim the right to prepare his soul for the reception of the mysteries of the great God Osiris. At the same time three priests, disguised in masks resembling the heads of jackals, and armed with swords, sought to frighten him, first

by their appearance and voice, afterwards by enu-
merating the dangers that waited him on his journey.
If his courage did not fail him here, he was permitted
to pass on to the hall of fire. This was a large
apartment lined with burning stuffs, and whose floor
was a grate painted to flame color; the bars of this
grate were so narrow that they offered scarcely room
enough for him to cross. Through this hall he was
obliged to pass with the greatest of speed to prevent
being burned and avoid the intense heat and flame.
He next encountered a wide channel fed from the
waters of the Nile. Over this stream he was
obliged to swim, with a small lamp, which furnished
all the light that was afforded him. On reaching the
opposite side, he found a narrow passage leading to a
landing place about six feet square, the floor of
which was made movable by mechanism underneath;
on each side were walls of rough stone, and behind
wheels of metal were fixed; in front was a gate of
ivory opening inward and preventing any further
advance. On attempting to turn two large rings
annexed to the door in hopes of continuing his
journey, the wheels came into motion, producing a
most terrific and stunning effect, and the floor gave
way, leaving him suspended by the arms over appa-
rently a deep abyss, from which proceeded a violent
and piercing current of cold air, so that the lamp
was extinguished, and he remained in complete
darkness. In this process of trial, it will be observed that the candidate was exposed to the action
of the four great purifying elements—Earth, Air,
Fire and Water. After the risk of falling into an
unknown depth, continued for a moment or two, the
floor resumed its original position, the wheels ceased
to revolve, and the doors of ivory flew open, disclos-

ing the Sanctuary of Isis, illuminated with a blaze
of light, where the priests of that goddess were
assembled, drawn up in two ranks, clothed in ceremonial dresses, and bearing the mysterious symbols
of the order, singing hymns in praise of their
divinity, who welcomed and congratulated him on
his courage and escape from the danger which had
surrounded him. The entrance to the Sanctuary
was constructed in the pedestal of the triple statue
of Isis, Osiris and Horus, and the walls were orna-
mented with various allegorical figures, symbols of
the Egyptian mysteries, among which were particularly prominent, 1st, the figure of a serpent throwing
an egg out of its mouth, a symbol of the production
of all things by the heat of the sun ; 2d, a serpent
curled up in the form of a circle, holding its tail in
its mouth, an allusion to eternity, and to the uninter-
rupted revolution of the sun ; 3d, the double tau,
which is meant to represent the active and passive
power of nature in the production and generation of
all things. Then he was made to kneel before an
altar, and required to pronounce the following solemn
obligation : " I swear never to reveal to any uninitiated person the things I have seen in this Sanctuary,
nor any of the mysteries which have been or shall
hereafter be communicated to me. I call on all the
Deities of earth, heaven, hell, and the infernal
regions, to be witness of this oath, and I trust that
their vengeance will fall on my head should I ever
become a villain so base and perjured." He was
then retained for a period of several months in the
Pyramid or Temple, where moral trials and physical
tests awaited him. The object of this was to bring
out all the powers of his physique and traits of his
character, thus testing his fitness for a vocation.

F

After he has passed through this trial, then came
what was called his Manifestation. This consisted
of a number of ceremonies of which the novice or
neophyte was the subject during the space of twelve
days. He was then dedicated to Osiris, Isis and
Horus, and decorated with the twelve consecrated
scarfs, (stolæ,) and the olympic cloak. These
scarfs were embroidered with the signs of the Zodiac
and the cloak with figures that were symbolic of
the starry heavens, as the abode of the Gods and
happy Spirits. A crown of palm leaves was placed
upon his head and a burning torch in his hand.
Thus prepared he was again led to the altar, where
he renewed and took additional oath. Now came the
time when he had the right to appear as victor
before the people, and to this end they prepared for
him a solemn procession, called the triumphal
march of the initiated, which was proclaimed by
heralds in every quarter of the city. On the morning of the day appointed for the ceremony, the
priests assembled in the temple, when the most
precious treasures belonging to the Sanctuary were
displayed, and repaired to the Chapel of Isis, to bring
sacrifice to the Goddess, covered with a veil of white
silk, embroidered with golden hieroglyphics, and this
again concealed beneath a black gauze. After this
service the procession left the temple and moved
westward. First in the train came an image of Isis
seated upon a triumphal car drawn by six white
horses, next to which walked the priests in the order
of their rank, dressed in the most gorgeous attire,
and carrying the sacred symbols, the utensils of the
temple, the books of Thot, and the sacred tablet of
Isis, which was a silver plate with the hieroglyphics
that referred to the mysteries of the Goddess engrossed

on it. The priests were followed by all the native
and foreign adepts dressed in white linen garments.
The newly initiated walked in their midst distinguished by a white veil, which extended from the top
of his head to his shoulders. All the houses of the
streets through which the procession passed were
decorated as on festal occasions, flowers and perfumes
were everywhere thrown over the person of the
novice, and his arrival greeted with shouts of
rejoicing. After his return to the temple he was
placed upon an elevated throne, before which immediately afterwards a curtain descended, while the
priests chanted during the interval hymns in favor
of the Goddess. He divested himself of his holiday
suit and assumed a white linen garb, which he was
henceforth to wear. The curtain was now again
raised, and the renewed shouts of the spectators
greeted him, as an adept. The ceremonies concluded
with a festival (banquet) which lasted three days,
during which the newly made brother occupied the
seat of honor.

At a subsequent period the mysteries were aug-
mented by the introduction of the Tragedy of
Osiris. This ceremony consisted of funeral rites
expressive of the wildest grief on account of his
death, a search for his body, which is at last found,
the return of Osiris to life, and the capture and
death or destruction of Typhon, his assasin. Osiris
was a symbol of truth, fortitude and goodness, one
who would sacrifice or lose his life rather than
betray his trust. Typhon was the symbol of error
or evil—the murder of Osiris signified the temporary
subjugation of virtue or truth.

This was the parent, or source of all the Grecian
or other rites which represent a death and a resur-

rection of the body, and whose principal features are perpetuated in the legend of the Sidonian builders. These mysteries exercised a powerful influence over the Egyptian mind. They gave unity to the Egyptian character, and consistency to their religious doctrines or establishments, stability to their political institutions, and vigor and directness in the pursuits of philosophy, science and art.

Edition of 1875, page 242, Mackey Encyclopedia, Egyptian Masonry: Egypt has always been considered as the birthplace of the mysteries; it was there that the ceremonies of initiation were first established. it was there that truth first veiled in allegory and the dogmas of religion were first imparted under symbolic forms. From Egypt, the land of the tongued globe, the land of science and philosophy, peerless for stately tombs and magnificent temples, the land whose civilization was old, and nation before other nations, since called to empire, had a name. this system of symbols was disseminated through Greece and Rome, and other countries of Europe and Asia, giving origin through many intermediate steps to that mysterious association which is now represented by the institution of Freemasonry.

To Egypt, therefore, Masons have always looked with a peculiar interest, as the cradle of that mysterious science of symbolism whose peculiar mode of teaching they alone of all modern institutions have preserved to the present day. The initiation into the Egyptian mysteries was, of all the mysteries practiced by the ancients, the most severe and impressive. The Greeks at Eleusis initiated it to some extent, but they never reached the magnitude of the

forms nor the austerity of its disciples. The system
had been organized for ages, and the priests, who
alone were the hierophants, the explainers of the
mysteries, or as we should call them in Masonic
language, the Masters of Lodges, were educated
almost from childhood for the business in which
they were engaged. That learning of the Egyptians
in which Moses is said to have been so skilled was
imparted in these mysteries; it was confined to the
priests and to the initiates, and the trials of initiation
which the latter had to pass were so difficult to be
endured that none but those who were stimulated by
the most ardent thirst for knowledge dared to
undertake them or succeed in submitting to them.
The priesthood of Egypt constituted a sacred court
on whom the sacerdotal functions were hereditary.
They exercised also an important part in the government of the State, and the Kings of Egypt were but
the first subjects of the priests. They had originally
organized, and continued to control the ceremonies
of initiation. These doctrines were of two kinds,
exortem, or public, which were communicated to the
multitude, and esoteric, or secret, which were revealed
only to a chosen few, and to obtain them it was
necessary to pass through an initiation which was
characterized by the severest trials of courage and
fortitude.

The principal seat of the mysteries was at Memphis, in the neighborhood of the great pyramid
Cheops. They were of two kinds, those of Osiris,
the greater, and those of Isis, the lesser.

Those of Osiris were celebrated at the autumnal
equinox, those of Serapis at the summer solstice,
and those of Isis at the vernal equinox.

The candidate was required to exhibit proofs of a blameless life. For some time or days previous to the commencement of the ceremonies of initiation, he abstained from all unchaste acts, confined himself to an exceedingly light diet, from which all animal food was excluded, and purified himself by repeated ablutions.

Apuleius, (Met. lib. xi,) who had been one of the initiated into all of them, thus alludes with cautious reticence to those of Isis: " The priests, (all the profane having been removed to a distance,) taking my hand, brought me into the inner recesses of the Sanctuary itself, clothed in a new linen garment. Perhaps, curious reader, you may be eager to know what was then said and done. I would tell you if it were lawful for me to do so; you should know if it were lawful for you to hear. But the ears that heard those things, and the tongue that told them, would reap the evil result of such rashness. Still, however, kept in suspense as you probably are with religious longing, I will not torment you with protracted anxiety. Hear, therefore, but believe what is the truth: *I approached the confines of death*, and having trod on the threshold of Proserpine, I returned therefrom, being borne through all the elements. At midnight I saw the sun shining with its brilliant light, and I approached the presence of the Gods above and stood near and worshiped them. Behold, I have related to you things of which though heard by you, you must necessarily remain ignorant."

The first degree, as we term it, of Egyptian initiation, was that into the mysteries of Isis. What was its peculiar import we are forbid to say. Isis, says Knight, was among the later Egyptians the personification of universal nature. To Apuleius he says,

" I am nature, the parent of all things, the sovereign of the elements, the primary progeny of time."

Plutarch tells us that on the front of the Temple of Isis was placed this inscription : " I, Isis, am all that has been, that is or shall be, and no mortal hath ever unveiled me." Thus we may conjecture that the Isaic mysteries were descriptive of the alternate decaying and renovating powers of nature.

Higgins' Anacal, 11-102, it is true, says that during the mysteries of Isis, were celebrated the misfortunes and tragical death of Osiris in a sort of drama, (like H∴ A∴ of the Masons.) And Apuleius asserts that the initiation into her mysteries is celebrated as bearing a close resemblance to a voluntary death, (like that of Cleopatria, in Shakspeare,) or with a very precarious chance of recovery. But Higgins gives us no reference or authority for his statements or conclusions, while that of Apuleius cannot be contravened by any resemblance or reference to the enforced death of Osiris. It is, therefore, says another, probable that the ceremonies of the initiation were simply, like the Apprentice and Fellow Craft, preparatory to the Master or Osiris, and taught by some of the instructions in the physical laws of nature, the necessity of moral purification, the theory of which is not incompatible with the mystic allusions of Apuleius, in which he hints at his own initiation.

The mysteries of Serapis constituted the second degree of the Egyptian initiation. Of this Rite, we have but a very scanty intimation or knowledge. Herodotus is entirely silent in the description of them—either he did not understand them, or, if he did, he feared to make them known ; and Apuleius, calling them " The Nocturnal Orgies of Serapis, a God of the first rank," only intimates that they followed those of Isis, and were preparatory to the last and greatest initiation.

Serapis is said to have been only Osiris while in Hades; and hence the Serapian initiation might have represented the death of Osiris, but leaving the resurrection for a subsequent or higher initiation. This however is merely a conjecture.

In the mysteries of Osiris, which were at first the consummation of the Egpytian system, the lesson of death and resurrection was symbolically taught, and the legend of the murder of Osiris, the search for the body, (not in the several apartments of the temple,) its discovery (not by the acacia,) and restoration to life, is scenically represented. This legend of initiations was as follows: Osiris, a wise King of Egypt, left the care of his kingdom to his wife, Isis, and travelled for three years to communicate to other na· tions the arts of civilization. During his absence, his brother, Typhon, (the Devil, or God of Pandemonium,) formed a secret conspiracy to destroy him and to usurp his throne. On his return, Osiris was invited by Typhon to an entertainment, in the month of November, at which all the conspirators were present. Typhon produced a chest inlaid with gold, and promised to give it to any person whose body it would most exactly fit. Osiris, against the entreaties of his wife, Isis, was tempted to try the experiment, but he had no sooner laid down in the chest than the lid was closed and nailed or fastened down, and the chest containing the body thrown into the river Nile. The chest containing the body of Osiris was, after being a long time tossed about by the waves, finally cast up at Byblos, in Phœnicia, and left at the foot of a tamarack tree. Isis, overwhelmed with grief at the loss of her husband, set out on a journey and traversed the earth in search of the body. After many adventures she at length discovered the spot where it had been thrown up by the waves, and returned with it in triumph to Egypt. It was then proclaimed with the most extravagant demonstrations of joy, Osiris was risen from the dead and had become a God. Such, with slight variations of details by different writers, are the general outlines of the Osiric legend which was represented in the drama of initiation. Its resemblance to the Hiramic legend of the Masonic system will be readily seen and understood. Osiris and Typhon are the representatives of the two antagonistic principles—good and evil, light and darkness, life and death.

There is also an astronomical interpretation of the legend which makes Osiris the sun, Typhon the season of winter, which suspends the fecundating and fertilizing powers of the sun or destroys its life, to be restored only by the return of invigorating Spring.

The sufferings and death of Osiris were the great mystery of the Egyptian religion. His being the abstract principle and abstract idea of the divine goodness, his manifestation upon the earth, his death, his resurrection, and his subsequent office as Judge of the dead in a future state, look, (says Wilkinson,) like the early revelations of a future manifestation of the Deity converted into a mythological fable. Into these mysteries Herodotus, Plutarch and Pythagoras were initiated, and the former two have given brief accounts of them. But then our knowledge of them must have been extremely limited; for, as Clement of Alexandria, (Chron. Vol. 7,) tells us, the more important secrets were not revealed even to *all* the priests, but to a select number of *them only.*

F*

The following is a synopsis of the preface to the first edition of the History of the Egpytian Masonic Rite of Memphis:

This book is written for the purpose of showing what the Egyptian Masonic Rite of Memphis really is; as some of the Craft have not had the advantages of Masonic libraries, and have been made to believe that it is an innovation on the other Rites or Systems, and particularly as there has, at this late day, arisen a new system of Masonry—or humbug called Masonry—entitled Ancient and Primitive Rite of Memphis, of 33 Degrees. The writer has taken the Introduction to the First Volume of the Ritual and prefaced it with an article from one of our ablest and highest Masons, which we commend to all true Masons, and which will well pay for the reading. We therefore submit the same, together with a few quotations from the Ancient Customs, Edicts, and Laws of the Order. Hoping it will serve to allay any feeling of alarm about the Egyptian Masonic Rite interfering with our present system, we submit it to the candid reader and inquirer after truth.

Since the issue of the first volume of the Ritual of these Degrees, the writer has been pleased to see the spirit of kindness shown by eminent Masons of every branch of the Institution toward the Egyptian Masonic Rite of Memphis, and who seem to be pleased with its rapid progress and wide-spread popularity among all classes of Masons, especially among the learned and eminent in the Craft. And when it is known that the original Egyptian Masonry is propagated by this Jurisdiction, they all seem eager to embrace it; so much so that it has been a great labor on the part of the Officers of the Sovereign Sanctuary to supply the necessary papers and Rituals. And as an evidence of its appreciation by the Craft, an article from *The Mystic Star*, of August, 1867, is here copied, and which commends itself to all true Masons:

"RITE OF MEMPHIS.—This branch of Free Masonry is acquiring a firm foothold among the learned and skilled of the Craft in the West. To those who are well informed in the York and Scotch Rites, the Memphian lectures are of peculiar interest, and their impression can not easily be destroyed. The question of precedency of these Rites is well established, but which of them ultimately is to prevail, in the West especially, is for the future to make known to us. While each of the legends is rich, alike with interest and freighted with truth, fortified with great and good morals, the inharmonies in philosophy and chronology in the two former are corrected and reconciled in the last.

"These systems have come down to us from remote ages, and each has had attentive ears and faithful breasts, and will probably be handed down to other generations with little if any improvement by us. While there is a disputation as to which is the better historic standard, we have no desire to dwell long on the question of antiquity, leaving that entirely with the records which are within the reach of every Master Mason in the country. The high grade of morals taught in every step of Masonry, in each line of march from the Master upward to the Knight Templar, the 33d Degree and 96th Degree are worth more to the world now than the fact as to which of these systems Hiram and King Solomon gave their patronage. It is more probable, in point of expenditure of time in the life of all Master Masons, to cultivate themselves up to the moral gauge laid before them in

the Third Degree than to be diverted from their
teachings by the confusion of Degrees and mixing of
systems. The beautiful illustrations of truth and
fidelity can nowhere be better displayed than in the
first three Degrees of the Order, and as in them there
is *something* not clearly understood, and for the finding of which we are pointed by the whole lesson to
look forward; an earnestness for mastery and observance of the principles taught should characterize
the whole life of the aspirant; the multiplication of
advancement, instead of relaxing the first obligations,
should endear them stronger and warmer to the
hearts of all true Masons.

"From the Third Degree we find three avenues of
advancement, and the Master Mason is sole umpire
of which he shall take, or all if he so determines.
Each of these branches have their friends; all will
doubtless live; one is destined to take the lead in the
United States, and appearances are very much in favor
of the Rite of Memphis. The continuation of the moral
lessons, the faithful following of the illustrious characters, and the harmony and beauty of the history,
as given in this Ritual, are certain to draw around
it everywhere warm friends and faithful adherents.

"We are informed that strong Chapters and Senates have already been formed in Illinois, under the
auspices of the Grand Orient, and that they are doing active and good work. A movement is also on
foot in Chicago for the same purpose. Believing that
this branch of Masonry possesses elements for doing
much good among Masons, and therefore making
society better and the world happier, it has our un-
qualified support and best wishes wherever its presence may be made known and invited to dwell.

"If Masonry has any mission in the world more

than to bring reputed good men together upon a common level of recognition and equality, it is to foster and exemplify the soundness of a life in the service of truth and righteousness, and to influence, at all points in life, the suppression of vice and crime, to strengthen the faltering, cheer the sorrowful, and soothe the afflicted. This being the province of the Order so faithfully cherished by the worthy and wise of antiquity, and the influence of its teachings marked with so many evidences of good to the world, let its custodians and pupils of this age see that its jewels are kept bright, and that its great designs are not diverted from their true intents. While this is presented to mankind as the outgrowth of the doings of Masonry, its prosperity will be measured by the march of civilization, and its greatest eulogy will be the examples of its membership throughout the world. With this view, let Masons remember that ' the end of a thing is better than the beginning thereof: and the patient in spirit is better than the proud in spirit.' "

Thus it will be seen that the regular Degrees, from the 3d to the 96th, are here endorsed; and Masons will remember that there can be no Rite of Memphis of less than 96 Degrees, (90 Degrees of Science and 6 Official,) as any Monitor, Lexicon, or Masonic History will show, and when we again call to mind all the Ancient Charges and Constitutions, which clearly teach and affirm that it is not in the power of any man, or body of men, to make innovations in Ancient Craft Masonry, what scorn and contempt must they unavoidably feel for any man, who, for the sake of gain, or other cause, should seek to deceive the Craft by an attempt to palm off as true Masonry of the Egyptian order, a system of 33 Degrees, and call it the Rite of Memphis ?

The Author issued the following as an introduction to his first edition, and as it contains much historic information not embraced herein, is reprinted, although repetition, viz:

In the following brief History of the Egyptian Masonic Rite of Memphis, the compiler does not claim to present a new theory or history, but merely to call up long established historical facts, and bring to mind Ancient Systems and Rituals long since neglected, and of more ancient origin than our present system of Masonry. And this is not for the purpose of throwing obstacles in the way, nor with any view to impede or discourage other systems; but only to supply anything which those systems shall fail to provide for, and also as additional embellishments, which the York Rite, the Scottish Rite, and our present form of Masonry, seem to make no provision for—one of which is the Religious test, or *Christian* Religious test, known to the York Rite, the Scottish Rite and the Templar system. Not that the Egyptian Rite requires no religion; but merely a belief in God, and that religion in which all rational men agree.

The writer does not wish to speak egotistically, but merely mentions the fact that he has taken all the Degrees of Symbolic Masonry in a regular and constitutional manner; has regularly passed the Chairs; been exalted to the Sublime Degree of the Royal Arch; dubbed and created a Knight of the Red Cross, of the Temple, and of Malta; has been permitted to view the beauties and learn the mysteries of a Sovereign Prince of the Royal Secret; has viewed the Veiled Statue of Osiris; and obtained the Secrets of the Chair of the Sovereign Sublime Magi, 96°, of the Egyptian Masonic Rite of Memphis, for the Continent of America. He therefore claims to look upon Masonry and its institutions from a standpoint well calculated to show its perfections and imperfections in the very best possible light. At all events, he ought to be in a position to judge of those matters better than those less advanced.

The writer, therefore, will only cite a few authors, and make a few quotations, which will tend to prove the fact that the Egyptian Masonic Rite is not only the oldest Rite, but is the fountain, or source from whence all Masonry was derived. And for the purpose of establishing this fact, the writer will ask the candid reader to examine the Masonic works and writings of Clavil, Pluche, Herodotus, Oliver, Mackey, and other Masonic writers, who affirm that Egypt was the cradle of all the mysteries; that she at one time was in exclusive possession of all the religious and mysterious learning in the world; and from her extended, not only all the influences of religious ceremonies, but also its sacred rites—its secret doctrines, and its esoteric rituals. "The importance, therefore," says one of the above writers, " of a full knowledge of the Egyptian mysteries, must be obvious to every Masonic scholar or inquirer after truth and knowledge;" and "the antiquity and importance of the Egyptian mysteries," says Mackey, "entitles them to a more diffusive examination, study, and explanation, than has been awarded them by most writers on Masonry."

We learn from sacred and profane history, that the priesthood of Egypt was a sacred caste, and the sacerdotal functions were hereditary. They also held an important position, and exerted a powerful influence on the government of the country; so much so, that even the King on his throne was in actual subjection to the Priests, and had an inferiority of rank with them—a fact which is also shown in the York Rite, for there the High Priest in the Chapter is the presiding officer, and the King his inferior officer, which plainly shows where that system of Masonry, or mysteries, sprang from. "They were also," says the same writer, "the originators, and controlled the ceremonies of *all* initiations. They had two doctrines—one public, for the masses; the other was private, or secret, which was only communicated to a chosen few, and that few obtained them only by the forms and ceremonies of initiation, which were always characterized by trials of courage and fortitude, (as in the initiations of the present day.")

The principal center or seat of the Egyptian mysteries was Memphis, (in and) near the Grand Pyramid. They were originally of only three kinds : 1. Those of Osiris. 2. Those of Serapis. 3. Those of Isis. The first were always celebrated at or near the Autumnal Equinox, about the 23d of the Egyptian month Shamenoth, (answering to the month of September with us.) The second in the Summer Solstice, about the 24th of the Egyptian month Chocac, (answering to the month of June with us.) The third at the Vernal Equinox, about the 21st of the Egyptian month Thoth, (answering to the month of March with us.) In all cases, the candidate was required to exhibit proofs of blameless life. (In our language, be properly vouched for and examined.)

First, in the mysteries of Isis, he is stripped of his outward clothing, and after the proper time of fasting and purification, is subjected to frightful and terrifying scenes, well calculated to exhibit his courage and prove his fortitude, as well as his belief in the Supreme Ruler of the Universe ; and if, after a severe trial, he overcomes obstacles and seeming

dangers, accomplishes the usual peregrinations, per-
ambulations, and allegorical journeys, over rugged
roads, and through darkness, and arrives at the place
of light, he is formally baptized, receives a new
name, and obligated to secresy, and is then put upon
a more severe trial, passing over rocks, through dark,
dismal caverns and passages, in which he sees, by
the flitful and vivid flashes of lightning, emblems of
mortality, in the shape of skeletons, etc., and hears
the fearful crash of thunder reverberating through
the caverns, mingled with the howling of wild
beasts which he has to encounter, (they being the
initiated clothed in the skins of wild beasts, and who
strenuously oppose his progress.) He is also made
to swim rivers and leap over fearful chasms, till,
finally, if he possesses the courage and perseverance
to overcome and surmount all these and other
obstacles, he is received into the second secret place,
or place of light, and invested with a robe of spotless
white, instructed in the mysteries, which can only
be done after he has exhibited his courage, been
baptized, given a new name, and passed through the
four elements—Earth, Air, Fire, and Water—by
which he is said to be purified and made a new
man—in the words of the Apostle, has put off the
old man, and put on the new—to which the Apostle
Paul doubtless alluded. He is then, for the first
time, permitted to view the veiled statue of Osiris.
He then is subjected to a period of fasting and
prayer; is instructed and makes suitable proficiency
in the mysteries, history, signs of recognition, and
words of the Order.

After a suitable lapse of time, he is proposed for
the Second Degree, or Mysteries of Serapis, which
are performed in the dead hours of night. In the

midst of human bones and ghastly emblems, he enters alone a cavern, in which is a taper shedding just light enough to magnify the terrors of the place; there he makes ablution, and deciphers the questions in hieroglyphics on the wall, and writes on a scroll the answers with an instrument dipped in his blood. If the questions are correctly answered, he is again obligated to secresy, makes a libation to the Gods to seal his obligation by drinking wine out of the top part of a human skull; after which he is conducted to a more magnificent chamber than the first, invested by the Hierophant with the secrets of the Degree, and clothed in a robe of azure blue.

After a proper period of time had elapsed, if the candidate could exhibit a suitable proficiency in the ceremonials and degrees of the Order, he was prepared for the third and highest grade of the Rite— the Mysteries of Osiris, which was then the summit of the Egyptian Mysteries, or Masonry. In this Degree, the murder of Osiris by his brother Typhon, and also the death and resurrection of the god Osiris, is represented by the candidate, the legend of which is familiar to all Masons; and although Osiris was looked upon by his followers as a god, he here represents, like Hiram Abif, Gedaliah, and Zerubbabel, the picture or type of a good man, who would sacrifice his life sooner than betray his trust, or forfeit his integrity. The legend of the murder, burial, and resurrection of Osiris, is there acted. Osiris having reformed all the bad habits of his own subjects, made a journey around the earth to reform the other nations, and to teach them the mysteries of Egypt, the arts and sciences, extend the blessings of civilization, and the art of agriculture; and, as the legend runs, he left his wife, Isis, a very wise

and beautiful woman, to take charge of the kingdom
in his absence. Having performed this arduous and
benevolent task, he returned to his own country, and
was shocked to learn that in his absence his brother
Typhon had seduced his beautiful and accomplished
wife, Isis, and demoralized his subjects to such a
degree that his wise laws, rules and maxims had
been entirely disregarded. Osiris attempted to re-
monstrate with his brother for the unbrotherly and
unmasonic act, when Typhon demanded that he
should acquiesce in his adulterous and wicked conduct, and upon his refusal Typhon flew into a
passion, and killed his brother Osiris, whom he cut
in pieces and packed them in a chest, and then threw
the chest into the river Nile. When it was found
that Osiris had been thus brutally murdered, his
wife and the subjects repented, and search was made
for the body, which was found cut in pieces, but an
important part of which was missing, viz : the
Phallus, or *Membrum Virile*. The body was given
to the Priests, and by them transformed ; and Osiris
became a god. Isis substitutd a piece in place of
the missing one, and named it *Phallus;* and it
became the emblem of fecundity in the mysteries
which are said to have been established or improvis-
ed to commemorate Osiris' death and sufferings by
the foul deed ; and the candidate goes through a
representation of the sufferings, death, and resurrec-
of Osiris, and is then declared free from sin and
regenerated.

The secret doctrines of the mysteries were Astronomy and Mythology, in which Osiris represents
the sun, Isis the moon. Typhon was the symbol
(darkness and evil) of winter, which destroys the
fertilizing power of the sun, depriving him, as it

were, for a time, (during the winter months,) of light and heat.

The other doctrines of the Rite related to the gods, the creation of the world, and the immortality of the soul. These traditions were not permitted to be written, except in hieroglyphics, understood only by the Priests, and handed down from one to the other of the initiated to secure secresy, (and as they claim,) from Adam, the first man, to Seth, Enoch, etc., etc., to the present day. The candidate, when he had passed through initiation, was given one of the names of Deity, and a name of the Deity was also used as password of the Order; secresy was the most binding part of the obligation, which was enjoined under fearful oaths. Their lessons were inculcated and illustrated by symbols. Thus, a point within a circle was Deity surrounded by Eternity, etc., etc. The conclusion of some of the obligations they took were: "I call to witness my promise, the gods of heaven and hell, and I invoke their vengeance on my head, if ever I willfully violate my oath or vow." Another conclusion was: "May my departed spirit wander in eternal misery, in immensity of space, without a place of rest, should I break my vow. Amen, Amen, Amen."

Thus I have briefly given some points in the Ancient Egyptian Masonic Rite, which the intelligent Mason will at once discover to be the chief and leading points of Masonry of the present day. And can there longer exist a doubt but they were the very essence of Ancient Masonry, and that they were the foundation and chief corner stone of the present institution? Now, the curious reader is referred to the several other writers on the subject, which want of time and space prohibit a further examination of

here, but which will well pay for the perusal, and
may be found in any of the authors before cited, and
especially in that valuable and reliable work by
Brother Mackey, viz., his Lexicon, which should be
in the library of every Mason or Masonic body.

As a matter of course, these mysteries have,
during the long period of time they have existed,
undergone changes; and as history shows, they have
been worked or practiced for more than three thous-
and years, and their date indicates and claims 25,000
years. As the manners and customs of the people
changed, and the memory of the devotees failed, new
systems have in part been adopted; hence, the different work among Masons at the present day, yet all
tending to the same result and having in view the
same object. Should our Ancient Brother and Grand
Master, King Solomon, come upon earth to-day, I apprehend he would find no little trouble in working
his way into his Blue Lodge, or proving himself a
Mason. But all the changes in Masonry are in im-
material points, and those parts have, for some good
cause and wise reasons doubtless, been changed. But
no person can deny but that the Egyptian Masonic
Rite to-day contains all and every principal element
of true Masonry. And the work has been to a
greater or less extent worked even before and since
the building of the Pyramids, and long before
Solomon's Temple was even thought of, and is now
extensively practiced in all foreign countries, and is
fast spreading itself over this land. It has, in addition to its liberal doctrine of that religion in which
all men agree, no contradictions or inconsistencies;
its traditions, history and record agree, as to time and
place, with all writers of sacred and profane history;
it teaches morality, the immortality of the soul, a

knowledge of God and His attributes, without endorsing or denouncing sects or creeds, eschews politics and teaches patriotism, worships God in spirit and in truth, and adopts the law of doing unto others whatsoever ye would that others should do unto you.

I have thus quoted liberally from this authentic history and the latest authors, for two reasons, viz: First, it proves most conclusively that Egyptian Masonry is the oldest and most systematic, and that all other Masonry, and in fact all other secret societies, had, to a greater or less extent, their origin in the Egyptian Mysteries, *or Masonic Rite;* and Second that the Masonry of the present day has, in its esoteric and exoteric ritual, the same end or object in view; and while, perhaps, the *modus operandi* or work of the degrees may differ, yet the real germ is discoverable, in the entire practice or work. And that from *these three* degrees of their operative work or Masonry and performance, have grown the entire speculative and symbolic ritual of our Rite, called the York Rite, and also fully prove that the popular form of religion has also been borrowed from Egyptian Masonry, as the death and resurrection of Osiris and his coming to life or transformation, is in full parallel with Christian doctrine, of the Saviour, Jesus Christ, and also the resurrection of the dead and the immortality of the soul of man, or the new birth of the Christian, as well as the reputed immaculate conception, and the instance of the assassination of H.·. A.·. at the building of King Solomon's Temple. Compare the ritual of the York Rite, and the catechism of the orthodox churches of to-day, and you, in each, can see cropping out the same doctrines and teachings. Thus also in the degrees of the A. & A., or Scotch Rite; the Royal Arch, the Council of Royal and Se-

lect Masters, and the Knight Templar. In each of
these again you see the *main* and strong points are
similar, and seem founded on the same analogy; then
again, if the searcher after truth will read the ancient
histories of the different religious creeds, and the histories of Freemasonry, he will be forcibly struck
with the similarity of views, language and teachings,
and the close analogy existing in all of them. Even
Christ, when His disciples asked him to teach them
to pray, says: " Enter into thy closet, and when thou
hast shut the door, pray to the Father in *secret*, and
He shall reward thee openly." (Matt. vi : 6.)

The secret or esoteric portion of the religious teaching has been thrown off in a measure, but not in all
of them, as there exists to-day, secret or esoteric
teaching in some of the churches at *least*, if not in
all of them; and although called by different names,
they are, to some extent, proof to the unprejudiced
mind, similar and alike. I could cite in proof one or
two instances; they are those of the confessional to
the priests, and others, and the doctrine of all of the
non-orthodox, and some of the orthodox churches or
societies of the world. In our endeavor to connect
the Egyption Masonry with the York Rite, or all the
Masonic teachings of to-day, we have far less trouble,
as they are so strikingly similar that I have only to
make this suggestion to the posted Mason, who will
at once recognize them, and the fountain of their
origin. And as this book is written *only* for, and in
the interests of Masonry, I am not going to take any
more space in my remarks to prove the similarity on
this part of my argument, but leave the few and
mere suggestions to be enlarged and finished in the
fruitful and natural product of the intelligent imagination of the reader, who will think of and apply

things that I am forbidden to write here, or to explain only in a well tiled Lodge, and show some of
the reasons why, and the benefits of these humani-
tarian societies. When the reasons are so much better
described in one and all of the lectures of *this* Rite,
than I can describe them, I quote freely from
them. Thus, in the Degree of Discreet Master, we
have this lecture, viz: a

BRIEF HISTORY.

In the Degrees of the Egyptian Masonic Rite of
Memphis, you will be forcibly struck with the great
dissimilarity between them and the degrees already
taken. When you were initiated into the first symbolic degree, called Apprentice, you swore not to
write, &c., any part of the secrets or mysteries of
those degrees. Under this impression, you will no
doubt be surprised that we have the degrees in manu-
script. It is therefore necessary to give some explanation of the difference.

Masonry was founded in those dark and rude ages
when civilization was yet in its infancy, and the arts
and sciences had shed but few and imperfect rays
across the gloom of barbarism; mutual wants and
necessities impelled our primeval brethren to seek
for mutual aid and assistance. Diversity of talent,
inclinations and pursuits, rendered each dependent
upon the other; thus society was formed, and as a
natural consequence, men of the same habits and
pursuits were associated more intimately together,
not only with a view of mutual improvement and
advantage, but from that natural impulse felt by congenial minds. In this manner societies were formed,
as civilization began to extend through the world,
and the minds of men became enlarged from the con-

templation of the works of nature; the arts and
sciences were cultivated by the most ingenious of the
people. The contemplation of the Planetary System,
as the works of an Almighty Artist, and the attributes
of their God, gave rise to religion, and the science of
astronomy, the measurement of land and the division
and marking of their property gave rise to geometry,
and these to the society into whose mysteries you
now desire to be introduced.

If we should look upon the earth with its produce,
the ocean with its tides, the coming and going of
day, the starry arch of heaven, the seasons and their
changes, the life and death of man, as being merely
the accidents of nature, we must shut up all the
powers of judgment, and yield up ourselves to the
darkest folly and ignorance.

The august scene of the planetary system, the day
and night, the seasons in their succession, the animal
frame, the vegetation of plants, all afford subjects of
astonishment the greatest, too mighty but for the
hand of Deity whose works they are; the least, too
miraculous but for the wisdom of their God.

It is no wonder, then, that the first institutors of
our Society, who had their eye on the revelation of
Deity from the earliest ages of the world, should hold
these sciences hallowed among them, whereby such
lights were ordained by man in the discovery of the
great wisdom of our adorable Creator in the beginning.

This Institution, which was originally founded in
the mysteries of religion and science, is now maintained by us on the principle of rendering mutual aid
to each other, as well as to preserve our adoration to
the Almighty Artist, and to improve our minds with
the principle of science.

G

How should we be able to discern the brethren of the great family, but through such tokens as should point them out from other men? Language is not provincial, and the dialects of different nations would not be comprehensible to men ignorant and unenlightened. Hence, it becomes necessary to use an expression which should be cognizable by people of all nations.

So it is with Masons; they are possessed of that universal expression, and of such remains of the original language, that they can communicate their history, their wants, and their prayers to every brother Mason throughout the globe; from whence it is certain that a multitude of lives have been saved in foreign countries, when shipwreck and misery overwhelmed them; when robbers had pillaged, and when sickness, want and misery had brought them to the brink of the grave.

The degrees of Ancient and Primitive Masonry being of still higher importance, as containing the real secrets and principles of the mystic institution, were to be guarded in a more particular manner, both from the knowledge of the world, and of those who may be unworthy of receiving them.

Consequently, it was ordained that the first three, or blue degrees, which are only symbols of the sublime and true degrees of Masonry, should be committed to memory, that it might be thereby known from the manner in which a symbolic Mason discharged the duties of those preparatory degrees, whether he was capable of being entrusted with the real and important secrets of the craft.

Again, the history of Masonry, as contained in the higher degrees, gives an account and authentic detail of occurrences found only in the records and archives of the sublime institution, and which are so lengthy that they fill many volumes, which it would be impossible to commit to memory, unless the whole of our lives were dedicated to it in the lecture.

Attention is called to the brilliant Delta, enclosing certain Hebraic characters, from which emanate nine beams of the Shekinah, bearing each an initial of a divine name, as derived from an attribute, and the whole surrounded by a great circle.

The meaning. of the Hebraic characters in the Delta, describe the ineffable name of the Grand Architect of the Universe, which was forbidden to be spoken by a law of Moses.

The initials of the names in the nine beams of the Skekinah, are those which God gave himself when he spoke to Moses on Mount Sinai, intimating to him at the same time that his future issue should one day know his real name.

The serpent forming a circle represents Eternity and the immensity of the power of God, which hath neither beginning nor end.

In the Sanctum Sanctorum a luminous circle, enclosing a brilliant star of five points, with the letter G in the centre, the meaning of which is thus described :—Glory, Grandeur and Gomel; from which we understand by Glory, God; by Grandeur, the man who may be great by perfection ; and by Gomel, a Hebrew word, which signifies thanks to God for His supreme power. It it the first which Adam spoke on discovering the adorable Eve.

There is also in the Sanctum Sanctorum, the Ark of Alliance, the Golden Candlestick with seven branches, having a lamp in each, also a table. The Ark of Alliance was placed in the middle of the Sanctum Sanctorum, under the brilliant star and the shadow of the wings of the cherubims, which represents the alliance which God made with His people.

The Ark of Alliance was of the form of a parallelogram, of which Solomon's Temple was an exact model, and also every Lodge of Masons, being a double cube and situated due East and West, extending from North to South, (see page 44, Monitor or Book of the Lodge by Mackey,) two cubits and a-half in length, one cubit and a-half in breadth, and the same in height, made of shittim wood, covered within and without with gold, decorated with a golden crown, and borne by two cherubims of gold. The cover of the Ark had a name; it was called the Propitiatory, a place that served to appease God's anger. Said Propitiatory contained the testimony which God gave to Moses, the tablets of the law. These tablets were of white marble, and contained the Decalogue, written in Hebrew characters. The commandments taught were disposed on the tablets as follows: The four first pointed out the duty of man to his God, and were engraved on the first tablet. The remaining six pointed out the obligations of man, and were engraved on the second tablet.

The name of the Sanctum Sanctorum in Hebrew is Dabir, denoting speech, and it was there the Divinity resided, and where He delivered His oracles.

Moses, by the help and command of God, constructed the Ark, and for that purpose he chose to assist him Bezaleel, of the tribe of Judah, son of Uri and Miriam, sister to Moses and Aholihab, of the tribe of Dan, the most learned of the people. The Israelites testified so much ardor for the works, and offered with so much zeal to carry on the same, that Moses proclaimed by sound of trumpets that he wanted no more. They worked after the model

which God had given unto Moses, who also instructed him in the number and form of the
sacred vessels which were to be made and placed in
the tabernacle to serve in the sacrifices.

The hangings of the Sanctum Sanctorum are Purple, Blue, Scarlet and White, implying Awe and Reverence, Truth and Constancy, Justice tempered with
Mercy, and Purity.

The seven branched candlestick alludes to the seven
planets, and was composed of seventy parts, which
alluded to the Decani, or seventy divisions of the
planets. The eye over the door of a Chapter or
Lodge, represents the eye of God, to whose name our
works are dedicated, and from whose inspection our
actions can never be concealed.

The Shekinah All Seeing Eye in a Delta or Triangle, signifies visible glory. which was a symbol of the Divine presence, but in our Ancient and
Primitive Rite we are taught to regard it as the cultivated mind which disperses Ignorance.

It will be remembered by those who are conver-
sant with Masonic literature and teachings, that when
Moses was but a youth, he by reason of his position
in Pharaoh's family, and being the adopted son of
Pharaoh's daughter, was given rule over certain of
the workmen, who were compelled to do the most
servile and degrading service for the Egyptians.
And Moses being a Hebrew by birth, naturally took
sides and sympathized with the Israelites, and remonstrated with the task masters, who compelled the
Jews to make brick without straw, a difficult and
slow operation. And they were also compelled to
make the same quantity or number of brick as the
Egyptians, who had straw, and complete the same
amount of material as the Egyptian workmen, al-

G*

though deprived of the principals. And straw being the most useful material used in the construction thereof, and by the use of which the bricks were held in place, and the shape not injured by handling before burning or hardening them. Hence, Moses seeing this and other great hardships his kinsmen were subjected to, began reproving the task masters for the cruel injustice and barbarous treatment they were subjected to, and remonstrated with the masters; and from words came blows, in which one of the Egyptian task masters was by Moses slain, while in the performance of duty. This becoming known next day, Moses was obliged to flee from the place; and journeying for several days in a north-western direction, came to a well, in Media, near the city of Hellopolis, in the vicinity of the great pyramid Cheops. When, armed with a pass from his foster mother, Pharaoh's daughter, he escaped the wrath and express commands of Pharaoh that he should be executed, or put to death; and he there married the priest of Midian's eldest daughter, Zipporah, where he dwelled forty years, and became learned and possessed of all the mysterious learning of the priests of Egypt, which gave him a high position among the Jews, and the dread of the Egyptians, of which he was High Priest, or Sublime Dai, in the mysteries or Masonry of the Egyptians, And being a levite or priest, by Jewish birth and parentage, gave him also a high position among the Jews, and rendered him a fit and proper person to undertake the liberation and freedom of his people, who had long remained in bondage with the Egyptians, and who inhabited a clay, barren and desolate portion of the Egyptian dominions, called Pithom and Raamses. (See Exodus i: 11.) And there were over six hundred thousand able bodied men under his charge. And being possessed of this mysterious learning, it was this also that fitted him for a ruler and leader of the million of souls over whom he presided, and enabled him to introduce that system of esoteric learning or Masonry, that raised the tabernacle by the command of God and the help of Ahohiab and Bazaleel, before mentioned, being the pattern of and after which King Solomon's Temple was built, and as we have before noticed, of which every Lodge is a pattern.

These degrees or mysteries were worked in the country of the Egyptians, as has been shown by our former quotations, many thousand years, and used and worked for two purposes, viz: Religious worship and Masonic ceremonies, and were of three kinds in the first or operative division, viz: First, those of Isis, second, those of Serapis, and third, those of Osiris, and from which every system of Masonry, operative and speculative, has been taken, as well as all the modern systems of secret associations or societies, and were the systems that built the pyramids, Cheops and others, and in which the building of Solomon's Temple was a comparative modern instance compared with those stupendous remains of edifices that exist in ruins of the ancient cities of Rome, Heliopolis, Liberi, Alexandria, Memphis, Tiberias and other stupendous works of the mystic art, reared by the ancient brethren who have gone before us into that Lodge not made with hands eternal in the heavens.

And as the writers before quoted, together with Herodotus and others inform us, had their origin at or about the time of the birth or introduction of civilization of Egypt, and these three degrees of ISIS,

SERAPIS, and OSIRIS, were the original three degrees of the present so-called York Rite. Although they have been changed, altered and abridged, yet they contain sufficient points and landmarks to satisfy the careful reader, or the educated craftsman, that these three degrees have been drawn out and added to, till they represent in numbers what is called 3, 7, 9, 10 and 12 degrees, being attached to, and containing when attached together, three in the Master Mason, seven in the Royal Arch, nine in the Council, and twelve in the Knight Templar, while in every other part of the world the York Rite contains but three degrees, the Royal Arch and Council being side degrees, and the Templar Degrees being forbidden, on account of the doctrine of Christianity embraced in them. They, (the Egyptian,) when being worked, are dramatized and are descriptive of Masonic and historic events that occurred or transpired before and at the destruction of the first and the building and destruction of the second Temple, and as such are worked in the Memphis Rite only.

Therefore, it may not be amiss in this connection to briefly explain that while the Memphis Rite contains all the Masonic learning in the world, yet, the possession of it, or any other system of Masonry, does not, iff itself, enable or give admission to the particular degrees that are worked in the other Masonic bodies, or admission to any but the regular initiates or members of that or those particular institutions where initiated; for it is in Masonry, as it is in other societies, masonic or religious, that the particular system has its particular tenets and its peculiar dogmas, so much so, that if one is in possession of all the mysteries of the Royal Arch, Master Mason, Knight Templar, &c., &c., yet unless this person has been

regularly initiated into each of these societies, he can
no more claim the right or gain admission to them
than a profane; and he must become a regular initiate
and member of the body before he can claim its protection, its charities, its fellowship, or right to visit
that particular body.

But, such is the law, rules and regulations and
edicts of each, that he may be subjected to discipline
and trial, suspension or expulsion, in any of the
bodies of the York Rite, within whose jurisdiction
he may be, either as sojourner or resident. And, as
a general rule, suspension from one branch or body
of this Rite works suspension or expulsion from all.
This is also, with some few exceptions, the law of
the Scotch Rite.

But a very different rule prevails in the Memphis
Rite. That Rite does not take the hearsay acts, say-
ings and decisions of other Rites, or even the doings
of the inferior bodies of this Rite, as conclusive evidence of the conclusions arrived at, or the decisions
therein pronounced, but require, unless the decision
is from a State or United States Grand Body, as conclusive evidence against a member denying his guilt,
a showing *de novo* in the body of the Rite
having jurisdiction, which a careful reading of
the printed constitutions and extracts from its decisions will show, and as we are taught in Masonry,
the right, and it is made the duty of visiting brethren
to know fully or examine closely into the legality
and authority of the bodies working Masonic degrees
or holding assemblages; and we, having shown our
charter, our constitution and organization, will now
briefly attempt to show our antiquity. Not that this
is really or absolutely necessary, but merely because
the fact exists. And as many good and learned Ma-

154

sons have said to the writer that the Masonic institution would be quite as good, and perhaps better, if it was of no more than one year's existence, yet the fact is that Egyptian Masonry is of very ancient date, and its birthplace is not very certain; but many writers and historians say:

The cradle of Masonry is placed by the most judicious historians in that country which was first inhabited, namely, the plateau of Tartary, and it is said that it was transmitted to us by the sages of India, Persia, Ethiopia, and Egypt.

It is evident that Masonry had its birth in India, and that it was transmitted to Europe by the sages of Ethiopia and Egypt, where the hierophantes and the patriarchs of this venerated order formed those great men who spread throughout the whole world Light and Truth.

The Masonic order of Memphis is, therefore, the sole depository of high masonic science, the true primitive rite, the supreme rite, that which has come down to us without any alteration, and consequently the rite that justifies its origin with a constant exercise of its rights by constitutions whose authenticity it is impossible to call in question. In fine, the Rite of Memphis is the true masonic tree, and all other systems, whatever they may be, are only detached branches of this institution, rendered respectable by its vast antiquity.

The mysteries were divided into two classes, the smaller and the greater.

The smaller had for its object the instruction of the initiated in the humane sciences; the sacred doctrine was reserved for the last degree of the initiation. This is what they called the great manifestation of Light,

Between the knowledge of humane science and that of the divine doctrine, there were symbolical degrees that had to be gone through. All the mysteries turned on three principal points, the morale, the exact sciences, and the sacred doctrine. From the first object they passed to the second without intermediary; but once arrived at the second degree, long preparations were necessary; these were the object to be attained by three other symbolic degrees; the first ended and completed the smaller mysteries, the other two opened the greater.

It was not till the first symbolic degree, the third of the initiation, that the fables were exposed, and in following the two other degrees, they strove to penetrate into the sense of these fables and to become worthy of the great manifestation of Light.

The general division included the preparations, the voyages and symbols, and the autopsie. The preparations were divided into two classes; the first had as symbolic title the word "wisdom," and for object the morale. The initiated were called Thalmedimites or disciples. The second had as symbolic title the word "strength," and for object the humane sciences. The initiated were called Heberemites or companions.

The voyages and symbols were divided into three classes. In the first, called the Obsequies, the initiated bore the name of Mouzehemites; in the second, called Vengeance, they took that of Bheremites; and in the third, called Emancipation, that of Nescherites. The autopsie was the grand completion of the initiation, the crowning of the edifice, the keystone of the arch.

The Antique Legends of Masonry, which date back 1,000 centuries, having descended to us fortified by unquestionable authenticity, through the Patriarchs

of our Ancient Rite, Priests of the Most High God,
who officiated in the Temples of Israel and of Judah,
and of Hierophants of Egypt, that land of mystery
of science, and of practical, operative Masonry, where
to this day wonders of Masonic Act, still towering to
Heaven their gigantic heads, exist as incontrovertible
proofs of the antiquity of our Order, inform us that
the Patriarch Noah was born in the year of the world
six hundred and twenty-two, that he lived three
hundred and sixty-five years, and that he walked
with God, and that he was not; for God took him.
We are also informed that Enoch, filled with the love
and fear of T. S. A. O. T. U. strove to direct the
minds of men in the paths of honor, truth and wisdom, but in vain; for the wickedness of man was
great in the earth, and every imagination of the
thoughts of his heart was only evil continually.
Enoch, overwhelmed with grief on account of the
wickedness of mankind, supplicated God to bring
them into the paths of Light and Truth; that they
might know, fear and love the Holy Name of Deity.

While thus pondering how to rescue the human
race from their sins and the punishment due to their
crimes, he dreamed that the Deity in visible shape
appeared unto him, saying, "Enoch, thou hast long
yearned to know my true name; arise, follow me,
and it shall be revealed to you?" Then it appeared
to Enoch as if he was taken up on the wings of the
winds, and transported to the summit of a high mountain, whose top was hid in the heavens; and appeared
to reach the stars. There he perceived amidst the
clouds, in letters of brilliant light, the Mysterious,
Omnific Word, whose pronunciation was then and
there made known to him. Suddenly he found himself descending perpendicularly into the bowels of

the earth, passing through nine subterranean apart ments, each roofed with an arch, the apex of each forming a keystone, having inscribed on it mysterious characters, emblematic of nine names or attributes, by which Deity was known to our ancient brethren.

In the ninth and lowest arch he perceived a pedestal of marble, on which was a triangular plate of gold, surrounded by rays of brilliant light, on which was engraven the same Mysterious Omnific Name, revealed to him upon the mountain. Upon awakening, Enoch accepted his vision as an inspiration from Heaven, and traveled in search of the mountain he saw in his dream. Way-worn and weary, he rested in the land of Canaan, then already populous with the descendants of Adam. With the assistance of his son Methuselah, he constructed in the bowels of the mountain nine apartments, each roofed with an arch, and having a keystone with mysterious characters upon it, even as he beheld them in his vision.

This labor being completed, he made two deltas of purest gold, engraving upon each two of the mysterious characters. One of the deltas he placed upon a pedestal of marble, which he erected in the deepest arch, as had been shown him in his dream—the other he retained.

Having accomplished this labor, he closed the aperture at the top with a square stone, having engraved on its sides the hieroglyphics which you have this day had interpreted to you. He also erected over the Royal Arch a roofless temple of huge, unhewn stones, to the glory O. T. S. A. O. T. U.

That the knowledge of this sacred spot and the treasure it contained might survive the flood, which Enoch knew would soon overwhelm the world in one

H

vast sea of ruin, he raised two columns on the hill—one of brass, to resist water, the other of granite, to withstand fire. On the column of granite he inscribed a description of the subterranean arches, on the other the rudiments of the arts and sciences. The column of granite was swept into a shapeless mass by the flood, but that of brass stood firm for ages after the Deluge.

This mountain was in the Holy Land opposite Mount Moriah, where King Solomon erected the Temple many thousand years afterwards; it was in later days named Zion, and it was there that the Ark of the Covenant was placed, in the Sabbitical year 1045 before the Christian era, when it was brought from the House of Aminadab, at Kirjathjearim, by King David, and sixty thousand choice men of Israel.

Enoch having finished the Sacred Vault, gave to his son Methuselah the Delta which he retained, with strict charge to give it to his grandson Noah; this was accomplished according to his desire. In the year of the world 1656, Noah entered the Ark, with his three sons, and, with their families, were, by Divine will, preserved from the deluge that destroyed the rest of the human race.

About the year 1200, before Christ, Mizraim, the grandson of Ham, led colonies into Egypt, and laid the foundation of the Kingdom of Egypt, which lasted 1,663 years. Mizraim carried with him the sacred Delta of the Patriarch Enoch, which he confided to the care of the Hierophants or Priests, who carefully preserved it in their splendid Temples on the banks of the Nile.

Hermes Trismegistus, who was looked upon by the Egyptians as the Interpreter of the Gods, was one of the most learned of the Hierophants; he deciphered the sacred characters upon the brazen obelisk erected by Noah, and was the inventor of many useful arts ; to him was ascribed the reformation of the Egyptian year. He prophesied that there would arise in the East a King, who would erect a magnificent Temple to the glory of the S. A. O. T. U., whose renown should penetrate to the remotest parts of the earth, and charged the Priests that when this great King should arise, that they should give into his keeping the Sacred Delta of the Patriarch Enoch.

This prophecy was fulfilled in the person of Solomon, during the reign of Hiram of Tyre, who initiated him into the mysteries of Masonry, and gave him the Sacred Delta, which Solomon caused to be suspended in the E. of his Hall of Audience.

From the time of Enoch the true pronunciation of the sacred name remained unknown, until the Almighty, many thousand years after, was pleased to reveal it to the prophet Moses, when he commanded him to go unto Pharaoh, and cause him to send forth the children of Israel out of bondage, saying unto him :

"I have sorely seen the affliction of my people which are in Egypt, and have heard their cry, by reason of their task masters—for I know their sorrows."

" And I have come down to deliver them out of the hand of the Egyptians, and to bring them out of that land unto a good land and large —unto a land flowing with milk and honey ; unto the place of Canaanites, and the Hittites, and the Amorites, and the Perrizzites, and the Hivites, and the Jebusites."

" Come now, therefore, and I will send thee unto Pharaoh, that thou mayest bring forth my people, the children of Israel, out of Egypt."

"And God said unto Moses, I AM THAT I AM ; and he said ; Thus shalt thou say unto the children of Israel, I AM hath sent me unto you.

"Moreover, he said, I am the God of thy father, the God of Abraham, the God of Isaac, and the God of Jacob."

Moses revealed the sacred name of Aaron to Joshua, the son of Nun, and atterwards it was communicated to the High Priests. The word being composed of consonants only, was lost, except to the few favored by the Almighty, and was entirely lost to Masons by the death of our operative Grand Master.

It is a historic fact that this rite has for its foundation and legends the truth of sacred and profane history, as well as the science of Philosophy, Architecture and Geometry, and they clearly and distinctively prove that the Egyptian Masonic Rite of Memphis is the most Ancient Freemasonry known to mankind, from which all Masonry of modern times has been derived, or originated, and all other systems are but off-shoots of the original tree, and contain only scintillations of the important and divine truths contained in the primitive teachings of this Ancient Rite, as taught, promulgated and practised by the Patriarchs Enoch, Noah, Mizraim, Sesostris, Hermes. Zoroaster, Plato, Socrates, Pythagoras, Lycurgus, Solon, Alcibades, and many other great and good philosophers; those great lights of antiquity, whose teachings guided and improved the rude barbarism of antiquity, and upon which all Masonry is founded. The Masonic Order of Memphis has but one Thought —to do Good; but one Banner—that of Humanity; but one Crown—it is for Virtue. Its origin is lost in the night of time. The most judicious historians assign as its birthplace the plains of Tartary, and trace it to our day through the sages of India, Persia, Ethiopia and Egypt.

In an immeasurable antiquity, according to Indian monuments, sages sought the light on the banks of the Ganges, and in the countries of Lower India. Like us, they worshiped Truth, and propagated it unostentatiously. Their doctrines were simple, and devoid of superstition. They adored an Eternal God! Creator of the world, who preserves its existence, and causes destruction to give birth to reproduction.

This simple theology of the Brahmins spread throughout Persia. It was cultivated by the Magi. It changed, as everything changes in the world, and was reduced to its primitive simplicity by a second Zoroaster. Its faithful disciples still exist in Ethiopia as well as in India, among nations not now classed in the ranks of civilization. Its votaries assembled in the Isle of Merve and gave freedom and happiness to the nations which they governed. Followed by a body of his countrymen, Osiris descended from the mountains of Ethiopia, and by the most glorious conquests brought Egypt, still barbarous, into subjection to his laws, conferring on them the blessings of civilization.

These benefactors of the human race deemed it impossible to present the true light to rude and uncultivated minds. They veiled under emblems which the multitude construed literally, the Truth, which had her devotees in the Temples of Sias, Thebes, Heliopolis and Memphis. Thus, as in China, Greece, and Ancient Rome, as also among enlightened people of the modern world, there were two religions in Egypt; that of the multitude, which mostly addresses itself to objects of the external world, and that of the enlightened, who, disregarding such objects, or viewing them only as important in an allegorical sense of sublime significance, and covering great moral truths, or great features of nature. Each city of Egypt had its peculiar symbols. Memphis, the eloquent, assumed for herself the "Raven." Thebes, which elevated thought to heaven, decorated her banners with the "Eagle with the eye of fire." Canapa chose the " Incense Vase," emblematic of Divine worship. The Sphinx, couching at the gate of the Temple, denoted the Sages that watched over Egypt. These Sages, educated in the solemn mysteries of Heliopolis, Thebes, and Memphis, were the conservators of the Divine Fire. The Sacred Fire of Masonry glowed during a thousand years, and no attempt was made to extinguish or weaken it.

The archives of the Egyptian Masonic Rite of Memphis can reckon among its votaries, such men as Orpheus, Homer. Pythagoras, Thales, Virgil, Hippo·crates, Socrates, Plato and many other great names of Greece, that intellectual daughter of Egypt Whilst on the banks of the Nile, the august guardians of the Traditions veiled them from contemporary eyes, and communicated them only to the few whom they deemed worthy of initiation; other adepts in the interior of Africa, assembling barbarous nations, polished their manners, propagated knowledge, and, in short, founded our secret mysteries among the burning sands of Nubia and Ethiopia Meroe, on one hand, gave light to her Gymnosophists, on the banks of the Ganges and the Indies. Zoroaster founded the Magian School in Persia and Media. Orpheus established the mysteries of Samothrace, which were consecrated to Cabiri, and spread among many nations.

Triptolemus gave laws to Greece, and laid down the principles of agricultural knowledge, and founded the Temple of Eleusis. Abaris carried the light into the North. The mysteries of Memphis were instituted everywhere, even among the frozen plains of Scythia.

In the early ages of mankind, all branches of science, and especially the architectural, were intrusted entirely to the Priests, or to such as they might admit by initiation; but religion, as explained by the mysteries, was the grand object,—science a subsidiary one. Such certainly was the case in the Egyptian mysteries; and as those of Eleusis were brought to Greece from Egypt, shortly before the departure of the Israelites, there is no reason to suppose that they were founded on different principles.

But after a period of four hundred years, during which Greece had advanced much in civilization, some of the initiated attached themselves more to one branch than to another; while some devoted themselves to religion, others followed up more closely the paths of science; and about the year 1060. B C, a portion emigrated to Asia Minor, and gave to that country the name of Ionia. Here the Rites received the name of the Dionysian Mysteries and were no longer practiced chiefly for inculcating religion, but as a necessary initiation or purification of the mind, before the candidate could be admitted to the privileges of an Architect;—for building was so peculiarly the object of this association, that its members were in after time known as the Dionysian Artificers. One of their chief cities was Byblos, the Gebal, or Gabbel of the sacred volume, and the Hebrew word Gibblim, translated (*1 Kings*, v : 18,) stone-squarers; in another place, (*Ezekiel*, xxviii : 9,) rendered (ancients of Gebel,) which means the inhabitants of or workman from Gebal, indicates with sufficient precision that the artists sent by Hiram, King of Tyre to Jerusalem, were a party of these famed artificers.

After the ceremonies of initiation, the candidate was led to the Presiding Priest, and instructed in the mystic science of the institution—Theology, Morals, Philosophy, and Politics being embraced in these instructions. He was baptized, and as in the Christian Church, received a new name. This was engraved, together with a mystic token or sign, upon a small white stone, which thus prepared was presented to the initiated. He preserved it as a sacred talisman, and carried it with him wherever he went, as a means of recognition, it being efficacious to procure him relief from distress and security from danger. It was at the same time the emblem of victory over fear, darkness and error, and the means of enjoyment and peace.

St. John, of the Apocalypse, was an initiate of the Cabiria; and alludes to the mystic stone just noticed, when he says: "To him that overcometh will I give to eat the hidden manna, and will give him a White Stone, and in the stone a new name written which no man knoweth, saving him that receiveth it." (*Rev.* ii: 17.) The Apostle means to say, as the initiate in the Cabirian mysteries, who with a brave heart and an unfaltering step, passes boldly through the terrible ordeal appointed to try his patience, receives a White Stone, with a new name and a mysterious inscription upon it, which is a powerful resource against misfortune, and gives him immunity from danger; so shall be given to the man who overcometh his passions, and triumphs over vice, security from sin and misery. It will raise him to a divine companionship, in a celestial fraternity, and to a full participation hereafter in the mysterious enjoyments of the Secret Pavilion above. These Rites were spread through all the cities of Syria. Hiram, King Tyre, was a High Priest of these mysteries.

This institution existed in Judea in the time of Christ, and it is a notable fact, that while he denounced in the severest terms, the Pharisees and Sadducees, he did not say a word against the Essenes, the faithful depositaries of the Ancient Cabirian Rite. That he was familiar with this Rite was certain, for it cannot be supposed that a mind like his could pass over without due consideration, a society like theirs, admired for amiability and gentleness of manners, and dignified with so many virtues. Besides the moral sentiments, the social maxims, the idea of liberty, fraternity and equality which distinguished the Order, differ in no respect from the teachings of Christians regarding the same things.

Though the Lodges in Judea were chiefly composed of Jews, yet they admitted into their Order, men of every religion and every rank of life, and like the Priests of Egypt, the Magi of Persia, the Gymnosophists of India, they united the study of Moral with that of Natural Philosophy. Although patronized by the great, and respected by all men for the correctness of their conduct, and the innocence of their lives, they were persecuted by the Romans until the abolition of their Rite, about the middle of the fifth century.

The mysteries of Eleusis were abolished by Valentinien, A. D. 396. Dispossessed of the pre-eminence of their worship, the Druids in great numbers took refuge in Britain; others retired among their brethren in the North. Egypt was equally troubled by the successors of Alexander. The initiated were

H*

obliged to hide themselves in the deserts, or to expatriate themselves. * Surrounded by barbarians, they felt more than ever the necessity of a rigorous secret. But they were initiates of different degrees; all were not equally instructed; there were no writings; the great part were ignorant of the oral traditions; few could read the hieroglyphics of the institution.

The real secret of Masonic principles, written in Chaldean, is preserved in the Venerated Ark of the Memphis Rite. A part of it is in the Grand Lodge of Scotland, in Edinburg, and in the Convent of Marmonites on Mount Lebanon. It has come down on the stream of time, pure and unchanged, as it was when from the Temples of Thebes and Eleusis, it excited the veneration of the world.

Whilst the ordinary man is content with the appearance of mystery, and is satisfied with pronouncing some words, of which he knows not the meaning, the Masonic philosopher roams through antiquity, and ascends to primary causes in the study of our institution. Whatever success may crown his toil, if the lamp of study has guided him through the labyrinth of Ancient Mystery, still eager to learn, he will knock at the gate of our Temples.

[The history of this Rite is so very closely connected with the sciences, that it cannot be well separated. So I will give them together as I find them, allowing the reader to cull out or separate for himself.]—AUTHOR.

The teachings of these degrees are of the highest antiquity. The Magi who were the founders, drew their science trom the Gymnosophists of India. There was in the ancient city of Hipparenum, a celebrated school, worthy of the concentration of all human virtues, of the chapters, which heaven designed to become the instructors of the world. But it was particularly in Media that the Magi celebrated their mysteries, and doctrines which spread through the world those floods of light and truth which the Supreme Architect of the Universe had placed in the hearts of the learned Hierophants of Egypt.

Plato attributes to the word Magi a mystic meaning, which signifies "the most perfect culture of all things." The principal object of this degree is to render man perfect, and to draw him nearer to the Divinity, from whom he emanated; that is to say, his re-habitation and re-integration in his primitive rites of rank. There is within us two natures, the animal and the angel, and our labor is to combat the one that the other may dominate, until that moment, when disengaged of its heavy envelope, it shall take flight to better and higher regions. It is perhaps in this sense that the universal dogma of the redemption of mankind should be explained. In the mysteries of this degree it was said that when man, by a new and exemplary life, and by useful work, has reinstated himself in his primitive dignity, he approaches his creator, is animated by a Divine breath, and is initiated. In the instruction, the occult sciences are taught; the secrets of this grade can only be acquired after the prescribed studies, and severe trials, which are in reality but a course of religious and moral ideas, divested of all superstition. To gain admission to this venerated institution, it is necessary to join to an elevation of soul and intelligence—a great purity of morals; and we should bind ourselves by a most solemn vow, to follow the precepts of the most severe virtue in the new life on which we enter.

The forms of this grade are few and simple, and recall the origin and arrangement of the Universe. The object is to render to the Supreme Architect of the Universe the homage which is due to him; to elevate man above his fellow creatures, and to place him beyond those passions which so often trouble his existence.

In the Spring of every year a festival was celebrated, "the regeneration of Light," to represent the primitive equality, and the present connection of mankind. Kings exchanged their vain pomp, and freely mingled with the humblest of their subjects, who were seated at the same table with their kings and princes, a custom calculated to imprint a salutary lesson on the minds of the young princes.

These doctrines, adopted long before by the Chaldeans, were perfected by the sage King Darius Hystaspes, who, having penetrated into most of the regions of India, found the Gymnosophists in the solitary forests, where deep tranquillity favored their profound labors. It was of them he learned the laws which govern the Universe, and the journey of the Stars. They revealed to him the Sacred Rite, which he knew to agree with the doctrine of the Magi. During several centuries these were transmitted to posterity through their descendants; and from time to time men of vast and profound genius in penetrating into the sanctuary of science, have dissipated the clouds which hid the truth from the eyes of the profane, and taught them how, by the force of perseverance, they might elevate temples to virtue, and dig graves for vice.

The ancient initiates have transmitted the science of calculation, a measurement so closely connected with Geometry, and which has been so frequently

pointed out as a necessary study. It begins with the
knowledge of figures, the key to which we derive
from the Egyptians. This consists of a perfect
square divided into four parts by a perpendicular
line, and a horizontal one ; then by two diagonal lines
from angle to angle, by which the square is divided
into triangles. Hence we find the cyphers from one
to ten. The ONE is a perpendicular line. The TWO
is formed by the two horizontal lines, and one of the
diagonal. The THREE is formed by the two horizontal lines of the great square, and by the right half of
the diagonal ones. The FOUR is formed by the right
perpendicular side of the great square, half the diagonal and half the central horizontal lines. The FIVE
is formed by the northwest half of the diagonal line,
the right side of the central horizontal, the lower
half of the right hand perpendicular of the great
square, and the right hand side of the lower horizontal side of the square. The SIX is formed by a line
extending from the right superior angle to the left
inferior one, thence horizontally to the right inferior
angle, thence diagonally to the centre. The SEVEN is
formed by a line drawn horizontally from the summit
of the middle, perpendicularly to the right superior
angle, thence horizontally to the left inferior angle.
The EIGHT is formed by two diagonal lines, making
a cross of St. Andrew, and uniting them above and
below by two horizontal lines. The NINE is formed
by a line drawn perpendicular upwards from the
centre of the square, thence horizontally to the right
superior angle, thence diagonally to the left inferior
angle. The AUGHT is the square itself. The ancient
figures were angular; but as nations became refined,
they gave their characters a more agreeable form,
curving the lines, which were originally straight ; and

thus formed what we improperly denominate Arabic characters. Geometrical studies led our forefathers to that of the inhabitable world, and they soon learned to fathom the ocean of immensity, and to pierce the azure vaults. Man devoted himself to mathematics; a noble science, known then but to the initiates of the Order. This enabled him to develop almost the organization of nature, noting the Solar and Lunar causes, the Astral periods, and the changes of the seasons. The ancient astronomical system is represented in the square; the four compartments of which are the four presumed regions of the world. By observing the sun's course, the four cardinal points were fixed East, West, North and South. The four squares served as angles of divisions for the seasons, making ninety-one days for each, nearly, or three hundred and sixty-four days for the whole, one or two days being added at determined periods.

The Magi studied every department of nature with attention, with a view to arrive at a knowledge of its essence. The immensity of the aerial fluid filled those fires, which they regarded as so many small Suns, and afterwards as Stars. The power of the atmosphere upon all things, and the harmony of the organic laws, caused them to admire the wonders of nature, and sharpened their energies to inquire, and to discover the vivifying principle, the soul of the Universe.

They recognized by their work, the Deity, as the sole origin of organization. They adored the Supreme Being in all the productions of the earth. They concealed their discoveries from the people, and gave fictitious significance to those emblems, which they made known to the public. They decomposed air and matter; salt, sulphur and mercury appeared to be its constituent elements. These three substances were figured as a triangle, which form became, for this reason, more intimately blended with their religious worship, as an emblem of the great motive, God, whom the Hebrews named Jehovah, or the soul of nature. The Triangle was placed in the centre of the divers circles and squares, to denote the vivifying principle which stretched its ramifications over all things. The Magi foretold eclipses and comets, thereby extending the influence of religious ideas, and leading to those of a metaphysical research. The several planets, which are represented as making their course round the common centre, announce the antiquity of the great personages who govern the earth, and were deified by admiring mortals.

Apollo, the God of Light, was synonymous with the sun; this deity also presided over the arts and sciences of antiquity. The Moon represented the Goddess Diana, the sister of Apollo; she was the nocturnal luminary, or light of the second order. Mars presided over the battles and was styled the God of Heroes and Patriots. Mercury, the interpreter of Divine Light, was also the patron deity of Eloquence and Virtue. Jupiter, the chief among the Gods, and the personification of divine intelligence and power. Venus, the Goddess of Beauty, and the Mother of Love, are names which the genius of Greece and Rome have transmitted imperishably in a language which will be preserved by the polished and the educated of mankind through all time.

So, also, these classic pages preserve the renown of the God who, personating Time, was said to have devoured his children, even as time consumes all to whom it gives birth—Saturn.

The two semi-circles are emblematical of Divinity and Nature, which to the true Mason are synonymous terms; everything in nature being governed by fixed laws, and consequently, periodical in its movements, announces the existence of a Grand Master, which attracts our veneration, and convinces us that nothing can be superior to Him. The Flaming Star is a symbol of Divine Providence, of that great and good Being whom Masons adore as the Supreme Architect of the Universe.

Among the mathematical sciences, Geometry is the one which has the most special reference to Architecture, and we can therefore understand the whole art of Freemasonry. The whole being of the Order is comprehended in it. Freemasons, therefore, ought to make themselves intimately acquainted with Geometry. It is not absolutely necessary to be able to delineate Geometrical figures, but it is necessary to be able to deduce all our actions, works and resolutions from Geometrical principles.

Freemasonry is a science which requires both time and experience, and more time than many brethren can devote to it; the only time in fact they can devote to it being during their hours of recreation. Therefore it is good that it is communicated by degrees, according to the regulations of the Order, or the candidate's power of comprehension.

As in Geometry, so in Masonry, there is no royal road to perfection; a knowledge of its science can only be acquired by long and diligent study. To the candidate who rapidly passes through the degrees, Masonry is as incomprehensible as the veiled statue of Isis, and he becomes either a useless drone in our hive, or retires in disgust from all participation in our labors. But the candidate who by slow and painful steps has proceeded through each apartment of our Mystic Temple, from its porch to its Sanctuary, pausing in his progress to admire the beauties and study the uses of each, learning as he advances, line upon line and precept upon precept, is gradually and almost imperceptibly struck with so much admiration of the institution, so much love of its principles, so much appreciation of its design as a conservator of Divine truth, and an agent of human civilization, that he is inclined at last, on beholding the whole beauty of the finished building, to exclaim as did the wonderful Queen of Sheba, " A most excellent Master must have done this !"

In the Degrees of the Rite of Memphis, it is explained to you that the builders of the Temple of Jerusalem, the Tyrians, the men of Gebal, were a colony of our ancient brethren, who had brought the Arts from Egypt to the shores of Asia Minor. They were famed for their skill in working metals, in hewing timber and stone, in a word for what was solid, great and ornamental in architecture.

They had already built the Temple of Hercules, at Tyre, and many magnificent edifices in Asia Minor; and the Israelites, who disregarded mechanical arts, applying themselves to agriculture and the feeding of cattle, had no professed artificers who could undertake the work of the Temple.

Solomon requested Hiram, King of Tyre, to send him men capable of constructing it; also an architect to superintend the work.

This person was found in Hiram Abiff, who was the most accomplished designer and operator on the earth. His abilities were not confined to building only, but extended to all kinds of work in gold, silver, brass or iron. Whether considered as an architect or designer, he equally excelled.

From his designs and under his direction, all the rich and splendid furniture of the temple and its several appendages were begun, carried on and finished. Solomon in his zeal to have the Temple finished, convened those masters who had distinguished themselves by their genius, capacity and devotion, and formed them into a Lodge to effect it. As these were no longer to be confounded with the rest of the workmen, he commanded that the distinct mark they had worn should be changed, and that they should in future have the right of entrance to the Sanctuary, having previously been placed on the letter "G," and the flaming star, and binding themselves by promises such as you have entered into. And may you many years enjoy this happiness among us.

Many remarkable circumstances occurred near Mount Horeb, where Moses received the Divine command to lead forth the Israelites from Egypt. This mountain was remarkable for seven memorable transactions. First, the Burning Bush; second, the striking of the rock with the rod of Moses; the lifting of Moses' hands by Aaron and Hur, which caused the slaughter of the Amelekites; fourth, the delivery of the Law; fifth, the forty days' abstinence of Moses; sixth, the erection of the Tabernacle; and seventh, the punishment of Korah, Dathan, and Abyram, for disobedience.

The Tabernacle was constructed on the plan of the Egyptian Temples. It is true that, strictly speaking, it ought not to be looked upon as a piece of architecture, being only a large tent. But by reflecting on it more closely, we shall perceive that the Tabernacle had a great relation with architecture. In the government of the Hebrews, the Supreme Being was equally their God and their King.

The Tabernacle was created to answer the double purpose of a Temple and a palace. Many symbols were represented on the Tabernacle and the Temple. Moses placed in the former two cherubims, or sphinxes, as well as ornaments; and decorations of flower work, and figures of cherubims were embroidered on the Vail of the Holy of Holies, on the hangings of the Sanctuary, and probably the curtains also. It is evident, therefore, that Moses never intended to prohibit the use of symbols; nor was such a thing understood by the Jews in any age.

Here Moses opened his Holy Lodge about two years after the exody of the children of Israel from Egypt into the wilderness of Sinai. Here the Almighty delivered to him the Decalogue, with the forms of the Tabernacle and the Ark; and here he dictated those peculiar forms of civil and religious policy which, by separating His people from all other nations, consecrated Israel a chosen vessel for His service.

Over this Lodge presided Moses, the great and inspired Lawgiver; Aholiab, the curious carver and embroiderer; and Bezaleel, the famous architect, until Korah, Dathan and Abyram raised up a sedition against Moses and Aaron, saying unto the children of Israel, " Ye take too much upon you, seeing all the congregation are holy, every one of them, and the Lord is among them. Wherefore, then, lift ye up yourselves above the congregation of the Lord ?"

And the Lord spake unto Moses, saying, "Speak unto the congregation, saying, Get you up from about the Tabernacle of Korah, Dathan and Abyram."

And Moses said, "Hereby ye shall know that the

Lord hath sent me to do all these works, for I have
not done them of my own mind.

" If these men die the common death of all men, or
if they be visited after the visitation of all men, then
the Lord hath not sent me.

" But if the Lord make a new thing, and the earth
open her mouth, and swallow them up, with all that
appertain unto them, and they go down quick into
the pit, then ye shall understand that these men have
provoked the Lord."

And it came to pass, as he had made an end of
speaking all these words, that the ground clave
asunder that was under them.

And the earth opened her mouth, and swallowed
them up, and their houses, and all the men that ap-
pertained unto Korah, and all their goods.

And thus Aaron was no longer to have the priesthood by the favor of Moses, but by the public judgment of God.

[Perhaps this is a digression, but in order that the
reader may see the difference between the York Rite
and Memphis Rite in its application, I here insert a portion of the lecture in one of the Degrees of a Senate.
I also append a Lecture on Coptic Worship, taught
by the Egyptians, and in some measure explaining
the use of the Serpent in Masonry.]—AUTHOR.

This Lecture supposes the Neophyte to have taken
the preceding Degrees of Symbolic Degree Nomen-
clature, and his guide, the Grand Marshal, answers
for him these questions :

Q. Illustrious Knight Marshal, tell me what qualities were ascribed by our venerated Patriarchs to
the Seven Planets ?

A. Saturn, cold and dry ; Jupiter, warm and
moist ; Mars, hot and dry ; Sun, fiery and dry ; Ve-

nus, moist and warm; Mercury, warm and dry; Moon, cold, moist and changing.

Q. What is the power of numbers?

A. Unity is the symbol of identity, existence and general harmony; Binary is the symbol of diversity and separation; the Ternary, the image of the Supreme Being, uniting in itself the properties of the two first numbers.

To the Pythagoreans it represented not only the surface, but the principle of the formation of bodies.

It applies to the three chemical principles, which give animation to the whole world, Salt, Sulphur and Mercury, belonging to the three kingdoms of Nature, Life, Soul and Body, Birth, existence and Death, Dryness, Humidity and Putrefaction; from all times, the ancients held the Ternary in great respect.

The number Four is found in time and space; there are four Cardinal Points and four Seasons.

The number Five was considered as a mystic number, composed of the Binary and Ternary. As a Pentalpha, it is an emblem of fellowship.

The number Six was in the ancient mysteries a striking emblem of Nature, North, East, South, West, the Zenith, and Nadir.

The Double Triangle is the emblem of the Sentence of Hermes, who said: "That which is below is like that which is above." This figure is emblematic of Deity.

The number Seven, according to the Sages, governed the Universe.

The number Eight is a symbol of perfection, and its figure indicates the perpetual and regular course of the Universe.

The number Nine was regarded by the Sages with veneration, for reasons already given.

The Hermetic Cross. The Cross mystically corresponds with the secret teachings of the high mysteries, and contains all the sacred numbers; it is the base of Geometry. This symbol existed in the Isle of Cazumel, on the coast of Yucatan, nearly four thousand years before Christ, and was revered as the divinity of rain, allegory of fertility.

Quetzalcoate, the legislator of the Indians, was represented in a robe with crosses. It was used anciently to indicate the roads. It was consecrated in China to the adoration of the Supreme Architect of the Universe.

In Northern Asia, and in some parts of America have been found large stones in the form of a Cross, adored by the ancient people. Many mythological ruins in Greece have had the same form.

Also we learn that in Egypt the Thos, (land-marks) were often in wood, and in the shape of a Cross. On the transverse pieces were inscriptions relative to science and the arts; and to multiply those inscriptions, they sometimes placed on three cross-pieces, which made double or triple Crosses, which are frequently seen on ancient monuments, as well as single crosses; again, it is considered as the key of the Nile, to which that country owes its fertility. We have seen how general was the veneration for this sign, with different motives.

It is to be remarked, with as much pleasure as interest, how natural good sense knew when science was but little advanced, how to represent by so simple a sign as two sticks laid across at right angles, the course of the sun and the progress of the seasons. It is not astonishing that to fix better the attention of the people on those great phenomena to which we owe the production of the earth, and to excite them to a pious gratitude towards their author, their representative sign was made a religious symbol.

The horizontal line represents the Equator, and the vertical, the Meridian; we have thus four extremities of the Equator, and the two solstices of Summer and Winter at those of the Meridian; consequently, the four seasons. By analogy, they unite to Spring, youth and morning; to Summer, ripe age and noon; to Autumn, age and evening; and to Winter, death and night.

The Alchemists added to those four points, which they called the four generative elements, Fire, Air, Earth and Water, which they expressed by conventional signs.

The Red Cross is the symbol of the life to come; the origin of this Cross is of the highest antiquity.

To form this Cross, commence by tracing a circle of three hundred and sixty degrees, in which design a Cross of twelve equal squares, which represent the twelve signs of the Zodiac, or the twelve months of the solar year; one-half in ascending from January to the end of June, indicates the progression of the days; and the other half, July to the end of December, the declination of the sun. This Cross essentially marks the line of meridian from South to North, and indicates at the same time the strong heat of Summer, in opposition to the frosts of Winter.

A horizontal line traverses the entire world from East to West, and shows us equal days and nights in the zone which it divides; this line is called the Equator.

In casting the eye of imagination over the four quarters of the globe, we discover in this Cross the principle of life, which is the Air, or the East; the beginning of vegetation, or Spring, which announces to us the awakening of Nature; infancy should be placed on this side, for man finds himself in the Spring of life, as the horizon of morning indicates the appearance of day in this quarter of the world, and the sun rising in the East enriches it with its beneficent rays.

Let us now look to the top of the Cross; we shall find there fire, which is the soul of life, according to many philosophers, who symbolized by this element the Creator of the Universe. The Summer by its great heat characterizes the second part of the year. Man, in adult age, is remarked by the desire of re-production of his kind, and by the strength of his physical faculties. Noon is naturally found in this part of the Cross, because the sun is at its highest point, which makes the meridian.

If we look at the West, we shall find that part of the world contains more atmospheric humidity. Autumn, which is the third season of the year, shows us that all the productions of the earth have arrived at their maturity. Man, in this division of the Cross, is placed in his decline, which we denominate age—third period of life—that in which he should live happy, if he has known how to profit by the preceding years of his labor. This division of the Cross indicates, also, that the sun descends under the horizon of night in the West; it is the time when man prepares himself for rest.

In the North is found the earth, as being the most material and consequently the heaviest portion; it is also the reason why we place it at the bottom. Winter, where all is frozen from its distance from the sun, procures the fourth season of the year, when all nature seems to be completely inert. The portion of the globe to the North is found to be less peopled than the other portion of the earth, because it is an almost continual Winter. In this part of the Cross is indicated the death to which each creature is obliged to submit.

Man, as well as animals, returns to the ground; all of matter is decomposed to be reproduced under other forms and is annihilated by turns, according to the order of the Divinity and Nature. In the bottom of the Cross is the instant os sleep or night; which makes the fourth part of the day, composed of twenty-four hours.

In the centre of the Cross is found the Flaming Star, with a Delta in the middle, bearing in its centre the simple, but great character of ONE GOD! —the point signifying the Universe, which is governed by invariable rules.

The laws are indicated by twelve squares, which bear the names of the months, composing the Solar Year. Outside of this Cross there is another, announcing the lunar months of twenty-eight days, two hours, seventeen minutes and thirty-six seconds, which the Mahommedans still follow; their year is therefore composed of thirteen lunar months, which gives the same number of days as the solar year, which is three hundred and sixty-five days, forty-eight minutes and forty-eight seconds. The Lunar Cross is called the Hammer Cross. The Alchemists of the middle ages wore a ring with the initials I. A. A. T.—*Ignus, Aqua, Aer, Terra,*—Fire, Water, Air, Earth.

The Hebrew words for the four elements, were— *Iammin,* Water; *Nour,* Fire; *Rouaah,* Air; *Iabescheh,* Earth. Of these four letters were the following aphorisms: "*Igne Natura Renovatar Integra.*"

1

Nature is entirely renewed by fire. *"Igne Nitrium
Roris Invenitur."* Repel we ignorance by indefati-
gable efforts.

We might follow this course of instruction through
a large number of pages, and show to the curious
reader that which a search into many volumes would
fail to convey—instruction strange to the Masonic
scholar who had contented himself with a mere
glance, or very superficial idea of what real Masonic
teaching was, for in the age in which this system of
education was introduced, venerable sages searched
the pages of antiquity, and gleaned from them the
rarest gems of thought and expression, and sought to
convey them to the mind of the neophyte in the
most simple and yet in the most striking and impressive manner; and as this sample of antiquity is
all we intended to copy, we will briefly consider the
more modern Masonry, from the raising of the Tabernacle in which God was worshiped in the wilderness, and the lifting up of the Brazen Serpent, to
the building of Solomon's Temple, and certain events
in connection therewith, and the tracing of the Rite
to the present day. And I shall avail myself again
of some of the valuable lectures of the Memphis Rite,
of the Brazen Serpent, being a partial induction into
the body of a Council of Knights of the Brazen Serpent, as an illustration of the condition to which the
children of Israel were reduced by their persistent
deviation from the teachings of their fathers, and the
revealed will of God, who brought many afflictions
upon them because they forsook His Divine Law.
And we read from history that while journeying
through the wilderness, many left the camp of safety,
and were lost; others profaned the privileges God
had vouchsafed unto them, for the correction of which

His powerful arm was frequently required for their subjugation and restoration. Prominent among these was the infesting their tents with poisonous serpents, who bit the transgressors, so that many died.

To appease or subvert the evils produced by disobedience, Moses, at God's command, caused a Brazen Serpent to be made, and set up on a cross, or T, so that all who were bitten might look upon the Brazen Serpent, and, by Faith, be healed. Of this we have an account in the Book of Numbers, to which I would call your especial attention.

" And the Lord sent fiery serpents among the people, and they bit the people; and much people of Israel died.

" Therefore the people came to Moses, and said, We have sinned, for we have spoken against the Lord, and against thee; pray unto the Lord, that he take away the serpents from us. And Moses prayed for the people.

" And the Lord said unto Moses, make thee a fiery serpent, and set it upon a pole; and it shall come to pass, that every one that is bitten, when he looketh upon it, shall live.

" And Moses made a serpent of brass, and put it upon a pole; and it came to pass, that if a serpent had bitten any man, when he beheld the serpent of brass, he lived."

And you are here shown that thus far Masonry has taught you that in our Egyptian Masonic Rite, the Legends of Antiquity, which had their origin on the banks of the Nile, were by our Primitive Brethren disregarded, and viewed only as myths, veiling from vulgar minds, important truths. In the earliest ages, amongst rude and uncivilized men, the Serpent or Dragon, was regarded as sacred; according to the writers of Antiquity, the very foundation of Greece, that intellectual daughter of Egypt, was cemented by the blood of the Dragon or Serpent, when Cadmus, having slain him and plucked his teeth and sown them, there sprang forth from these seeds, armed warriors, from whom afterward were to be born the sages and heroes of antiquity. This, perchance, may refer mythologically to the advent of the ophitic worship into Greece, for we notice that after his death, Cadmus, like Toth among the Egyptians, was transformed into a snake, and adored under that form; still further, when the country began to be reduced to some order, Draco, that is the Dragon, was first monarch at Athens. In short, the histographers and logographers are replete with anecdotes and illustrations of the worship as it then existed, depicting in their sober sincerity, the same state of things which prevailed, even with the savage tribes of Africa; describing their serpents as the guardians or palladiums of the cities, and as beings reverenced with every expression of abject submission. Their entire mythology abounds with similar allusions and circumstances, wherein the serpent personates a most important character. Again, the adventures of Hercules in his childhood, the death of Laocoon, the gaolers in the gardens of Hesperides, and the thousand fabulous grottos defended by the snake in some one of his varied forms, are illustrations familiar to all. As to the Latin nation, religion had become so modified up to the period of their settlement, that their mythology embodies fewer circumstances expresssive of its ophitic origin than other nations springing more directly from the Orientals; still they appropriated much from the neighboring Greeks and Egyptians.

The rapid extension of Roman and Grecian power

and with it, an intercourse with the then known
world, afforded but so many facilities for the propagation of their religious ideas; and, although there
seldom enforced the unwilling acceptance of opinions
and beliefs upon their conquered nations, still, there
must have resulted from the mere communication a
reciprocal influence, as might be surmised, in favor of
the mightier minds. Thus the Muscovite and Pole
finally adopted the most debased form of worship,
adoring the serpent as a household divinity. like the
lares and penates of the classic world, decreeing it a
penalty of death to injure one, however venomous in
its character, and surrendering up to them the unrestrained freedom of their hearths. Almost all the
vipers obtained their protection and reverence in an
equal degree. But of the divisions of Europe,
Scandinavia, embracing the Swedes, Fins, Norwegi-
ans, Danes, &c., is particularly rich in the mysteries
and legends of this character. Its mythology
abounds in allusions to, and its fables are filled with
exploits of the serpent. Lok, the genius of evils, is
styled the father of the great serpent; the standards
of many exhibit the same emblem, and the few hiero-
glyphic remains that have been discovered, bear
witness of the prominent character it assumed in
their belief. The only difference to be remarked, is
the variation in the form of the reptile, which now
assumed the most monstrous and terrific powers,
breathing flames and pestilence from its distended
jaws, and expressing revenge and utter slaughter in
its looks. This fanciful form became a particular
favorite with the earlier Christian writers, whence
have resulted the heroic legends of St. Patrick, St.
Michael, St. George and St Margaret, and the extra-
ordinary wonders depicted in the stories of the Mid-
1*

dle Ages. That such was the policy of the founders
of most religions is not a matter of astonishment,
since, to the uneducated mind the awful and sublime
are to be represented less in things invisible than in
natural forms exaggerated into terrors, in physical
events, partaking of the purely tragic character; it
appeals, in short, rather to the eye than to the subtle
essence of the mind. Thus it seems to them that
God would rather afflict nations with His wrath, than
seek to raise up prophets in their midst to instruct
and forewarn them.

At length, we enter into Gaul and Britain with the
worship which, like the symbolical representation of
the Chinese, had literally encircled the earth. The
Druid worship, so famous in antiquity, was an off-
spring of the ophitic creed; the same familiar snake
was adored, not only as a symbol of light and life,
but independently, in its own animal nature, as a
serpent. So close, indeed, are the affinities of their
gods and goddesses, so perfect the exposition of that
creed, that many incline to the opinion that the intercourse between these isles and the ancient world
was far more intimate than we are accustomed to
think.

Their divinities are variously pictured under the
form of the snake, whilst still further to increase and
cement the connection of ideas, "draig" signifies
both serpent and a Supreme God. Their many
fables, among others that of "Uther Pendragon,"
contain explicit and conclusive evidence of their
worship, with its ambiguous reference to the "gliding
king" pursuing the "fair one," even as in the garden
of Eden, the treacherous angel followed the credulous
Eve. The same peculiarity to which we have referred in other nations, that of attributing healing

powers to the serpent, is abundantly manifested among the Druids.

As the Druid religion was established in Ireland and Gaul, there, no less than in England, were examples afforded of the old creed. The story of St. Patrick banishing the toads and serpents from Ireland, has, with a great deal of ingenuity, been referred to his opposition to the existing faith and his determination to eradicate its pernicious doctrines from the minds of the people; the ruling divinities in both countries are presented armed with the caduceus of Mercury, or associated in some distinct manner with the serpent, either as a symbol or attribute; the same low superstitions and their resultant cruelties and barbarism are reproduced.

The cycle is thus completed, but much remains untold, were it but the theory of the origin of the serpent worship or its practice as it exists in our own times. We have only to recall the numerous current stories of the fascination of the snake, its mesmeric and medicinal powers, the wondrous accounts of the ubiquitous sea-serpents that startle the world so frequently, and tales of a similar character, to understand that the old belief is not entirely dead nor the old terror entirely cast aside. The whole subject affords us a fine illustration of credulity, whether indulged by minds sottish and brutal, or active and refined. Unfortunately, in all religions, the element of fear has entered too largely; and to repent, in order to be saved, is a precept more attentively followed than to do, in order to have done. And so of old, it hung like a dark mist over the intellectual sight of the world, at the dawn of science. But the sun rose at last, blood-stained, it is true, and the glorious prospects began to be revealed. Far back lay the mountains, clad in purple and gloom, around all flashed a golden light, whilst forward, the unfathomless vistas of space were opened, glittering with worlds through all immensity. And that sun was the light of knowledge, and those growing mountain tops the past, and the golden glow and heat the present, and the future lies with those worlds dimly seen and known. For the past there is charity, for the present hope, for the future there is faith.

HISTORY OF MOSES MASONRY.

A good deal of the history of Moses and the journey of the Israelites through the wilderness is the connecting link in the quasi Egyptian Hebrew Masonry, called now York Rite, and more particularly the first three degrees of Operative Masonry, called in Egpyt, the Degrees of "Isis, Serapis and Osiris," and known to us as Apprentice, Fellow-craft and Master, the Royal Arch of the York Rite, together with the Royal and Select Master, or Council Degrees, being side degrees, and there communicated instead of being worked as they now are in America, they being better adapted to building and municipal government than the higher or philosophical degrees; therefore, when Moses undertook the arduous task, and had got through the Red Sea, he commenced to disseminate the work by Degrees of Operative Government or Labor.

After Moses had led the children of Israel through the wilderness to Mount Sinai, and had founded in some degree the secret mysteries of the Egyptians, among whom he had been educated, and of which he was one, except perhaps by blood and birth, he was allowed to see from Pisga's top, the land of promise, that land which had been the goal of his ambition, his hopes and aspirations. He had, although a man slow of speech, been a diligent officer, High Priest and King. He had rescued his people from the hand of the oppressor, and had taught them in all the ways of civilization then known; he had, above all things, learned them self government, the real spirit of Free-masonry, the art of benevolent society. He had made wise laws, and laid down in plain unmistaken terms the true principles of law and order; he had spent a long life of usefulness, and had acted as a mediator between God and man, and had lived to a green old age. Yet he was over one hundred years old, and with all his toil and care, including a life of over forty years in the wilderness, on a constant march, subject to all the changing seasons of such a varied life, and yet such was the care he had taken of himself, such had been the control he exercised over the passions and the inclemency of a life in the tented field, subject so the changing seasons, the cold wintry winds, and the heated months of summer; in all this we are told that his natural forces had not been impaired, his eye was not dimmed, or his nat-ural forces abated; he possessed all the vigor and alacrity of youth, coupled with the wisdom and ex-perience of the sage, fresh and vigorous in body and mind, just the pattern and type of a good Mason, one well calculated to rule and govern the Lodge, and to give good and wholesome advice on all subjects com-ing within his duty as Master, Priest, King and Scribe, to that million of Brother Masons' wives and children entrusted to his care. But he, for disobe-dience to his maker, was debarred the privilege of entering into that land of promise, that land flowing with milk and honey, that he had so long pictured and described to his brethren. When the storms of adversity and thick and dark clouds of doubt and distrust took hold on his people, when his Lodge remonstrated with him for bringing them into the wilderness to starve, (as they claimed,) when hunger and cold, and rain, hail and the thousand ills, that flesh is heir to set in, and discontent and dissatisfaction reigned supreme, yet he, like the true Mason, cheered them on, by his sage and good counsel, even when the serpent bit them, and they died by hundreds of the poisonous reptiles. And when they were perishing with thirst for the want of water, yet he with a firm belief in the immutable promises of Divinity, followed the pillar of cloud by day and fire by night, till he brought his Lodge within sight of the land that was to be the inheritance for them and their children forever—then and then only did he resign the gavel into other hands; and he was gathered to and slept with his fathers. And his works lived; they were confided to faithful breasts; and the Tabernacle, by Moses, with the help of Aholiab and Bezaleel, was the pattern of the Temple, and that pattern was one he had learned in Egypt, where Masonic usage and custom had taught its votaries, who to the present day follow its patterns. Although thousands of years have rolled into the dark vista, and generation after generation have passed away. yet its secrets to-day live in the hearts of every true craftsman. As the needle to the pole is true, so are the cardinal principles and landmarks of that institution, reared for wise, good and benevolent purposes in the hearts of good men; and although we no longer practice the operative, yet we do and should revere the speculative, and propose to trace, mostly by extracts from the several lectures of the degrees, the history of the institution through the temple

building period down to the present time, speaking
first of the Orders of Knighthood or Chevalier Degrees, as the French call them, and by which the
officers of the several degrees were instructed, it being a kind of Council or Court for the instruction of
Masons who had charge of the drawings and specifi-
cations necessary to the construction and design of
the edifice or superstructure that was to be raised,
and here it was that the principles of geometry and
its kindred sciences were discussed and unfolded;
here also it was that the higher branches of architecture were taught. And we as Masons, keeping in
full view the rules, regulations and principles of the
operative workman, teach the ardent Mason the
principles of speculative science, adapting its rules
and regulations, and applying its cardinal principles
to the good of society and the development of its
virtuous and benevolent principles, to explain which
we now begin with the temple building period.

In Egyptian Masonry and this Masonic Rite we
believe that there is no God but GOD, and all men are
His children. Then let us each endeavor to purify
our hearts, that we may be worthy of that heritage
hereafter, which our Father who is in Heaven has
provided for His children.

There is nothing stable in this world; the most
solid monuments, the institutions most revered, are
subject to this law. Virtue alone is immortal, and
renders the true Mason unshakable in the events of
life. In the great revolutions, the ordinary man sees
only the physical causes which have prepared and
produced them; but the sage knows there is a Providence in the secret council of His justice, which dis-
poses and directs events for the fulfillment of His
designs.

The Degrees through which you have passed have taught you what the Ancient Egyptian Masonic Rite expects from you. They have made you feel the necessity of purging your soul of vice, the passions and the prejudices which obscure the intelligence, and which deprive the soul of all its energy, They have been at the same time for us, the means of proving your zeal, docility, and love of the Order, and of mankind.

The Temple of Jerusalem is the Grand Type of Masonry. The revolutions it has undergone will recall to you those the Masonic Order has suffered at different times. The masonry instituted by the Chiefs of the workmen at the Temple of Solomon, rebuilt by Zerubbabel, presents but the solid principles, and the pure morality, which tends to make man better, and more useful to others; to teach him his duties, and to elevate him to the dignity of his existence. So long as it was practiced on this basis, the Order was and must be flourishing, and all its members respected.

Such was its first state, which is figured to you by the Temple of Jerusalem, which was in its splendor under King Solomon, and was the glory of all nations. But from the time that indolence was introduced into the Order, that members were admitted little disposed to follow its fundamental principles, they neglected the prescribed virtues, and introduced the vices, which had till then been banished; then was seen a mixture of worthy men, in manners, knowledge and benevolence, with others, who, having but the appearance of those virtues, with the insulting arrogance of vice, gave a mortal blow to the reputation which they had enjoyed. Envy, jealousy and calumny gave rise to powerful enemies; its ceremonies, and mysterious practices became suspected, and served as a pretext for graver imputations, injustices and persecutions, from which it has so often and so severely suffered. Pride, so familiar to the man who has lost sight of all that should humiliate him,—pride to belong to a body which had so long excited the admiration of all who knew it, was the source of all its evils. The vices which resulted therefrom burst on the entire Order; it was persecuted and lost all its *eclat*. The second state of our Order is renewed by the improper conduct of many of its members, and which is represented by the burning and sacking of Jerusalem and its Temple. But, as in that revolution, its foundations were preserved; even so the true Masons, yielding for a time to the torrent, have guarded carefully the precious deposit transmitted to them, and when they have seen a multitude of Masons, like the Israelites, repairing their faults, then they have again brought forth, in all their primitive splendor, those rules. Like Esdras of old, they have made the Masonic fraternity feel the necessity of purging their Lodges of innovations, which the second state of the Order had introduced. Thus the Temple has been re-edified; the Sacred Word has been again found, and Masonry has resumed its ancient lustre, which will be preserved, so long as Masons keep in view the invariable principle on which it was founded. This is the actual state of the Order, represented to you by the third epoch of the Temple re-established by Zerubbabel. For it must be remembered that during the reign of Zedekiah, Jerusalem was destroyed, her people driven in chains to Babylon by their conquerors, who carried with them those holy vessels of silver and gold which had adorned that

K

magnificent Temple, erected by our Ancient Grand Master, King Solomon, four hundred and seventy years six months and ten days previous.

After the city was destroyed, and the Temple demolished, several Knights of the Secret Vault bethought them of the Sacred Delta. On repairing to the ruins of the Temple at midnight, they found the entrance open; upon descending discovered in the cold embrace of death the body of Gedaliah, whom you to-day have represented, covering the secret place where he had concealed the precious emblem He, like Hiram Abif, nobly lost his life, rather than betray his trust to the unworthy. Thereupon, they erased the sacred characters from the Delta, and broke it into pieces. They then placed the body of Gedaliah by the cube stone, and having performed the rites of sepulchre over his inanimate remains, they filled the Vault with rubbish.

The Egyptian Masonic Rite is a religion that taught the patriarchs of antiquity to render homage to T. S. A. O. T. U. It has for its basis the belief in the existence of God, and the immortality of the soul; and for its aim the practice of benevolence and virtue.

It is the fraternal claim that links the brethren together in bonds of FAITH in GOD, who redeemeth; of CHARITY, which blesseth; and of HOPE in immortality.

These Degrees are founded on a knowledge, belief and adoration of the Sacred Word or name of God, which is the foundation of every branch of Masonry and religion, whether ancient or modern.

In the beginning was the WORD, and the WORD was with GOD, and the WORD was GOD.

This same word, however mysterious it may appear to the profane, has been held sacred by all Masons who have been exalted to the high Degrees throughout the world. The belief in the Eternity of the Godhead, being the foundation of every religion known to the world.

Our ancient Hebrew brethren recognized twelve mysterious or cabalistic names by which they expressed the attributes of Deity, which we cannot repeat or give here, but which Masons know and fully understand.

You are already acquainted with the fact that the true pronunciation of the name of God was revealed to Enoch, and that he engraved the letters composing that name on a triangular plate of gold. The name was represented by the four Hebrew consonants. The vowel sounds of this language being represented by points placed above the consonants composing the mysterious word, at different ages received different pronunciations. Hence, though the method of writing this word remained uniform, its pronunciation underwent many changes. These' changes constitute what are termed the different ages of Masonry. These are the three ages of Masonry, and are thus estimated. After the death of Enoch the Ineffable Name was pronounced by

Names	Pronunciation	Ages	Names	Pronunciation	Ages
Methuselah, Lamech, and Noah,	Juha, (Ye haw.),	3 ages.	Shem, Araphaxed, Salah, Eber, Peleg,	Jeva, (Ye-waw.)	5 ages.
Reu, Serug, Nahor, Terah, Abraham, Isaac, Judah,	Jova, (Yo-waw.)	7 ages.	Hezron, Ram, Abidah, Nasahon, Salmon, Boaz, Obed, Jesse, David,	Jevo, (Yay-wo.) Jevah, (Ye-way.) Johe, (Yo-hay.) Jehovah, (Ye ho-waw.)	9 ages.

The true pronunciation of the name was revealed to Enoch, Jacob, and Moses, and on that account are not named in this enumeration. The perfect number

is thus formed. The number of corrupted words is
9. The ages of Masonry, 3, 5, 7, 9—24, multiplied
by 3, gives the product 72; to this add 9, the number
of corrupted words, the amount is 81, which is the
age of a Knight of the Secret Vault. The mysterious words which you received in the preceding Degrees, are all so many corruptions of the true name
of God, which was engraved on the triangle.

Moses did not ask for the true name of God, but
for the true pronunciation of it, which had been lost
through the wickedness of mankind. It was enacted in the Mosaic Law, that if any one expressly
mentioned the name of Jehovah blasphemously, he
should be stoned to death. Upon this account the
name has always been called SHEM-HAM-PHERAUSH,
the unutterable name, or as it is sometimes called the
word of a Mason which I have before explained to
be the true name of T. S. A. O. T. U.; spoken in or
pronounced differently by different nations in different parts of the world.

It remains with me to explain the connection of
Hiram Abif with the Order. Hiram, the sublime
workman, endowed, according to the Holy Writings,
with intelligence and rare knowledge, surnamed Abif,
which, according to some, signifies "sent from God"
—this man, revered by Hiram, King of Tyre, as a
father; esteemed, cherished and honored by King
Solomon, who was guided by his counsel, is at once
the father and model of true Masons, and the particular type of the Order, and the three states, of which
I have presented to you the image. The history of
his death and assassination by three Fellow Crafts is
an ingenious fiction, favored by the silence of the
Holy Writings; it veils, however, great truths for
the Mason who would instruct himself. Each cir-

cumstance of his life, and the mournful event which Masons celebrate iu their works, teach the virtues they should practice, of which the example is now before you. Hiram, living respected, cherished, and directing all, represents the Order in its primitive state, when it was known only by its good deeds and the admiration it excited. Hiram, in the Temple, praying each night, when the workmen retired, teaches Masons that they owe more to the Supreme Being than to the profane. Hiram, assassinated by three Fellow Crafts, who would force from him the WORD, indicates the danger of violent passions, which may lead us to the greatest extremes, if they are not at once repressed; and the injustice of those, who, without taking the trouble to labor themselves, would tear from others their discoveries, and partake with them the fruits thereof.

The refusal of Hiram teaches that discretion should ever be the favorite virtue of a Mason. Lastly, his tragic death announces the second state of the Order, succumbing through the bad conduct of some of its members, designated by the Fellow Crafts under the characters of Avarice, Calumny and Injustice, Hiram, the particular type of the Masonic Order, and of the three epochs, is to-day presented to you as rising from the dead. Aid us to recall him to life, surrounded by the virtues he practiced, and which conduct to that immortality to which all should aspire who would imitate his truth.

This ends all of Masonry connected with the Temple erected by Solomon. At its commencement a Brother sealed his truth with his blood, and at its destruction, amidst the wickedness of the people, there was still found a brother whose integrity was equal to that of our first Operative Grand Master.

May you, and all Masons of our Egyptian Masonic Rite, emulate their courage in the cause of truth. So shall our beloved institution be honored by the world, and our Sanctuary be blessed by Heaven ; and the light of our truth shine forth as the morning star in the midst of a cloud ; as the sun shining upon the Temple of the Most High ; and as the rainbow giving light in the bright clouds ; as the flavor of roses in the spring of the year; as lillies by the waters, and as the frankincense tree in summer ; as fire and incense in the censer, and as a vessel of gold set with precious stones; as a fair olive tree budding forth fruit, and as a cypress which groweth up to the clouds. And when the robes of death are placed upon us, may they prove to be the garments of perfection to the All Seeing Eye of the S. A. O. T. U., Supreme Architect of the Universe, that He may appoint each of us Guardians of his resplendent Sanctuary of Truth, and to an everlasting lite, where is love, and peace, and joy unspeakable, in the Divine presence of Him who was, who is, and who ever shall be, world without end.

In conclusion, therefore, I have only to recall some of the main points of the former brief history, in order that the reader may not get embarrassed in the brief histories set forth; the first being a history of our organization, the second a brief history of the Rite in America, which was then called the Ancient and Primitive Rite, and the third a synopsis of the history of the Egyptian Masonic Rite of Memphis, with a brief outline of Moses' Masonry, or quasi Egyptian-Hebrew Masonry. And after completing the Temple, and drawing therefrom the moral, and exposing some of the myths and evils arising from the drawing out of a Rite of Three Degrees, with the Royal Arch as a side degree or honorary degree, and the Council of Royal and Select Masters as explanatory degrees, with the original signs and tokens changed, and other new ones substituted, which tend greatly to hinder and embarrass either the Neophyte of this country or of Europe, and which instead of making the degrees universal, makes them to seem contradictory and different. Thus the mission of the Memphis Rite, seems to be a sort of explanatory Rite, doing no harm. In that it *does not* interfere with any other, or in any way seek to dissuade or hinder the candidate from any, either the Scotch or the York Rite. In that it does not make Masons *ab initio*, but takes only those who have been made in the York Rite. And while this Rite works over and explains the York Rite, or the first three degrees, yet it makes the possession of those degrees, taken in the York Rite, a condition precedent to receiving the degrees of the Memphis Rite, so there can be no hindrance to the York Rite— on the other hand, makes it an inducement to the obtaining of the higher and universal Masonry of the world, the Memphis Rite. And the reason why I have taken the pains to say thus much on this seeming objection, is because some persons who happened to occupy high and honorable positions in the York Rite have taken it upon themselves to slander and traduce this Rite, and try to prevent persons from taking the degrees, as they say, (or this they advance as an objection,) that the Memphis Rite ought not to be patronized or worked, for two reasons. First, because it would have a tendency to injure the York Rite, and the institutions that they claim are attached to it, viz: The Royal Arch Chapter, Council and Commandery. And some go farther to

say, that it will injure the A. and A., or the Scotch
Rite ; and for a second and further reason they ad-
vance, the degrees are not worked in the Grand
Orient of France, where the Charter comes from.

But to return to the two objections, viz: that it
may tend to injure the Scotch or A. & A. Rite, I have
this to say, that I have conclusively shown ' that it
does not or cannot injure the York Rite of Three Degrees, because every one must possess them before he
can be taken into this Rite. And as to the other,
Royal Arch and Commandery, they are no part of
the York Rite except by adoption, and I cannot see
how it could by any possibility injure them, and I
am a past officer in each of them, and a majority or
nearly all our members belong to them. But, if the
assertion is true that the Chapter which has been
working in this country for ninety-five years, and the
Commandery that has also been working for over one
hundred years, can be injured by a Rite that has
been only fourteen years working in this country,
(see page 3 ante,) I for one would willingly consent
to its doing so, because either the high degrees of the
York Rite are meaningless and impotent, or that the
Memphis Rite is the better Rite, and if so, why not
adopt it; but the fact is in relation also to the A. &
A. or Scotch Rite, which originated in Charleston
in 1802, died out in 1805, revived again in 1845,
(Rebolt Hist. page 171,) and was refused a recognition by the Orient of France till 1841—cannot com-
pete with a Rite that had its formation and foundation, in fact, the previous organization having died
out in this country on the 17th day of June, 1867,
(see page 3 ante.) It shows very conclusively to my
mind, and I apprehend it does to the reader, that the
Memphis Rite must be the better Rite, and that the

A. & A. or Scotch Rite, ought to be injured or out-
run; thus again, the assertion that the Memphis Rite
is not recognized by or does not now recognize the
Grand Orient of France, ought to be in the Memphis Rite, for it is a fact that the Memphis Rite is
not worked by the Grand Orient of France, for the
very reason that no person can be made in this Rite
unless he believe to some extent in the Divine Revelation of the Holy Bible or Scriptures, and must
be obligated on the great light of Masonry, viz: the
Holy Bible. And as the French Masons, particularly
the Grand Orient of France, have eschewed and dis-
carded God's Holy Book from their Masonic Institution, and as the Memphis Degrees cannot be given
or worked except on the Holy Bible, they have tried
in every way to injure it by attempting to reduce the
degrees to 33, and then by calling it a dead Rite, and
that too after in the most solemn manner, and for
pay, giving us a Charter, (see pages 84 to 104, ante,)
to work the degrees; but we are free from them, and
are proud of the fact that they do not work the degrees. After having transmitted to us the rituals,
(that they never fully understood,) and given us the
entire jurisdiction, for we use the Bible, for we refuse
to acknowledge any Masonic Rite that refuses to use
the Holy Bible, for we believe that no person can be
made in this Rite, or legally in any other, except on
the Holy Bible, and for this cause did we in 1870,
dissolve all connection with the Grand Orient of
France; and they do not work the Memphis Rite
above the 33°, and for this reason solely. Another
reason why the Memphis Rite is much the best Rite,
and ought to succeed, no matter if the poorer Rite,
called A. & A. Scottish Rite, or called by any other
name, should not succeed in this land of light and

K*

liberty and knowledge, where true and undefiled Masonry should succeed, flourish and abound; and by the blessing of God I hope it may when the shafts of calumny, envy, ignorance, falsehood and malice shall be broken by the hand of truth, or fall harmless to the ground before the pure light of Masonry, and " the lion can then, comparatively speaking, lay down with the lamb, and a little child to lead them."

This is a millennium we need, especially in Masonry, and not that Michigan is any worse than other States. But for the late Masonry of Michigan, it must be said of a truth, (and I am sorry to say it,) that the high offices of the several departments of the York Rite have been filled more than they should have been with men who looked more to their own personal aggrandizement, than to the good interests of Masonry. And I must repeat it, that 1878 was one of the most disastrous and unfortunate and disgraceful of its years and history; and so much more the pity too, in a State embracing over 29,000 Master Masons, with over 300 Lodges, over 100 Royal Arch Chapters, 50 Royal and Select Councils, over 50 Commanderies, but with only about 332 Scotch Rite Masons. But the redeeming fact, we opine, is shown that in less working time than two years 2,731 90 degree Memphis Masons have been made here, and we have over 58 Rose-Croix chartered Chapters; and the grand officers elect are, some of them, good Memphis Masons, notwithstanding Finch's edict. And in conclusion of the edict matter, I refer you again to my edict or answer to John W. Finch's celebrated pronunciamento, which will be read with surprise by all intelligent men and Masons, and be a foul blot on the proud escutcheon of the Grand Lodge of Michigan. But I must again express my hope and wish that its East will never again be disgraced by such an edict or by such a person occupying its chair.

And yet the present Deputy Grand Master, Rufus C. Hathaway, of Ionia, Michigan, is, I am credibly informed, at the present time busily engaged canvassing the State trying to secure his re-election as Deputy, if he cannot be advanced to the Grand Master's Chair, but is trying hard for the Grand Mastership. Should he succeed, it will be a sorry day for the Masonic Fraternity in the Wolverine State, as the same Hathaway stands suspended in the Memphis Rite for the unmasonic offence of appropriating Rituals of this Order, and in being arrested for the offence of embezzlement, he was discharged for the technical reason that the taking of these rituals and refusing to return or to account for them, was not embezzlement. Such men would rarely hold Masonic offices, should the maxim of the wise and good Diogenes prevail, who searched for honest men even in the day time with a light, viz : that offices should seek the men, rather than men for themselves seek the office.

But to resume my recapitulation, and leaving Michigan Masonry to take care of itself, as I have said before this Rite is now worked by and under this Grand Body. Thus: A portion of this Rite was translated and worked in the Grand Orient and Grand Lodge of France as early as 1694, and its rituals, translated and untranslated, from the Egyptian Sanscrit, and other original languages deposited with that Body, with an arrangement that all bodies working these degrees should be chartered by that body, viz : the Grand Orient de France.

Accordingly, in 1856, Marconi De Negree formed a body with John Mitchell as Grand Maji. (See ante page 87.) This body was to be the head

center of the Rite, and held its office in New York
City. The neglect to elect officers caused the body
to lose its organization, i. e., charter, and a new body,
or council was formed in 1857, was also allowed to
forfeit its right to work. Again, in 1857, David
McLellan, a member of the Grand Orient of France,
locating in New York City, formed a Grand Council
90°, but this followed the fate of its predecessors
in 1861, when the Grand Orient of France issued
its dispensation for the formation of a jurisdiction to
be called the Sovereign Sanctuary, which was of
short duration really, although they professed to
keep up the organization (see ante page 87,) of this
Rite, a full copy of all documents, charters, &c., down
to the issuing of a consolidation of the Rite into 33°,
when the split between this and the A. & A. Rite
began, (again see ante page 90 to 106,) and given
full power and authority to charter Lodges, Chapters,
Senates and Councils, Areopages and Consistories and
Sovereign Grand Bodies under the jurisdiction of
State Councils General 90°, and from them subordinate bodies to conter the several degrees from Apprentice to the 90°, make Masons at sight, and to take,
assume, and maintain control, power and authority
over the entire craft for the continent of America, to
elect its officers, appoint its Deputies, and install
them and its officers for all time to come and forever
thereafter. To exact from and receive homage, and
exercise full, perfect and complete authority over
every and all bodies of Masons throughout its jurisdiction, as full, complete and perfect as the Grand
Lodges of England, Ireland, Scotland and the Grand
Orient of France could do; the first, only, real and
authentic depository of all Masonic records, Rites ;
Nom de Plume, Grand College, Lithurgique Rite de

Memphis Sublime, Images, Lepatua et Marconi; to install its officers for all time to come and forever thereafter; Supreme, Superior, Most Worshipfnl, High and Exalted, Most Potent, All Powerful and Augu st, Thrice Illustrious, *ne plus ultra* Royal Grand Sovereign Sanctuary and Repository of the Ancient and Sacred name; rank and title, Grand Magenties 96°, Patriarch, Grand Defender of Truth 95°, for its officers, members, &c., &c., and with the Sovereign Grand Magi, degree 96, for its Grand and Deputy Masters, for all time, and to the end of the world, and for this purpose full blanks and rituals were forwarded, which rituals, on examination, proved to be in the original Egyptian and Sauscirt languages with the exception of the first eighteen degrees, which were printed in French. A body was accordingly formed, but owing to the very poor and superficial manner in which the translation of the eighteen degrees had been done, it made very slow progress, and few persons were disposed to embrace the degrees or learn the work; and the whole other work in the original languages and hieroglyphics written upon highly and formidable looking rolls and parchments and vellum, which had become aged, musty, torn and soiled, almost beyond translation or interpretation, and so continued till about the first of November, A. D. 1861, when a committee consisting of a French Masonic scholar by the name of Baron De Brum, and a Jewish Rabbi, Raphelph, and the author, who at once set about translating and correcting the degrees of the Rose-Croix, degrees which, upon examination, proved to be a work of great antiquity and rare Masonic beauty, and in reality contained the history and source from which all the systems of Masonry had emanated, and had the full original work

of the first three degrees, and which, when
translated, was truly what it claimed to be,
the true source of all Masonic learning, and
those musty, dust-covered and soiled parchments
were rare literary and Masonic gems, and contained
some of. the most brilliant and beautifully dramatized
and instructive degrees ever seen in any symbolic or
other institutions, which were replete with histories,
Masonic learning and history, as well as a synopsis
of the science of philosophy, astronomy, geology,
alchemy and theosophy. Accordingly, in 1862, a
charter was obtained, (see page ante, 93,) a full record
of each charter organizations, and down to the 17th
day of June, A. D., 1867, when the degrees were
condensed from 96° to 33°, and then came a split
in the body by an edict purporting to come from the
Grand Orient of France.

The society formed in 1862, was called the Ancient and Primitive Rite of Memphis. The degrees
of this Rite were slowly and surely progressing in
interpretation, when, in 1863, the author, for a consideration, obtained possession of all the charters,
dispensations, rituals, &c., &c., with a view of forming bodies in the west and south. About this time
the war of the rebellion became general and peaceful pursuits gave way to the grim visage of war,
and absorbed the attention of most every one. Even
Masonry, except in the military camp, was abandoned,
or at least in part neglected. The work of this translating however, went slowly on ; the bodies mentioned before continued to hold occasional meetings,
but very few members were admitted. At this
period the war between the two factions of the A.
& A. Rite or Scotch Rite began, and the Scotch Rite
being very jealous as to higher degrees, and fearing

that the introduction of a new or higher system of Masonry might injure the prospects of the A. & A. Rite, they opposed this Rite with all the power they possessed, frequently giving hostile war to the Memphis Rite; and things were getting so hot in New York, (so to speak,) that more conservative fields of operation were sought after and the work was introduced into the western States of Illinois, Michigan, Wisconsin and Indiana, at various periods, from 1863 to 1867, when the A. & A. Rite began to oppose the progress of the Rite, notwithstanding which a large and eminent body of Masons in the Memphis Rite had been made, and a goodly number of societies formed.

At about this time, February, 1866, the then Grand Master of this Rite; H. J. Seymour, 96°, got into a controversy with the Grand Orient of France, and entered into an arrangement to reduce the degrees of this Rite to 33°, (see ante, page 114.) This being in the opinion of the most eminent Masons in this Rite, residing in the western States, a very great wrong and a violation of the first principles of the order, they, in a body, absolutely refused to accept the recommendation of the Grand Master, H. J. Seymour, 96°, or the Orient of France, and called for a convention of the brethren in the western States to meet at Chicago. Accordingly, on the 17th day of June, A. D. 1867, (see pages 3 to 15, ante,) such a convention met and which resulted in a general meeting of the ten Rose Croix Chapters, two Senates and one Council, and other unaffiliated Masons then working in the States, besides a large number of 90° and upwards Masons, who were assembled firmly resolved not to abide by the order, or the condensation of the degrees to 33, but formed a Constitution and Laws

for themselves, and changed the name of the body to
Egyptian Masonic Rite of Memphis, (see ante, page
4,) declared·themselves the only body of Masons on
the continent of America working the degrees, who
acknowledged the Rite of Memphis contains 96°, and
that it is not in the power of any person or body
of Masons on this globe to alter, change or reduce
or interpolate to any less number of degrees
after this Rite had been established; and this
body has been by that style and name known,
and is now at the head of this beautiful system of morality, veiled in allegory, illustrated by
symbols. The degrees will be found to be most beautifully dramatized, and contain the most exhaustive and
complete form and system of Masonry the world ever
saw. The teachings of morality are combined with
brotherly love, friendship and truth, that divine
attribute, the chief corner-stone of the superstructure,
In the original work, the various degrees of work,
90 in all, were divided into a large number of bodies;
and while each was well calculated to impress upon
the mind some important truth, and at the same time
to communicate lessons of Religion, Morality, Philosophy, Astronomy and Geometry; and while the
names of Geology, Alchema, are used to express and
represent and to challenge fortitude and brotherly
love, all tend to force upon the mind important
Masonic truths, and present to the symbolic craftsman toiling in the speculative quarries of Masonic
lore a full reward for his labors, not satisfied with a
superficial illustration of the terms of architecture,
but delving into the mysteries of the order, portray-
ing its beauties and filling and storing the mind
with useful knowledge by such a changing series of
mysterious knowledge as is only accessible to the true

craftsman holding the mystic key of translation. In the year 1866, the full translation of the entire work from the 1st to the 96th degree being completed under the last mentioned name, it was deemed advisable to procure the further recognition of the Grand Orient of France to this new organization by this new name. Accordingly, Dr. Johnson, a very influential Mason, residing in Paris, near the Grand Orient of France, was appointed representative of the Sovereign Sanctuary to the Grand Orient, and in return, Mons. John H. Blake, 95°, was appointed by the Grand Orient representative residing near the Sovereign Sanctuary in the city of Chicago. Applications for charters and dispensations were accordingly granted to the Masonic brethren residing in Illinois, Wisconsin, Michigan, New York, New Jersey, California, Oregon and other States, and the work went on for about two years, when a serious disturbance arose between some of the members of this Rite and the Scotch Rite and the Commandery of Knight Templars, each claiming a prior right to the working of some of the first degrees. Accordingly, a conference was held, and upon examination of the most prominent points of the work, principally names of the degrees, which were similar, it was found that they were entirely dissimilar, and did not collide or interfere with each other, and the Grand Orient of France, becoming satisfied that they were not then and never had been in possession of a real translation of the Egyptian work, and it being entirely too large for a body that was merely legislative and judicial to work all or even a part of the degrees by a grand annual meeting of Masonic deputies, they convened on or about the 1st of June, A. D. 1869, condensed the degrees of the Rite called the Ancient and Primitive

Rite of Memphis or the Ancient and Accepted Rite
of Herodem into 33°, and relinquished all other degrees to the care, custody, keeping, communication
propogation and diffusion of the Sovereign Sanctuary
of the Egyptian Masonic Rite of Memphis sitting in
America, which is the only true, legal and proper body
of Memphis Masons who are in possession of 96°, or
who have the right to communicate or work
them, and giving to this Grand Body full, complete,
and entire jurisdiction of all the entire Cosmos or
Masonic world, the whole habitable universe,
wherever civilization and the light of Masonry has
shed or shall hereafter shed its beneficent rays.
This Memphis Rite of 96 degrees has full power,
force, authority and Masonic command, although the
scoffs of the ignorant, the jeers of the prejudiced and
the taunts of the aspirant for Masonic power, rule
and influence may for a time seem to prevail. Yet
truth being a divine attribute and the foundation of
every virtue, must surely prevail. And, although
like our former craftsman, Zerubbabel, it may be
clouded with infamous reports or charged with the
assumption of false power, yet the King of Kings
will in due time issue his edict that the temple shall
be built with all its pristine beauty, the holy vessels
of silver, of gold and brass returned, and the tribute
due to its greatness paid within the porch of the
temple. There it will be ever as it is now, and
most of the enlightened and zealous Masons in the
order in search of light and knowledge may see and
know and fully understand that the perhaps seeming
devious ways of the Egyptian Masonic Rite of
Memphis and what in truth is claimed for it, are like
the visit of the Queen of Sheba to the first temple of

Solomon—the half of its beauties and virtues have not been told.

It has been greatly abused and villified, traduced without cause, but only by those who either did not know or could not understand or explain its mysteries. But it is like some great rock in a desert land, towering above the common things of earth and pointing the weary traveler or searcher after Masonic truth, or inviting the weary craftsman to enter its temples, examine its work from the 1st to the 96th degree harmoniously in keeping with the truth of history, the light of science and of knowledge shedding its rays across the path of life, at peace with itself and all the world beside, bearing on its banners the motto of peace on earth, good will to men, dispensing wisdom and Masonic lore without fear of reproach. And as none but Master Masons in good standing can enter its portals, interfering with none, but teaching pure Masonry, such as will enable the possessor of its degrees to work his way into any body of Masons in the world—eschewing priestcraft, sects, creeds and societies who use the holy Bible and who do not acknowledge God as God, and believe in the immortality of the soul of man, its future reward or punishment.

Such being the tenets of this Ancient Order, and it seemingly not being understood, or the attempt of designing men to injure its progress by the circulation of base falsehoods against the Rite and the writer, it has been considered best to issue this book containing a brief history of the organization of the present Grand Body, and a brief history of the Rite, in order that Masons may read and know what the Rite of Memphis really is. This being a short, condensed recapitulation of the contents of the book, the reader is earnestly requested to read the work carefully over, and then allow some brother, who may not feel able or inclined to buy a copy, to read this one. It is Masonry that will commend itself to every lover of the Art, and the reader will be amply repaid for the time spent, if only by the reading borrowed from other books by the author, and compiler, as it is not in the power of every Mason to own a large Masonic library, and as they are scarce even in the hands of wealthy Masons. This, by numerous quotations of other authors, may awaken in the reader a desire to follow up the subject, and examine for himself the source from which these quotations issue.

And in conclusion of this branch of history, I wish to express my sincere thanks for favors and assistance in books and other help from Brother Masons, among whom are R. W. Bro. C. W. Strait, 95°, Deputy Grand Representative for Michigan, Past Grand Warden of the Grand Commandery of Michigan, and Past Grand Principal Sojourner of the Grand Chapter, and Deputy Grand Master of the Grand Council, as well as a member for some years past of the Committee on Appeals of the Grand Lodge of Michigan. Brother Strait is a very zealous Mason, understands the work of the Lodge, Chapter, Council and Commandery as well as any, if not much better than any other Grand Officer of my acquaintance in this State. Brother Strait is a good worker in this Rite also, and was a very efficient officer at the last meeting of the Grand Body of this Rite, of which he is now an honorable member. With his assistance the writer has formed forty-two Chapters of Rose-Croix in Michigan and five in the State of New York, also a Senate and one Rose-Croix Chap-

ter in Ohio, and several others are under process of
construction in this and other States. I must also
return my sincere thanks to R. W. Bro. W. B. Lord,
95°, of Utica, N. Y., who, as Deputy Grand Representative for New York, has formed many Chapters
in that State, and assisted me on this book by proof
reading, &c., &c. Bro. W. B. Lord, 95°, has proved
himself a valuable member of this order. I. also
wish to return my thanks for favors to other members of the Rite. Hoping this will be the means of
making more plain the principles of this order, and
of doing good generally, is the sincere wish and desire
of the author.

CHAPTER II.

Having devoted perhaps more time and space to
the first chapter or section of this book, viz: the record of our organization, the brief existence of the so-
called Ancient and Primitive Rite, and a partial history of the Egyptian Masonic Rite of Memphis, I will
now briefly introduce the reader to a short description of the degrees, as a sort of Monitor or Book of
the Chapter, calculated in some measure to assist in
working the degrees in the Chapter as well as to give
the uninitiated Mason an idea of the character and
dramatic work on which certain portions of the history of events upon which they are founded, taking
care not to repeat anything before said, or to publish
anything forbidden or not proper to be seen or told
outside the Tiler's door, which will be followed with
the three public degrees of Installator, Consecrator
and Eulogist, and a few forms for Masonic documents
and records in this Rite.

And the writer wishes to say in this connection
that the publication of this work has been greatly
delayed and all parties have been greatly embar-

rassed by the fact that the brok has been written at
the great distance of 500 miles from the printer, and
that they have been unable to see each other or compare notes, but that the work has been written
and forwarded by mail under the Act of Congress
allowing such matter to be sent registered, and in
consequence some parts have been delayed till a former part has been received by the printer, which will
account for the seeming and perhaps real unconnected
reading of the sections, a thing the writer will endeavor to obviate in a future issue of the work,
should this production be found worthy of it.

Therefore, in the presenting of this Monitor, or
further history and description of the Memphis Rite
Degrees, the only apology the writer and compiler
deems it necessary to make, is that there is or was
no other person acquainted with its peculiar forms
and ceremonies who was willing to spend the time
and money that must necessarily be spent and given
to a work like this.   And as we are expected to use
all just and honorable means in our power to disseminate the true light and to bring good Masons into
the Order, and having a few spare hours, I have un-
dertaken what generally is a thankless duty, of re-
peating in some degree a thrice told tale, for it makes
very little difference on what branch of Freemasonry
we write or speak, some one who has written or
spoken on the same subject before, has perhaps had
the same ideas, the same thoughts, or perhaps had his
mind drawn by the same ideas written or spoken by
others on the same or analogous subjects.   But inasmuch as it has become a sort of practice or custom
for authors to make some introductory and explanatory remarks before they begin the main part of their
discourse, and also as there has been and perhaps

now exists in the minds of many of those who may read these lines, a feeling of prejudice against anything written about Masonry, there may also be a feeling in the minds of some against the institution itself, in any of its various phases or forms, and they are ready to embrace every argument advanced tending in the slightest degree to injure its influence or prevent its truths and useful forms; for such I have no word of apology or care for their judgments. Another class are so self-confident in their opinions of its merits or demerits, that nothing new can be produced from the old, well worn and established forms, and who view every word written or spoken outside of the tiled chapter, as an innovation or disclosure of its hidden mysteries.

But for the fair minded honest searcher after truth, light and knowledge, and those who are willing to search into and weigh well everything pertaining to the institution, for the mere love of the institution, or for the acquirement of light and knowledge, no matter from what source it may emanate, and those who are not content with a mere superficial knowledge, but wish to drink deeply of the perennial spring, this work is written and to them is dedicated, in the zealous and honest desire that they may derive benefit, light and knowledge of its degrees, lectures and teachings, for I am well aware that before this branch of Masonry can succeed, it must in a measure meet and overcome some at least of the very many prejudices existing in the minds of the public and also among even the fraternity. The former, as before stated, are usually prejudiced in a great measure against any new or secret organization, not merely because it is wrong, but with them because they do not know whether it is right or

wrong, but because they think that it is not right
that anything secret should exist, and the very
fact of its being secret is to their minds evidence that
it is wrong, or the secret would not exist. Forget-
ting for the moment, perhaps, that very many of the
best things derive their force and usefulness fro n
the very fact that they are not public. The uncov-
ering or bringing to light produces the highest evidence of their utility and success—for them the evidence of their usefulness. But suffice it to say that it
is not the object or intention of the writer or of this
book to bring to light or to expose any of the esoteric
part of Masonry, but merely to enlarge upon what
has long ere this become exoteric to many who have
given their time to searching out its seeming mysteries, and those who have been in a position to or
who have had access to those writings and teachings
of men learned in the ancient Masonic law, and have
devoted a great portion of their lives to its study, as
we have had occasion to say in a former part of this
work. We need but allude to the mere fact that the
forms and ceremonies of our Masonic institutions
cannot be materially altered or changed. That they
have become in a great measure the landmarks, and
that there is a great difference in or between learning and changing things; not merely are things
changed because they are new to the reader, or the
discoverer, and the very best evidence of their being
ancient and not new, remains in the fact, that they
are found by the searcher, otherwise they would not
have been found, or not have been to be found. All we
ask of the candid Mason or reader is a fair and dis-
passionate examination of the work, being well
aware that there are very many good and conscien-
tious Masons who believe that there is no Masonry or

good Masonry, above or not contained in the first (as they are called) three degrees, and that all above or outside of these three degrees of Apprentice, Fellow-craft and Master Mason, is not true Masonry at all. Others believe that the Royal Arch, in addition to the other three, is the apex or summit of the Mystic Art, while not a few contend that the whole thing is a matter of very modern date, and has in fact existed but a very few years in even the first three degree form, but that the Rose-Croix chapter is more ancient than any of them, and in fact there are very many strong points of evidence that go to sustain that position ; while others again contend that the Masonry of the original (as they claim first three degrees) was the form of religion that existed prior to the Christian era. Be this as it may with the first three degrees or York Rite, as it is called, yet no respectable historian, I think, can be found, who does not admit that the mysteries such as are and were practiced in Egypt and the countries of the East have existed for a much longer period than either the first three degrees or the Christian Religion, and in the work which we present to the Fraternity and the public, we shall not so much contend for antiquity as for universal general instruction and consistent Masonry.

For many years it has been the desire, and the author has labored in the various Rites and branches of the Order with an eye single to the advancement and prosperity of the Egyptian Masonic Rite of Memphis, and during the past fifteen to twenty years, has, at a great sacrifice of time, labor and money; struggled to bring before the public and get into practical and useful working order, this, to his mind, the most beautiful, instructive, and useful branch of Free

L

Masonry, and the publication of such works as would challenge the careful and candid Mason to examine; and he now, after years of toil and research, with many forebodings and doubts, introduces this work, in addition to the short history that precedes it, as a working monitor, or book of the Egyptian Rite, which he is confident will, to a great degree, assist the members and officers in the Rite in working the degrees and conducting its ceremonies, and preserve in such form as may, at least, assist future generations in the work of the different degrees and bodies of the Rite. The presiding officers, as well as the craftsmen, will find that the exoteric work has been arranged in perhaps as good a form as could be in so small a book. As it is not the intention of the writer to make a very large work or to explain every part of the ritual, but merely as a guide in conferring of the degrees; and as this is the first monitor or book of the Rite ever published, to the knowledge of the author, he has not been able to draw forms or suggestions from others, but has had to depend on his own knowledge of the actual work for subject matter and material. He therefore hopes and confidently expects, that great allowance will be made for these reasons; and he also hopes to allay any fear or prejudice that may have been, or does now exist in the minds of those not so familiar with what is sometimes termed high decrees, against their usefulness and utility, but that it may, in a measure, be instrumental in bringing good Masons into the Order. But should the work fall into the hands of any whose better judgments are still clouded by the calumnies of by-gone days, we beg to assure them that in the following pages they will find the best refutation of the various misstatements that have so long been banded about the world in regard to this high and intellectual branch of Freemasonry.

However anxious and restless the busy and invidious may be, and whatever attempts they may make, to traduce our institution or discover our mysteries, all their endeavors will prove ineffectual. They will still find that the only means to attain to the knowledge of our mysteries are abilities, integrity, firmness, and a due and constant perseverance in the great duties of moral and social life, in principles of religion and virtue, and whatever is commendable and praiseworthy. These are the steps and this the clue, that will lead and direct the practicers of such excellencies to the heights of Freemasonry, and while they adhere to them, will effectually secure them favor and esteem from every able and faithful Brother, and the warmest approbation and satisfaction from their own hearts.

Masonic assemblies were anciently called lodges, and in the ancient and original acceptation of the term, were composed of a certain well-known number of Masons, duly assembled, having the necessary furniture, ornaments and working tools. When thus convened, each body was perfect in itself and acknowledged no higher Masonic authority. In this respect Masonry differs from all other institutions of a like nature. The reason is obvious. Dating its commencement from a remote period, its government naturally became assimilated to that of the times and country where it arose; hence, we find its office bearers invested with the high sounding titles of the earlier ages of the world, and its ceremonies emblazoned with the gold and purple of antiquity; but with time, which traces its progress on all material things, the world changed, empires and kingdoms

flourished and decayed, stately palaces and gorgeous
temples now marked the habitations of earthly grandeur, or enclosed the altars whence arose the oraisons
of the faithful, and anon—they crumbled into dust.
The golden age encompassed the world with joy and
the age of darkness spread over it like a funeral pall;
yet amid all these circumstances and changes Masonry remained intact. The ceremonies that were
practiced in the beginning are still observed, the
laws that first governed the craft are still obeyed.
Every zealous Mason should therefore keep steadily
in view the ancient rules, customs and ceremonies
which, by long continuance, have been stamped as
portions of those landmarks which our fathers
charged us not to remove. One of the most important of these is UNIFORMITY. Too much care cannot
be exercised in this respect; every craftsman must
acknowledge it as one of the safeguards of our institution, as one of the means by which it has out-
lived the pitiless storms of malice and persecution,
that have so often burst upon it, the means by which
it will be communicated in all the freshness of its
original purity to the latest posterity.

Many ways of attaining this desirable end, have,
at different times, been suggested to the Fraternity;
but none seems to have met with more favor than
the system of printing in whole or in part, the work,
which zealous Masons will guard and take care of so
there can be no difference in the work and ceremonials. Brethren selected to fill so important a station
should be men of education, tact and address—well
skilled in the lectures, and capable of winning the
hearts as well as the attention of those whom they
may be called to instruct. Assiduous attention to
lectures, work, and a desire to learn on the side of

the members, cannot fail of producing the happiest results.

Another method tending to the same end, enjoined in the charges and constitutions (portions of which we subjoin) is, that each Lodge in a jurisdiction shall appoint some of its members to visit the others. Apart from that knowledge which is to distinguish us from the profane, thus obtained, is the interchange of fraternal greetings—the formation of friendship cemented by our mystic ties, producing the most beneficent effects.

Much also devolves upon the craft in the selection of competent officers for the various stations in the Lodge. "The possession and exercise of authority is a matter of honorable and proper ambition in every Brother who really prizes the Institution into which he has been initiated, and who wishes to render his Masonry productive of its legitimate fruits, the moral improvement of his mental faculties. To maintain his authority the Master of a Masonic Body must possess talent, moral virtue, and courtesy, blended with firmness. He must teach both by precept and example; Faith the most lively, Hope the most pure, Charity the most unfeigned. He must inculcate Temperance, unmoved except by the delights of science; Fortitude unshaken alike by prosperity and adversity; Prudence united with inflexible Justice; and he is bound to instruct the Brethren in the development of that mysterious and important fact, that man was not created to promote the selfish purposes of his own interest alone, but to use his best endeavors to advance the welfare of others; and above all, to elucidate that leading secret of Freemasonry—the absolute necessity of acquiring a practical knowledge of ourselves.

" If, then, it be the Master's province to instruct
others, he must be conscious that ignorance in himself is totally inexcusable. He cannot enforce on
the younger Brethren the necessity of ruling and gov-
erning their passions—of keeping a tongue of good
report—of practising all the duties of morality and
social order, unless he exhibit an example of these
virtues in his own person. If he be insincere, his
praise of Truth will stand for nothing; if he be not
charitable, he cannot consistently recommend the
practice of relief; nor if he be factious, can he di-
late, with any effect, on the exercise of the most
beautiful feature in the Masonic system, Brotherly
Love or Charity; that glorious emanation of the
Deity, divested of which, Freemasonry would be unworthy of attention. Without these essential qualifications, the Chair will be bereft of its influence;
the Master's authority will be disregarded by the
Brethren; and disorder and disunion, though delayed,
will not be the less certain to ensue."

If these remarks may be truly applied to the
Brother whose distinguishing jewel is the " square,"
they have also their relation to the officers of a
Lodge; both Master and officers should always be .
punctual in their attendance; and observe the hour
of meeting with scrupulous exactness; for correct
conduct in officers will invariably produce a corres-
ponding accuracy in the brethren. If there be not
absolute certainty that the Lodge will be opened at
the proper hour, it must be expected that the members will visibly relax in point of punctuality. If
the system is to be kept vigorous and healthy, ac-
tivity and address, perseverance and energy are required on the part of its principal functionaries.
Let the superior officers diligently and conscientiously

perform *their* duty, and then there will be little fear
of irregularity or defection on the part of the
members.

A proper administration of the various ceremonies
connected with our ritual is of the first importance
and worthy of our serious consideration. The rites
and ceremonies of Freemasonry form the distinctive
peculiarity of the Institution. In their nature they
are simple—in their end instructive. They naturally
excite a high degree of curiosity in a newly initiated
brother, and create an earnest desire to investigate
their meaning, and to become acquainted with their
object and design. It requires, however, both serious
application and untiring diligence to ascertain the
precise nature of every ceremony, which our ancient
brethren saw reason to adopt in the formation of an
exclusive system, which was to pass through the
world unconnected with the religion and politics of
all times, and of every people among whom it should
flourish and increase.* In order to preserve our
ceremonies from the hand of innovation, it is essentially necessary that every officer should be thor-
oughly acquainted with them, and that a firm de-
.termination should exist among the craft to admit
no change. A few words here or there may not in
themselves appear of much consequence, yet, by frequent allowance we become habituated to them, and
thus open the door to evils of more serious magnitude.
There is, there can be, no safety but in a rigid ad-
herence to the ancient ceremonies of the Order.

The first of these that claim our attention are
those employed in opening and closing the Lodge;
much might here be said in relation to them did they
in our opinion admit of written elucidation, but as

*Philosophy of Freemasonry,

they are necessarily kept within the body of the Lodge, nothing but vague and unsatisfactory hints could be given respecting them; we therefore prefer to pass them in silence, reiterating our previous recommendation to visit each other as the best method of keeping out innovation and preserving uniformity.

In connection with this ceremony a variety of charges have, at various times, been used by the Order; from the number, we cull the two following, as well for their simple beauty as for the wholesome truths contained in them.

SELECT READING BY THE ORATOR OR PRELATE AT OPENING.

The ways of virtue are beautiful. Knowledge is attained by degrees. Wisdom dwells with contemplation. There we must seek her. Let us then, Brethren, apply ourselves with becoming zeal to the practice of the excellent principles inculcated by our Order. Let us ever remember that the great objects of our association are, the restraint of improper desires and passions, the cultivation of an active benevolence, and the promotion of a correct knowledge of the duties we owe to God, our neighbor, and ourselves. Let us be united, and practice with assiduity the sacred tenets of our Order. Let all private animosities, if any unhappily exist, give place to affection and brotherly love. It is a useless parade to talk of the subjection of irregular passions within the walls of the Chapter, if we permit them to triumph in our intercourse with each other. Uniting in the grand design, let us be happy ourselves and endeavor to promote the happiness of others. Let us cultivate the great moral virtues which are laid down on our Masonic Trestle-board, and improve in every-

thing that is good, amiable and useful. Let the benign Genius of the Mystic Art preside over our councils, and under her sway let us act with a dignity
becoming the high moral character of our venerable
Institution.

Brethren : You are now to quit this sacred retreat
of friendship and virtue, to mix again with the
world. Amidst its concerns and employments, forget
not the duties you have heard so frequently inculcated and forcibly recommended in this Lodge. Be
diligent, prudent, temperate, discreet. Remember
that around this altar you have promised to befriend
and relieve every brother who shall need your assistance ; remember that you have promised to remind
him, in the most tender manner, of his failings, and
aid his reformation. Vindicate his character, when
wrongfully traduced. Suggest in his behalf the
most candid and favorable circumstances. Is he
justly reprehended ?—Let the world observe how
Masons love one another.

These generous principles are to extend farther.
Every human being has a claim upon your kind offices. "Do good unto all." Recommend it more
" especially to the household of the FAITHFUL."

By diligence in the duties of your respective call-
ings; by liberal benevolence and diffusive charity ;
by constancy and fidelity in your friendships, discover the beneficial and happy effects of this ancient
and honorable Institution.

Let it not be supposed that you have here "LA-
BORED in vain, and spent your STRENGTH for naught;
L*

for your work is with the LORD and your RECOM-
PENSE with your GOD."

Finally, Brethren, be ye all of one mind,—live in
peace, and may the God of love and peace delight to
dwell with and bless you!

The ancient manner prescribed for the admission
of candidates also claims our attention, and we here
insert it, least in this age of new invention any
method should be found supplanting that which has
for ages been the practice of the Fraternity.

ADMISSION OF CANDIDATES.

By the regulations of the Fraternity, a candidate
tor the mysteries of Masonry cannot be initiated in
any regular Lodge, without having stood proposed
one regular meeting, unless a dispensation be obtained in his favor. All applications for initiation
should be made in writing, giving name, residence,
age, occupation and references.

The petition, having been read in open Lodge, is
placed on file. A committee is then appointed to investigate the character and qualifications of the pe-
titioner. If, at the next regular meeting of the
Lodge, the report of the committee be favorable, and
the candidate is admitted, he is required to give his
free and full assent to the following interrogations:

1. "Do you seriously declare, upon your honor,
before these gentlemen, that, unbiased by friends, and
uninfluenced by mercenary motives, you freely and
voluntarily offer yourself a candidate for the mysteries of this Chapter?

2. "Do you seriously declare, upon your honor, before these gentlemen, that you are prompted to solicit
the privileges of Masonry by a favorable opinion con-

ceived of the Institution, a desire of knowledge, and a sincere wish of being serviceable to your fellow-creatures?

3. " Do you seriously declare, upon your honor, before these gentlemen, that you will cheerfuly conform to all the ancient established usages and customs of the Fraternity ?"

The candidate, if no objections be urged to the contrary, is then introduced in due and ancient form.

Having thus spoken of the Lodge and its officers, a few words to the craft themselves might not be deemed out of place; but we prefer to speak to them in the plain yet eloquent language of the following charges, worthy the attention of all men, and particularly the zealous inquirer for MASONIC TRUTH.

ANCIENT CHARGES.
THE PRIVATE DUTIES OF MASONS.

Whoever would be a Mason should know how to practice all the private virtues. He should avoid all manner of intemperance or excess, which might prevent his performance of the laudable duties of his Craft, or lead him into enormities which would reflect dishonor upon the ancient Fraternity. He is to be industrious in his profession, and true to the Master he serves. He is to labor justly, and not to eat any man's bread for naught; but to pay truly for his meat and drink. What leisure his labor allows, he is to employ in studying the arts and sciences with a diligent mind, that he may the better perform all his duties to his Creator, his country, his neighbor, and himself.

He is to seek and acquire, as far sa possible, the virtues of patience, meekness, self-denial, forbearance, and the like, which give him the command over himself, and enable him to govern his own family with affection, dignity and prudence; at the same time checking every disposition injurious to the world, and promoting that love and service which Brethren of the same household owe to each other.

Therefore, to afford succor to the distressed, to divide our bread with the industrious poor, and to put the misguided traveler into the way, are duties of the Craft, suitable to its dignity, and expressive of its usefulness. But, though a Mason is never to shut his ear unkindly against the complaints of any of the human race, yet when a Brother is oppressed or suffers, he is in a more peculiar manner called to open his whole soul in love and compassion to him, and to relieve him without prejudice, according to his capacity.

It is also necessary, that all who would be true Masons should learn to abstain from all malice, slander and evil speaking; from all provoking, reproachful and ungodly language; keeping always a tongue of good report.

A Mason should know how to obey those who are set over him; however inferior they may be in worldly rank or condition. For although Masonry divests no man of his honors and titles, yet in a Lodge, pre-eminence of virtue and knowledge in the art, is considered as the true source of all nobility, rule and government.

The virtue indispensably requisite in Masons is—SECRECY. This is the guard of their confidence and the security of their trust. So great stress is to be laid upon it, that it is enforced under the strongest obligations; nor, in their esteem, is any man to be accounted wise who has not intellectual strength and ability sufficient to cover and conceal such honest secrets as are committed to him, as well as his own more serious and private affairs.

DUTIES AS CITIZENS.

A Mason is a peaceable citizen, and is never to be concerned in plots and conspiracies against the peace and welfare of the nation, nor to behave himself undutifully to inferior magistrates. He is cheerfully to conform to every lawful authority; to uphold on every occasion the interest of the community, and zealously promote the prosperity of his own country. Masonry has ever flourished in times of peace, and been always injured by war, bloodshed and confusion; so that kings and princes, in every age, have been much disposed to encourage the craftsmen on account of their peaceableness and loyalty, whereby they practically answer the cavils of their adversaries and promote the honor of the Fraternity. Craftsmen are bound by peculiar ties to promote peace, cultivate harmony and live in concord and Brotherly Love.

DUTIES IN THE LODGE.

While the Lodge is open for work, Masons must hold no private conversation or committees, without leave from the Master; nor talk of anything foreign or impertinent; nor interrupt the Master or Wardens, nor any Brother addressing himself to the Chair, nor behave inattentively while the Lodge is engaged in what is serious and solemn; but every Brother shall pay due reverence to the Master, the Wardens and all his fellows.

Every Brother guilty of a fault shall submit to the Lodge, unless he appeal to the Grand Lodge.

No private offences, or disputes about nations, families, religious or politics, must be brought within the doors of the Lodge.

DUTIES AS NEIGHBORS.

Masons ought to be moral men. Consequently they should be good husbands, good parents, good sons and good neighbors; avoiding all excess, injurious to themselves or families, and wise as to all affairs, both of their own household and of the Lodge, for certain reasons known to themselves.

DUTIES TOWARDS A BROTHER.

Free and Accepted Masons have ever been charged to avoid all slander of true and faithful Brethren, and all malice or unjust resentment, or talking disrespectfully of a Brother's person or performance. Nor must they suffer any to spread unjust reproaches or calumnies against a Brother behind his back, nor to injure him in his fortune, occupation or character; but they shall defend such a Brother, and give him notice of any danger or injury wherewith he may be threatened, to enable him to escape the same, as far as is consistent with honor, prudence and the safety of religion, morality and the State; but no farther.

REASONS FOR DESCRIPTION OF DEGREES

As the Rose-Croix Chapters have now become almost as universal as Masters' Lodges, of which summary descriptions are to be found in the various monitors published, and in use in all the Bodies of the York Rite, and inasmuch as this system of Masonry has been for the past century worked only in foreign countries, we deem it advisable to put into this book (which is only written for, and expected to be sought after or purchased by Masons,) a brief description of the collection of 18 degrees that are worked in a Rose-Croix Chapter. Therefore, in Masonic parlance or language, I wish merely to write of the prominent and material points of the non-esoteric part of the degrees, and briefly at that, viz :

The first degree of the Chapter is called Discreet Master, and is the 4th degree of Masonry; and is, together with the eight degrees that follow it descriptive of and explanatory to the Master's degree, and is founded on events that took place before and at the building of the first temple, and completes the tragic description of the integrity, fortitude and virtues possessed by some of the ancient members of the craft whose virtues we should endeavor to perpetuate and emulate, as well as commemorate, as a fitting tribute to the memory of those who have gone before us into that undiscovered country whence no traveler will return ; and as it exhibits a trial of fortitude through which all who seek after truth, must, in some measure, obtain it, and an impression upon the mind that will never fail so long as reason sits enthroned upon its seat, or the windows of the soul continue to reflect shadows of passing events. Here the Neophyte is for the first time introduced unto the unfinished Holy of Holies, the unfinished sanctum sanctorum of that magnificent, and at that time most stupendous Temple that has ever been built by the Jews or by any other nation on the earth; the fame of which Temple erected on Mount Moriah, and on the celebrated reputed threshing floor of Ornan the Jebusite, and the place of the offering of Isaac by his father Abraham, and which had for ages been known as the place where the Almighty made his name known to man. This Temple had been contemplated by King David while he was king of Israel, and was by Solomon, his son, when Israel's King, and Hiram, the Tyrian King, with the assistance of the widow's son, made the most costly and magnificent structure that at that day had been erected, the renown and wonder of which spread itself all over the civilized world. It is here in this degree of Discreet Master, that a representation of a case of unparalleled fortitude and integrity is manifested, and a pattern of the person who would rather lose his life than sacrifice his honor or integrity, and here the proper and fitting ceremonies of honor and respect are paid to the exalted worth and true Masonry. In this degree the M∴ M∴ then for the first time beholds the reward paid to virtue, fortitude and integrity, and views the Holy Shekinah, the representation of visible glory, which is to dispel ignorance and vice and symbolize truth and righteousness. Here the seeker after light is taught to prove himself worthy of immortality, and learned to form habits and associations acceptable to the S∴ A∴ O∴ T∴ U∴ his country, his family, his neighbor and himself; to learn that man is created for virtue and to know himself; and that the Deity has created all men to be happy; to that purpose he has bestowed upon mankind a mind stored with intelligence and reasoning power, which is full and conclusive evidence of its immortality, and by which we know that if our minds are well employed and our energies well directed, we are the more capable of rendering that perfect adoration that is due from a creature to his creator, and thereby better fitted to appreciate the greatness of his power, the goodness of his grace and his munificent blessing daily bestowed on and dispensed to the creatures of his creation, causing them to thereby become more fit subjects to inherit the crown of glory laid up for those who render to the Supreme Architect that true adoration and worship him in spirit and in truth. And the degree closes with a great moral lesson of the instability of human affairs, and a fitting tribute to the illustrious character of the truly good man who would rather lose his life than betray his trust.

The Orator reads from the Monitor the following:

The Lord reigneth; let the people tremble. He sitteth between the Cherubims; let the earth be moved; praise ye the Lord; praise, O ye servants of the Lord; praise ye the name of the Lord.

Blessed be the name of the Lord from this time forth and forevermore. From the rising of the sun unto the going down of the same. The Lord's name is to be praised. The Lord is high above all nations and His glory above the heavens.

Praise ye the Lord; praise ye the name of the

Lord; praise Him, O ye servants of the Lord. Ye that stand in the house of the Lord in the courts of the house of our God; praise the Lord; for the Lord is good; sing praises unto His name, for it is pleasant; for the Lord hath chosen Jacob unto Himself, and Israel for His peculiar treasure; let them praise the name of the Lord, for His name alone is excellent; His glory is above the earth and the heaven.

Thy name, O Lord, endureth forever; and Thy memorial throughout all generations. Bless the Lord, O my soul, and all that is within me, bless His holy name.

The Fifth, or Degree of Perfect Master, illustrates in a striking and signal manner the noble and truly commendable traits of character practiced and inculcated by the faithful Mason, transmits to posterity a lesson of intelligence venerating old age, and the perpetuation of the good deeds of a long and useful life, devoted to Friendship and Brotherly Love, a full knowledge of which can only be known and appreciated by the actual exemplification of the degree by those who desire to join in the perpetuation of them by an actual participation in the mysteries, to whom only this can be imparted by permission of their fellows within the vail and in due form.

In the Sixth Degree, or Sublime Master, there is expressed and exemplified a striking illustration of the effect of good government, and the reward of a laudible curiosity that has for its attainment the desire to protect our friends, superiors and brethren from the claims of avarice, or the knife of the assasin, and a check upon the avarice or cupidity of dishonest intercourses. In this degree the Neophyte is taught to appreciate the fact that he is *(Filius*

Dei,) the Son of God, and therefore entitled to
Divine Love. He here perceives the intimacy between the creature and the Creator, between divine
and human nature, and his alliance with his Heavenly
Father, and now for the first time realizes the fact
of his celestial origin. He learns the fact with joy,
adheres to it with gratitude. God is his soul, his
light, his companion; they unite through a mutual
force of attraction, from whence is derived the glory
of God, and the perfection of man before his fall.
He also witnesses the alliance with which the true
Mason, armed with true fortitude, exhibits his power
to stay evil and do good, which is perfection, and
gives the true meaning of B. * * * N. * * * * S. * * * *
which closes the Degree.

The Seventh, Eighth, Ninth, Tenth, Eleventh and
Twelfth Degrees can only be learned by the Initiate
within the double guarded Chapter, as they allude to
and exemplify subjects that I am neither permitted
to write or to speak of outside the Chapter.

The Thirteenth Degree of Sacred or Royal Arch,
represents scenes that took place in the Holy Mountain shortly after the landing of Noah's Ark, and are
decorated by the Pillars of Strength and Beauty, together with nine of the signs of the Zodiac, viz:
Aries, Taurus, Gemini, Cancer, Leo, Virgo, Scorpio,
Capricorn and Pisces; the other three or winter signs
of Libra, Sagittarius and Aquarius are omitted, they
being the dead or winter signs of the Egyptians.
Besides which are the nine names by which Deity
was known to our Ancient Brethren, and were by
Enoch engraven by divine command on the Delta, to
preserve the same for the craft, and from destruction
in case the world should again be destroyed by flood,
and which is explained (ante page 156 and 157.)

And there should not be found a family like Noah's, to whom the Almighty should give warning in time to prepare an ark of safety for their preservation, with some of their descendants who could explain the same. This of course is not like the Royal Arch of the York Rite. This Degree also rationally explains and accounts for in an intelligent manner the various blessings conferred upon the children of man, and historically shows the age in which the flood took place, during which the Orator reads and explains the following scripture, viz:

My son, if thou wilt receive my words, and hide my commandments with thee;

So that thou incline thine ear into wisdom, and apply thine heart to understanding;

Yea, if thou criest after knowledge, and liftest up thy voice for understanding;

If thou seekest her as silver, and searchest for her as for hidden treasures, then shalt thou understand the fear of the Lord, and find the knowledge of God;

For the Lord giveth wisdom; out of His mouth cometh knowledge and understanding.

Canst thou, by searching, find out God? Canst thou find the Almighty to perfection? He is high as Heaven. What canst thou do? He is low as Hell. What canst thou know?

O God, let thy work appear unto thy servants, and thy glory unto the children of men.

Let the beauty of the Lord be upon us, and establish the work of our hands, O Jehovah, establish thou it.

God is the Principle, the source of all things, the great Supreme Cause, and Universal Father.

God is existence; in Him we live and have our being. Go on.

God is eternal; without beginning and without end; unto Him, the past, the present, and the future are one. Go on.

God is immortality; He was, is, and ever shall be, world without end. Go on.

Fortitude is from God; His mercy and His truth giveth the weight on one side and the other, and His judgments are perfect. Go on.

There are two Jewels belonging to this Degree. The intersecting Triangles forming a six pointed star, with the mysterious characters, is a perfect representation of the Signet of Solomon, of Israel, which for ages has been the object of profound veneration among the nations of the East.

The Intersecting Deltas are emblematic of Fire and Water; Prayer and Remission; Creation and Redemption; Life and Death; and of Resurrection and Judgment; and denote that the Mason who is worthy of this Sacred Degree, should fulfill his duty to God and to man; and fill with justice, truth and honor his place in creation wherein T. S. A. O. T. U. has pleased to place him.

The second Jewel is a representation of the Hieroglyphics upon one side of the Cubical Stone, which was discovered, closing the aperture to the sacred vault, and is the particular mark of this Degree. It is the Triple Tau, a figure of five lines, thus ————, as T. upon H.; it is symbolical of the union between the Father and the Son, the letter H. representing Jehovah, the Father. Again, the T. H. is explained, Templum Hierosolyma, Temple of Jerusalem; meaning a treasure, or the place in which the Treasure is deposited. The true interpretation of this symbol is Key to knowledge, or the intellectual searching into the physical mysteries, and obtaining revelation of truth.   *   *   *   *   *

Amongst the Egyptian Brethren it was named Nilometer, and was used to measure the height of the waters of the Nile at their annual overflowing.

It also signifies Clavis ad Thesaurum, Key to a Treasure; and what more appropriate symbol can there be than the Cross or Key, to the unlocking of those mysteries which cease to be such when opened with the Key of Knowledge? The Cross is an emblem of science in the mind of man, and is the first object in every system of human worship. One of the secrets of Masonry is, that it passess by symbols from superstitions to science, and leads us to the Light of Truth.   *   *   *   *

He draws pictures to the mind and enables him to understand or readily to comprehend by Metaphysical reasoning.   *   *   Also upon the Cubical Stone certain other Hieroglyphics, which are used as a means of secret correspondence between Masons of this Degree, and are explained to the Neophyte in order that he may be thereby enabled to correspond with his fellows in that language which, although well known to the posted Mason, is meaningless to the profane, and in which he can without fear of being misunderstood, or in spite of prying eyes, or meddling outsiders, being able to read its language, to understand its meaning or comprehend its significance.

The Fourteenth Degree, or Secret Vault, is a continuation of the Arch Degree and belongs with the eleven preceding degrees to what is called the Master's Degrees, (see ante, page 195, 196,) and are to them a sort of compendium and contain all of the original work worked here, and such other work as is, at the present day, worked in all the symbolic

Lodges of Europe, and other foreign countries, and while it is a condition precedent that a man be a Master Mason, in good standing, before he can enter this Rite or any of the bodies of this Rite, yet, being in the possession of the Master's Degree, and being well posted and familiar with each and every of them is, in fact, no evidence that he is such a Master Mason as could prove himself such in any foreign country. Quite the contrary. A few words of explanation may not be improper in this connection.

Masonry, while it is general, existing in all parts of the world, yet, it is by no means universal in its workings and details, and while the Masonry taught (I mean the lecturers of course,) and worked in the symbolic Lodges and Chapters of this country, is not generally so universal as to be understood and practiced without much hindrance, yet the symbolic Masonry of other countries, where there are but three degrees in the York Rite, (or Symbolic Rite so called here,) must, of course, differ from the York Rite of this country with nine degrees. Consequently, the drawing out of the three degrees of the English York Rite, to nine degrees of the American York Rite, must necessarily tend to misplace and confuse those who practice the other way, and that too, when in this changing, some of the tests are left out or new ones put in. The posted Mason will readily understand this, and hence we say that the possession of the Memphis Rite becomes a real necessity,—especially to the Mason wishing to visit foreign countries. And should the recipient of these degrees never visit a working body he would be well paid and the attendant expense well invested, by the knowledge he will gain of his previously taken degrees, to say nothing of the light and knowledge imparted in the various and beautiful lectures that cannot be given here; to say nothing of the beautiful and sublime dramatic work embraced in the actual dissemination of the parts and the degrees.

The degree being founded on events that took place before and at the destruction of Jerusalem and the temple by Nebuzaradan, is the summit of symbolic or operative Freemasonry. During the conferring of the degrees the following is spoken by the Orator or Prelate, viz: (Is fully described ante page 197.)

Thus saith the Lord, the God of Israel: Behold, I will give this city into the hand of the King of Babylon; and he shall burn it with fire.   *

And thou shalt not escape out of his hand; but shalt surely be taken and delivered into his hand; and thine eyes shall behold the eyes of the King of Babylon; and he shall speak with thee mouth to mouth; and thou shalt go to Babylon.   *

The Babylonians have broken down the walls of Jerusalem, slain our young men and old men. seized upon our women, and have polluted the House of the Lord; and we fear that they will penetrate this Secret Vault and carry off our Sacred Delta.   *

Arise, Priests of the Temple; let not the Babylonians desecrate this holy place, nor enter within the Temple. •   *   *   *   *   *

A BRIEF DESCRIPTION OF KING SOLOMON'S TEMPLE.

This structure, for beauty, magnificence and expense, exceeded any building which was ever erected. It was built of large stones of white marble, curiously hewn, and so artfully joined together that they appeared like one entire stone. Its inner walls, beams, posts, doors, floors and ceilings, were made of cedar

and olive wood, and planks of fir, which were entirely covered with plates of gold, with various beautiful
engravings, and adorned with precious jewels of
many colors. The nails which fastened those plates
were also of gold, with heads of curious workman-
ship. The roof was of olive wood, covered with
gold; and when the sun shone thereon, the reflection
from it was of such a refulgent splendor that it daz-
zled the eyes of all who beheld it. The court in
which the temple stood, and the courts without were
adorned on all sides with stately buildings and clois-
ters; and the gates entering therein were exquisitely
beautiful and elegant. The vessels consecrated to the
perpetual use of the temple, were suited to the magnificence of the edifice in which they were deposited
and used.

Josephus states that there were one hundred and
forty thousand of those vessels, which were made of
gold, and one million three hundred and forty thous-
and of silver; ten thousand vestments for the priests,
made of silk, with purple girdles; and two millions
of purple vestments for the singers. There were also
two hundred thousand trumpets, and forty thousand
other musical instruments, made use of in the temple and in worshiping God.

According to the most accurate computation of the
number of talents of gold, silver and brass, laid out
upon the temple, the sum amounts to six thousand
nine hundred and four millions eight hundred and
twenty-two thousand and five hundred pounds sterling; and the jewels are reckoned to exceed
this sum. The gold vessels are estimated at
five hundred and forty-five millions two hundred
and ninety-six thousand two hundred and three
pounds and four shillings sterling; and the silver

M

ones at four hundred and thirty-nine millions three
hundred and fourty-four thousand pounds sterling;
amounting in all to nine hundred and eighty-
four millions six hundred and thirty thousand
two hundred and thirty pounds four shillings.
In addition to this, there were expenses for
workmen and for materials brought from
Mount Libanus and the quarries of Zeradatha.
There were ten thousand men per month in Lebanon,
employed in felling and preparing the timbers for the
craftsmen to hew them; seventy thousand to carry
burdens; eighty thousand to hew the stones and
timber; and three thousand three hundred overseers
of the work; who were all employed for seven years;
to whom, besides their wages and diet, King Solomon gave as a free gift, six millions seven hundred
and thirty-three thousand nine hundred and seventy-
seven pounds.

The treasure left by David, towards carrying on
this noble and glorious work, is reckoned to be nine
hundred and eleven millions four hundred and six-
teen thousand two hundred and seven pounds, to
which if we add King Solomon's annual revenue, his
trading to Ophir for gold, and the presents made him
by all the earth, we shall not wonder at his being
able to carry on so stupendous a work; nor can we,
without impiety, question its surpassing all other
structures, since we are assured that it was built by
the immediate direction of heaven.

The Fifteenth Degree, or Knight of the Flaming
Sword, is taken in part from the organization known
as the Knight Crusaders. (Referred to ante, page
191.) And is founded on events connected with the
liberation of the Jews from Babylonian captivity,
and the commencement or rather permission to the

Jews to rebuild the temple in spite of the Samaritans, and the compelling them to pay tribute to Judea as a tributary province, in which Zerubbabel and Cyrus, with Darius, kings in authority, are favorably impressed and render material aid and assistance to the Jews, to recover the vessels of gold and silver contained in the sanctuary of Solomon when he was King of Israel. During which is also produced a singular phenomena, and Zerubbabel is fully convinced of his divine and important mission, and during the interview with King Cyrus by Zerubbabel, who had been taken prisoner by the guards of the King, while traveling within his territory in search of the King, who was a friend of his youth, and had made a most solemn promise that should he ever become King, he would liberate the captive Jews from their Babylonian captivity, in which they had been held for seventy years, being the descendants of those ancient Jews whom Moses had liberated from Egyptian bondage, and who were in possession of Egyptian Masonry as taught their forefathers by the High Priest Moses; and Zerubbabel had been by the Jewish Synagogue and Sanhedrim Council, on account of his former and youthful acquaintance with Cyrus, deputed to do this great service, thereby incurring the risk of being taken a prisoner and spy, as he really was suspected to be, and arrested and brought before Cyrus for.

In this Degree is shown and exemplified one of the severest tests and trials of courage, integrity and Masonic firmness in the keeping of its secrets since the days of Huram and Jedediah, during which the following colloquy takes place and the King's dream is interpreted, and the King is called upon to pronounce sentence upon the spy, viz:

Q. Who are you, and why were you found in our territory and brought here as a prisoner and a spy ?

A. I am no spy.

Q. Who are you then ?

A. I am Zerubbabel, the first among my equals, a Mason of rank.

Q. What is your desire ?

A. An interview with your Majesty.

Q. What is your age ?

A. 70 years.

Q. What is the nature of your application ?

A. To remedy the condition of my brother Masons who are in captivity.

Princes and Rulers, this is Zerubbabel, my early friend. I have long witnessed the captivity of the Jews and have resolved in my mind to ameliorate their condition. I am greatly troubled in my sleep with dreams relative thereto, one of which I will relate, and as Zerubbabel is a wise man of the tribe of Judah, he may be able to interpret it, while you also will assist me with your counsel. This is my dream : (Reads from the Book of Esdras.)

In my sleep I saw a lion ready to spring upon and devour me, and at a distance Nebuchadnezzar and Belshazzar, my predecessors, chained in the garb of slavery; they were contemplating a halo of glory which Masons show as the name of the G. A. O. T. U., out of which is issued the words " Liberty to the Captives."

My tranquillity is disturbed; interpret, if thou canst, my dream.

" Blessed be the name of God, forever and ever, for wisdom and might are His; He giveth wisdom unto the wise, and knowledge to them that know understanding. He revealeth the deep and secret things;

He knoweth what is in the darkness, and the light dwelleth with Him."

Zerubbabel replies :

Oh, King! forasmuch as thy predecessors appeared to thee, captives, and in chains, beneath the sacred Emblem of Deity, and a lion was about to devour thee, this is the dream, and this is the interpretation thereof.

Thy predecessors being in chains, showeth the wrong they have done unto Israel. The lion is the wrath that will fall upon thee, if thou followest in their footsteps, and the halo of glory is the reward thou shalt receive hereafter, if thou wilt liberate the captive Jews.

King. The captivity shall be concluded. Zerubbabel, signify the favor you request.

Most Potent King, we request that you grant us our liberty, and permit us to return to Jerusalem, to assist in rebuilding the Temple of our God.

King. Arise! I have long witnessed the weight of your captivity, and the zeal and attachment you have for the Institution of Masonry, the secrets of which I am not in the possession of, though I have for a long time been anxious to be possessed of them without the trouble and fear of an initiation, and am ready to release you on the instant, if you will communicate to me the mysteries of Masonry, for which I have the most profound veneration.   *   *

Cond.: Most Potent King, your situation renders it desirable that you should become a Mason, as we are taught in Masonry that the wise, great and good are always acceptable candidates. But our obligations render it impossible that we can communicate its mysteries to you, or entrust you with its secrets, without a proper obligation to secrecy taken on your part, as we and all other Masons have done, before you can be entrusted with them; for our Grand Master Solomon taught the craft these principles, that FIDELITY, EQUALITY and BROTHERLY LOVE, were ever to be the criterions among us; your rank, titles and superiority are not incompatible with the mysteries of our order, but our obligations are unknown to you, our engagements with our brethren are inviolable, I will not reveal our secrets. If our liberty is only to be purchased at the price of integrity, we prefer captivity or death.

King. I admire your zeal and constancy. Princes and Rulers, this worthy Prince merits liberty for his attachment to his solemn compact. Our Archivist Semetius, will draw up a royal proclamation that people may return, unmolested to Jerusalem.   *   *

Thus said Cyrus, King of Persia: "The Lord God of Heaven hath given me all the kingdoms of the earth, therefore I give to as many of the Jews that dwell in my country, permission to return to their own country, and to build the Temple of God at Jerusalem, at the same place where it was before. I also send my Treasurer, Mithridates, and Zerubbabel, the Governor of the Jews, that they may lay the foundations of the Temple, and may build it sixty cubits high, and of the same latitude, making three edifices of polished stones, and one of the wood of the country, and the same order extends to the altar whereon they offer sacrifices to God. I give order that the expenses shall be given them out of the tributes due from Samaria; the Priests shall also offer their sacrifices according to the law of Moses in Jerusalem, and when they offer them, they shall pray to God for the preservation of the King, and of his family, that the Kingdom of Persia may continue.

By order of

CYRUS, *King of Persia.*

SEMETIUS, *Grand Chancellor.*

Take this epistle, Zerubbabel, and with it I arm you with this sword, as a distinguishing mark above your companions. It is the sword that Nebuchadnezzar received from Jehoiachim, King of Jerusalem, at the time of his captivity; employ it in the defence of your country, religion and laws.   *   *

Henceforth, you are to me, and I will be to you, a brother. Proceed to Judea, and rebuild the Temple. I appoint you chief over your brethren, with full powers to rule over Judea as a Tributary Province, and the annual payment shall be made within the porch of the Temple, of which you will forward me an exact model; but before you depart, I will entrust you with the necessary Signs and Pass Words by which you will be enabled to make yourself known to my Guards on this side of the river Euphrates.

  *   *   *   *   *   *

The Degree ends with a striking evidence of the Power of Truth.   *   *   *   *

The Knight of Jerusalem, or the Seventeenth Degree of the Egyptian Masonic Rite, is the conclusion of the former fifteenth degree, and is an illustration of the Order of Chivalry or Knighthood, as it existed in the early days of Jewish prosperity, and was kept up in commemoration of the Hebrew word that signified the 20th day of the 10th month, as well as the Hebrew word signifying the 23d day of the 12th month; these being the days in which the Second Temple was begun and when it was finished, and

had been kept sacred and held in great veneration by
Jewish Masons.   *   *   *   *

This degree also represents the two at that time
only civilized, except the Egyptians, nations who
possessed a knowledge to any great extent of the
doctrine of revealed religion, or a close acquaintane
with the revelations of God to mankind; one being
the Jewish Sanhedrim or Council of the twelve
tribes, and the other the Court of Cyrus, King of
Persia, to whom, by reason in part of religious faith
and by reason of Masonic ties, he complied with the
request and granted permission. And in this degree
is represented in connection with Temple Building,
the kind of embassadors employed by our ancient
brethren—and this being about the time of the death
of Cambyses, son of Cyrus, King of Persia, who had
been a sort of ally to the Samaritans, who were the
deadly enemies of the Jews, and who also were opposed to all Masonic societies. However, by the
wisdom and influence of Zerubbabel, the aid of the
great King Darius, King of the other provinces, the
Jews are enabled to build the Second Temple, and
dedicate it after the exact model and manner of the
First. For which purpose he obtained of Darius the
following interview and which, by the force of truth,
gained for them a decree to build and complete the
Temple.   *   *   *   *

The following discourse is introduced, viz: 1 Esdras 2d and 3d chapters, which after   *   *
in which a Masonic examination is had.   *   *

Oh! This is Zerubabbel, my early friend. Release
him. Your presence here is most opportune. Be
seated amongst our Princes; accompany us to and
partake of our banquet. Yesterday I found under '
my pillow these three questions: "Which is the

strongest, Wine, Woman, or the King ?" I promise him whose answer is the most agreeable to truth and the dictates of wisdom, a chain of gold, and a chariot shall be given him. He shall sit next myself, and be called my cousin.　　*　　*　　*

Let us retire to our banqueting hall, and after supper, we will discuss the questions. [Strikes ! ! !] Attention, Sir Knights. Form in line, facing the West. [The Senior Warden and Most Wise lead the procession, Junior Warden and Neophyte next, Orator next. Sir Knights form in double lines, in two divisions. Conductor takes the first division, Captain of Guard the second. They each give the command: "Draw swords! Carry swords! March!" They march to the table, one line each side. After the officers are seated in the following manner:
Senior Warden at the head, Most Wise on his right, and the Junior Warden on his left—the orders are given by the Conductor and Captain of the Guard: "Present swords! Recover swords! Return swords!" They are then seated. (See Tactics Book.) After supper, they return in the same manner, the Most Wise in the Orient, the Senior Warden being seated in the West, with Junior Warden, Orator and Captain of the Guard, Neophyte.] We will now discuss the questions, "Which is the strongest—Wine, Woman, or the King?" Sir Knight Orator, we will hear you—which is the strongest?

Orator: O, ye men! how exceedingly strong is Wine! It maketh the mind of the King and of the fatherless child all one; of the bond man and the free man; of the poor man and the rich. It turneth also every thought into jollity and mirth, so that a man remembereth neither sorrow nor debt. It maketh every heart rich, so that a man remembereth
M*

neither King nor Governor; and it maketh to speak all things by talents. O, ye men! is not Wine the strongest, that enforceth to do thus?

S. W.: Respectable Knight Junior Warden, what say you—which is the strongest?

J. W.: O, ye men! do not men excel in strength, that bear rule over sea and land, and all things in them? But yet the King is more mighty, for he is lord of all these things, and hath dominion over them, and whatsoever he commandeth them they do it. They slay and are slain, and transgress not the King's commandment; if they get the victory, they bring all things to the King. Likewise for those that are no soldiers, but use husbandry; when they have reaped that which they had sown, they pay tribute to the King. And yet he is but one man; if he command to kill, they kill; if he command to spare, they spare. O, ye men! how should not the King be mightiest, when he is thus obeyed!

S. W.: What say you, Zerubabbel—which is strongest?

Capt. Guard: [Speaks for Neophyte.] O, ye men! It is not the great King, nor the multitude of men, neither is it Wine that excelleth; who is it, then, that ruleth them? are they not Women? Women have borne the King, and all the people;—a man leaveth his father, and his country, and cleaveth unto his wife;—Women have dominion over you! Many have also sinned and perished for Women. And now, do ye not believe me? Is not the King great in his power, and do not all nations fear to touch him? Yet did I see APAME, daughter of BARTACUS, sitting at the King's right hand, and taking the crown from the King's head and setting it upon her own. And if she took any displeasure, the

King was fain to flatter, that she might be reconciled to him again! Woman is the strongest! Yet, O men! Wine is wicked,—the King is wicked,—Women are wicked. The children of men are wicked! But the TRUTH is strong, and endureth forever, There is but one true God. He is the strongest. Blessed be the God of Truth!

S. W.: Zerubbabel, ask what thou wilt and it shall be granted thee,—for thou hast been found the wisest.

Cond.: Mighty King! the Samaritans refuse to pay the tribute imposed on them by Cyrus, King of Persia, for defraying the expenses of the sacrifices which are offered on the Altar in the Temple we are about to rebuild. The people of Israel entreat that you will compel the Samaritans to perform their duty.

S. W.: Your request is just and equitable; I order that the Samaritans shall immediately pay the tribute imposed on them. I deliver to you my decree for this purpose. Go in peace!

Cond.: I deliver to you the decree of Darius, King of Persia, which we have obtained after defeating our enemies, and encountering many dangers in our journey.

M. W. [Reads.] "We, Darius, 'King of Kings!' willing to favor and protect our people at Jerusalem, after the example of our illustrious predecessor, King Cyrus, do will and ordain, that the Samaritans, against whom complaints have been made, shall punctually pay the tribute money which they owe for the sacrifices of the Temple—otherwise they shall receive the punishment due to their disobedience. Given at Shushan, the Palace, this fourth day of the second month, in the year 3534, and of our reign the third, under the seal of our faithful Sandram, Minister of State.   DARIUS."

M. W.; [To Zerubbabel.] The people of Jerusalem are under the greatest obligations to you for the zeal and courage displayed by you in surmounting the obstacles which you encountered in your journey.

After the   *   *   *   and the ode is sung   *   *   *   *   the degree is closed.
*   *   *   *   *   *

The altar of perfumes is raised and the tools by which all constructions are formed and without which they would be irregular. They are the *   *   *   Y∴ H∴ V∴ H∴ and a re- markable evidence of the assurance of divine ac- ceptance of the labor of men is evinced and an un- mistakable evidence of celestial favor which spread over the superstructure and proves a most happy au- gury for the craftsman and the *faithful believer *   *   *   The following from the Book of Esdras is repeated.   *   *   *

The following ode is sung, with solemn ceremony :

All hail to the morning,
That bids us rejoice;
The temple's completed,
Exalt high each voice.
The capstone is finished,
Our labor is o'er;
· The sound of the gavel
Shall hail us no more.

To the Power Almighty, who ever has guided
The tribes of old Israel, exalting their fame ;
To Him who hath governed our hearts undivided,
Let's send forth our voices to praise His great name.

Companions, assemble
On this joyful day;
(The occasion is glorious,)
The keystone to lay;

Fulfilled is the promise,
  By the ANCIENT OF DAYS,
To bring forth the capstone
  With shouting and praise.

(CEREMONIES.)

There is no more occasion for level or plumb-line,
  For trowel or gavel, for compass or square;
Our works are completed, the ARK safely seated,
  And we shall be greeted as workmen most rare.

Now those that are worthy,
  Our toils who have shared,
And prov'd themselves faithful,
  Shall meet their reward.
Their virtue and knowledge,
  Industry and skill,
Have our approbation,
  Have gained our good will.

We accept and receive them, Most Excellent Masters,
  Invested with honors and power to preside;
Among worthy craftsmen, wherever assembled,
  The knowledge of Masons to spread far and wide.

ALMIGHTY JEHOVAH!
  Descend now and fill
This Lodge with thy glory,
  Our hearts with good will!
Preside at our meetings,
  Assist us to find
True pleasure in teaching
  Good will to mankind.

Thy *wisdom* inspired the great institution,
  Thy *strength* shall support it till nature expire;
And when the creation shall fall into ruin,
  Its *beauty* shall rise through the midst of the fire.

" Now when Solomon had made an end of praying, the fire came down from heaven and consumed the burnt offering and the sacrifices ; and the glory of the Lord filled the house. And the priests could not enter into the house of the Lord, because the glory of the Lord had filled the Lord's house,

"And when all the children of Israel saw how the fire came down, and the glory of the Lord upon the house, they bowed themselves with their faces to the ground upon the pavement and worshiped, and praised the Lord, saying, For he is good; for his mercy endureth forever."—II Chron. vii : 1-3.

Our misfortunes are at an end and our success henceforth assured. By this sign of celestial favor, which spread itself over us, let us be firm and unshaken in the practice of those virtues which shall assure us its continuation.

You will now listen to the discourse of the Knight Orator.

Orator : Sir Knight, you have retraced an epoch forever memorable to the workmen of the second Temple and their successors. Redouble your attention to that which is yet to be made known to you, and learn to make of it a just application. The Supreme Architect of the Universe would punish the pride of a rebellious nation, without entirely casting them off.

The sacred fire of the Temple was hid, but not extinguished. During the captivity it meditated with more fruit than in the past, on the laws and ceremonies; its blindness ceased; it recognized the true cause of its misfortunes and after seventy years of bondage, recovered its liberty.

Zerubbabel, descended from the Princes of his nation, had the courage to return at the head of the people of Jerusalem, to re-establish the Temple on its foundation; to this end he bore the Sword in one hand and the Trowel in the other, because he was annoyed by his enemies. Many who were dispersed among the neighboring people, on learning the news of the rebuilding, came to offer their assistance ; but

they were not admitted till they had given proofs of
their zeal and courage in the rigorous trials to which
they were submitted. After many trials, the workmen succeeded in establishing the Temple on its
foundations; but it differed from the first, so far as
the sentiments it excited were also different. The
ancients who had seen the glory and splendor of the
first Temple, shed tears of bitterness; but the Supreme Architect of the Universe consoled them by
an event which proved to them that they had found
grace in His sight, and that He would again dwell
among them. In fact, the new Temple was finished,
the altar of sacrifice and that of perfumes had been
rebuilt, and the people instructed in the laws by Esdras. Nehemiah arranged everything for the solemn
dedication of the Temple, and knowing that the sacred fire had been hid in a deep dry pit, at the destruction of the Temple, he sent the priests to search
for it. Not finding any fire there, but only thick,
muddy water, he, full of confidence, took it and
poured it on the altar; it ignited at once, and consumed the sacrifice in the presence of the people, who
gave themselves up to the purest joy at the sight of
an event which again raised the glory of the nation.

This concludes the degree of Knight of Jerusalem,
and I congratulate you upon your advancement.

The Seventeenth Degree, or Knight of the Orient,
is in fact the ceremonials of dedication of the Second
Temple, and the investing of the Neophyte with the
orders of Knighthood and in a solemn manner offering his vows to the Supreme Ruler of the Universe,

*   *   *   *   *   *

with proper ceremonials and investments of the Order of Priestly Knighthood, by which he can prove
himself a Knight of the Temple of Jerusalem, but not

a Knight of the Christian Religion; for these degrees were worked in Palestine long before the birth
of Christ or the Christian Religion was thought of,
but from which all such degrees have been taken
and appropriated, and were worked over four
thousand years ago. Hence, as the Templar system
does not claim a record of over one hundred years,
and as the A. and A. or Scotch Rite has only existed
since 1802, it is very evident to the Masonic scholar
or posted Mason where these degrees come from.

This ends the Seventeeth Degree of the Memphis
Rite.

The Eighteenth, or last Degree of the Rose-Croix
Memphis Chapter, called Rose-Croix, or by some
Rose-Croix de Heredom, is perhaps older than other
of the Masonic Degrees, save perhaps the degree of
the York Rite called Master Mason. But it has undergone many and various changes and is now worked
with some differences in the Scotch Rite, the Rite of
the Three Globes and the French Rite. At one time,
however, it was a Catholic Degree remodeled and
furbished up by a pretender by the name of Stuart,
in the college of the Jesuits, at Clairmont, in 1754,
and mixed up with the Crusade or Ancient Templar
system, and adopted the Christian religion and the
Resurrection of Christ for its ceremonial, and which
had been taken from the Egyptian Rite of Memphis
in the main, and dedicated to the Christian instead
of the Jewish faith or Hebrew religion. The degree
is founded on events connected with the last days of
the ancient crusaders, and was not till after the
building of the Como in Italy, worked as a Masonic
Degree, and is now only so worked in the A. and A.
Rite as a religious festival degree, and in the Egyptian or Memphis Rite as a Masonic degree; and its

scenes are located at or near the great pyramid Cheops, and along the banks of the river Nile. Its lectures have with them a semblance of religious creed of that general or natural religion in which all men agree to worship the Supreme Architect of the Universe, and keep the moral law of doing unto others as we would others should do unto us.

The following among select readings are recited by the Orator, viz:

FIRST JOURNEY.

The Temple of Masonry is demolished; the Tools and Columns are broken; the blazing Star of Truth has disappeared; the Light of Philosophy is obscured; the darkness of Ignorance spreads over the earth; the Word is lost! Disorder reigns amongst us.

Solomon erected on Mount Moriah a Temple, in which to render that homage to the Supreme Architect of the World, due Him from His intelligent creatures.

Solomon received from God in Gabaon that which he was not able to preserve in Zion,—even Wisdom; and his errors and irregularities giving a taint to his glory, she constantly veiled from him her sacred Tabernacle.

This example, as striking as that of the conduct of the children of Israel, during the forty days that Moses went from them into Sinai, demonstrated the instability and blindness of the man reputed wise— and warns us to be on our guard against ourselves and others. Is it not written,—"If any man among you *seemeth* to be wise, let him become a fool, that he may be wise, for the wisdom of this world is foolishness with God."

Happy is the man that findeth wisdom, and the man that getteth understanding, for it is better than

the merchandise of silver and fine gold. She is more
precious than rubies; and all the things that thou
canst desire are not to be compared unto her. Length
of days is in her right hand; and in her left hand,
riches and honor; her ways are ways of pleasantness,
and all her paths are peace; she is a tree of life to
them that lay hold of her, and happy is every one
that retaineth her.

[The Neophyte, in charge of the Conductor, stops
by the Pillar of the Senior Warden. As the Senior
Warden commences his address, the Neophyte commences the six last Journeys, and gives the Signs.]

SECOND JOURNEY.

S. W.: ! ! Corruption has glided among our
work; darkness covers the earth; the pointed cubical stone sweats blood and water; the Word is lost.

The Temple of Jehovah, sullied, profaned and for-
saken in Zion, that of Ignorance watered with the
blood of human victims, burning upon its Altars the
incense due only to the true God, is not the only
stain upon the glory of Israel.

Despotism has reared her altars, which being ar-
rayed in glittering jewels and riches of the world,
dazzle the eyes of the weak-minded man, and Superstition opposes itself towards any approach to true
wisdom.

Be not led astray by false lights. The vapors that
arise from the mire of the Earth, gilded by the splendor of the Sun, have retired.

THIRD JOURNEY.

M. W.: ! ! ! Withdraw, ye dark phantoms of superstition that oppress the freedom of mind; withdraw, ye oracles of ignorance and delusion, that

would deceive and enchain the intelligence of him who searches after truth.

Ye purple-robed kings, ye false prophets, and still falser priests, who debase man by encircling his soul with the adamantine chain of despotism, vanish from before the pure spirit of Masonry.

FOURTH JOURNEY.

J. W.: ! ! ! ! The great Adonai, who is enthroned in every glory above the sphere of innumerable worlds, will render futile your sacrilegious efforts to enslave the minds of His creatures. The Sun of Truth will scatter to dim chaos your slavish teachings. True Wisdom, which Solomon in all his glory conceived not, shall revisit the earth.

FIFTH JOURNEY.

S. W.: ! ! ! ! ! Let us no longer lament over the misfortunes of Eden, nor of Zion; they will no longer obstruct the efforts of a free and absolute will. The Spirit of Evil, who contrived them, will remain a nullity in his abortive empire.

Eden, that antique garden, that visible paradise, will be but a weak image of the splendors of Heaven and the beatitude that the Eternal has created for those who love Him.

SIXTH JOURNEY.

M. W.: ! ! ! ! ! ! Now we know the wisdom of God—even the hidden wisdom which God ordained before the world to our glory.

The princes and rulers of the earth had not the knowledge we possess; if they had had it, they would never have slain Him who proclaimed,— "Peace on earth: good will towards men."

SEVENTH JOURNEY.

J. W.: ! ! ! ! ! ! ! The rule of conduct He proclaimed was, "Whatsoever ye would that others should do unto you, do ye even so unto them."

It is written : "Eye hath not seen, ear hath not heard, neither hath it entered into the heart of man to conceive those things which God hath prepared for those who love Him."

We will not despair—we will practice the new law, and, guided by its teaching, endeavor to recover the Sacred Word.

M. W.: This Sublime Degree was founded by a Philosopher of Egypt named Ormus, who purified the doctrines of the Egyptians by the precepts of the new law of doing unto others whatsoever we would they should do unto us. His disciples united with the Essenes, who had founded Lodges or Schools of Solamonic Science, and traveled from the East to propagate their secret doctrines in the West, where they instructed their pupils 'in the mysteries of religiou and philosophy.

Some of the brethren of the Rose-Croix attaching themselves to the crusaders in Palestine, in the year 1181, communicated their secrets to Garimont, Patriarch of Jerusalem, and having formed themselves into armed associations for the protection of the pilgrims who visited the Holy City, assumed the title of Knights of Palestine.

J. W.: Sir Knight Conductor, you will cause the Neophyte to travel by the North, East, South and West, that he may behold and approve the beauties of Eden, whence the new law is derived, even the law of love.

Orator : [Reads.] Faith is the substance of things hoped for—the evidence of things not seen. Through faith we understand that the world was formed by the Word of God. By Faith, Enoch was translated, so that he should not see death. By Faith, Abraham, when he was tried, essayed to offer up his son Isaac.

S. W.: Hope is the evidence of things not seen. Waiting for the redemption of our bodies from death ; for we are saved by Hope; but Hope that is seen is not Hope, for when a man seeth, what doth he then hope for ? But if we hope for that we see not, then do we with patience wait.

J. W.: Though I speak with the tongues of men and of angels, and have not Charity, I am become as sounding brass, or a tinkling cymbal ;—Charity suffereth long, and is kind ; Charity envieth not ; Charity vaunteth not itself; is not puffed up ; rejoiceth not in iniquity, but rejoiceth in truth ; beareth all things ; believeth all things; hopeth all things; endureth all things; Charity never faileth ; and now abideth Faith, Hope, and Charity, these three; but the greatest of all these is Charity.

Sir Knight———, what have you learned on your journeys ?

Three virtues, Faith, Hope, and Charity to be my guide. Teach me if there be any other to seek and follow.

We must inform you that those three words you have so often heard, have, among the Knights of the Rose-Croix, a more extended signification than is generally attached to them. You will observe that the chief virtue of a Mason is Charity—the first law he should obey. The Hope of improving our spiritual condition is an immediate consequence of Charity. Love and Hope united will give Faith in our labors for the promotion of happiness among brethren. Bigots, under the most fearful threats, compel men to believe in them—to have Faith in their doctrines, and

man becomes a tool in their hands. According to
their teachings, Faith consists in believing that which
is not always consistent with nature, science and
reason. Charity is a virtue; its object is to love and
assist our fellow beings, as well as an act of our own
free will. Masonic charity teaches the love of all
men, without regard to their religion or origin; so as
to be useful, kind and indulgent to every one—to
establish enlightenment and union where ignorance
and discord prevail. Charity is the love of God and
His creatures. To love is to know:—to love and to
know God are essentially the same thing. If we
know God, it must be as a father; and the idea of a
father conveys the idea of kindness, mercy and care
for the happiness of his children.

In the troubles and perplexities incident to human
life, we are bound by our nature to seek for help;
hence, we hope in Him for our happiness; have faith
in Him, and patiently bear that which sometimes to
us seems unjust, because we know that a loving
Father cannot deceive His children.

We do therefore proclaim it as a duty—Masons
must love each other. Their union will cause them
to hope for the better condition of humanity; and
with Faith in their cause, they will ultimately gather
all men under their fraternal banner.

It has been said that the degree of Rose-Croix has
but little to do with Masonry. Those who make
such declarations are equally ignorant of the principles therein taught, as they are those of Masonry, for
the diligent scholar will find them identical.

As Masons, we have nothing to do with the dogmas
of different religious sects—these are left for individual opinion. As a fraternity, we acknowledge but

one Almighty Parent; that all men are brothers, having a common origin and a common end.

And now, my brother, if it is your intention to follow the new law we have alluded to—that of doing unto others, as you would they should do unto you—take in our presence the solemn vow.

M. W.: Let the Triangle be formed.

[Conductor then places the Neophyte between the Columns.]

M. W.: Respectable Knight Senior Warden, what is the motive of our assembly?

S. W.: We seek the * * *

M. W.: What must be done * * *

S. W.: We must embrace the new law, and be convinced of the three Virtues, which are its pillars, base and principles.

M. W.: What are they?

S. W.: Faith, Hope and Charity.

M. W.: How shall we find those * * *

S. W.: By traveling three days in * * *

M. W.: Let us, then, travel from the East to the South, from the South to the West, from the West to the North.

Orator: Behold, I lay in Zion a chief corner-stone, elect, precious; and he that believeth, shall not be confounded. But ye are a chosen generation; a royal priesthood; a holy nation; a peculiar people; and though now for a season ye are in heaviness through manifold temptations, the trial of your faith being more precious than gold purified with fire, shall result in honors and rewards. Love the Brotherhood! Fear God! Honor the Most Wise!
*   *   *   *   *   *

Orator: Hear my prayer, oh Lord, and consider

my calling; hold not thy peace at my tears; oh, spare me, that I may recover strength to go hence.

Thou hast beset me behind and before; whither shall I flee from thy presence?

If I say, surely the darkness shall cover me, the darkness hideth not from thee; the night shineth as the day; the darkness and the light are both alike to thee.

Yet I beseech thee, oh Lord, to have compassion on the lowly, even though I walk in the midst of Death.

Oh Lord, haste to deliver me, for I am brought very low. Bring my soul out of prison that I may give thanks unto thy Holy name.

"And I heard a voice from Heaven saying—Blessed are the dead that die in the Lord, from henceforth, saith the spirit, they rest from their labors and their works do follow them." I am the resurrection and the life, saith the Lord; he that believeth in me, though he were dead, yet shall he live, and whosoever believeth in me, shall never, never die.

Cond.: A Knight of the Orient, who having penetrated the Womb of earth and the abode of Sin and Death, during three days, desires from you the Word as his reward.

J. W.: Most Wise, it is a Kninght of the Orient, who having penetrated to the Womb of the Earth and the abode of Sin and Death, during three days, desires from you   *   *   *   *

M. W.: Let him enter.

J. W.: Save me, oh God, by Thy name, and judge me by Thy strength. Hear my prayer, oh God! Give ear to the words of my mouth! For strangers are risen up against me, and oppressors seek after my soul. Behold, God is mine helper. I will praise Thy name, oh Lord, for it is good; for he hath delivered me out of all trouble.

M. W.: Worthy Knight, from whence came you ?

Cond.: Judea.

M. W.: By what place have you passed ?

Cond.: Nazareth.

M. W.: Who has conducted you ?

Cond.: Raphael.

M. W.: Of what tribe are you ?

Cond.: Judah.

M. W.: Give me the initials of the four names you have just produced.

Cond.:   *   *   *   *   *   *

M. W.: Sir Knights,   *   *   is found ; let the Neophyte   *   *   Advance, and receive the reward due to your merit.

LECTURE ON THE CROSS.

Orator : The sign or symbol of the Cross is a natural one. The ancient Romans had ensigns, flags, and crosses gilded and beautified. When a man, in the hour of overwhelming distress and sorrow, prays his Father to have mercy upon him, he extends his hands heavenwards, and makes precisely the same figure.

In Egypt, the illiterate gratitude of a superstitious people, while they adored the river on whose inundations the fertility of their provinces depended, could not fail of attaching notions of sanctity and holiness to the crosses which were erected along the banks of the Nile.

There is a Masonic legend that a Delta, in which was a cross encircled by the motto, " IN HOC SIGNO VINCES," was shown in a vision to the knight crusaders of Palestine on the night before a victorious

N

battle; and thus the motto became one of the Order.

It was held in the earliest ages among the Egyptians, Arabians and Indians, as the signification of "the life to come"—of "eternal life."

To us it has become, as in the days of the Egyptians, "the symbol of the life to come"—"of eternity;" and it will serve to remind all true Masons that they must always be ready to give even their lives for the perpetuation and triumphs of truth.

The Rose which you see on the Cross is the emblem of Discretion. Discretion is a necessity, lest those who are opposed to our principles, should shut up our Temples and disperse our institutions, as they have in former times. The death of one of us would not serve our cause. Martyrdom is fruitless in our days, and is not to be sought after.

All we have to do is to enlist good and honest men so that an army of true and practical Masons shall array themselves against tyrants, imposters and fanatics, and prove to them that their days of successful opposition are gone forever, and their only choice is to relinquish their useless weapons and join us.

Therefore, we must not discuss our principles outside of our Temples. We know human nature well enough to be satisfied that secresy is in itself attraction, and is a means by which we make it impossible for our profane enemies to assail us with their sophistry. For we are always right when we answer them by saying: "You speak of what you know not." To argue about Masonry, a man must be a Mason, and once admitted, he must certainly be a bad man if he does not love it with all his heart.

*   *   *   *   *   *

We must be particular in our admissions, especially in this degree.

Until then let us be prudent and act " sub rosa."

In the name of this Chapter, I sincerely congratulate you on your admission amongst you. In your further advancement you will find a more mysterious significance attached to the Cross, not revealed in the Chapter, and which can only be made known within a Senate of Hermetic Philosophers.

Believe me, that I am sure your good conduct, zeal, virtue and discretion, will always render you more and more deserving of the honor which you have this day received, and we most heartily and sincerely wish that your life may long be preserved to enable you to continue a useful member of our Ancient Rite, and a faithful and devoted Apostle of Truth, Science and Love.

This ends the Rose-Croix Degree and the Chapter lecture of the Rite.　　　*　　　*　　　*

This closes the description of the degrees and some of the lectures and quotations from Scripture used in conferring the degrees.

The following three degrees are public degrees and will be found useful in the conferring of degrees and in a convenient form, being separated from the esoteric work ; they will also be found instructive, and were it not for the fact that my time was very limited, I would have added the poetry and music ; as it is I put in such as I can find time to attend to.—AUTHOR.

PUBLIC DEGREES

OF

ADEPT INSTALLATOR, CONSECRATOR AND EULOGIST.

THE FORTY-THIRD, FORTY-FOURTH AND FORTY-FIFTH
DEGREES OF THE SENATE

OF THE

EGYPTIAN MASONIC RITE OF MEMPHIS.

INSTALLATION CEREMONIES.

The highest presiding officer of the body to be installed takes the Orient; and if the ceremony is to be private, opens the body in due form; if public, orders the officers to places, and proceeds thus:

Sub. Gr. Com.—Illustrious Senior Knight Interpreter, what is the cause of this assemblage?

Sen. Kt.—Most Wise, this is the appointed time when we should renew our vows to the Supreme Architect of the Universe, and perform the ceremonials of installation, according to the Regulations of the Egyptian Masonic Rite of Memphis, and our ancient customs.

Sub. Gr. Com.—This being so, let us ascertain if the officers are at their respective stations. Illustrious Knight Recorder, call the roll of officers of ———Senate, No.—.

[This is done, and if all are present and the offices are filled, the Sub. Gr. Com. says:]

Attention, Sir Knights. ! ! ! We, as Masons, are taught, before entering upon any important duty, first to invoke a blessing from Deity, to bless us and our works. Let the Triangle be formed. Illustrious Knight Prelate, invoke the blessing.

Prelate. —Oh Thou Almighty Father of the Universe! Behold here Thy children standing in Thy court, invoking Thy blessing! Be pleased, oh Lord, to smile upon us and bless us. Give us wisdom to so order and direct these ceremonies of installation, that they may prove acceptable in Thy sight. Be pleased to bless this congregation, this Senate, this place, and its institutions. Look with favor, we beseech Thee, upon the officers that are to be here installed. Bless the Grand Master of this Rite and his officers. Bless, we pray Thee, oh Lord, the Sublime Dai and his officers, and all others in authority. Bless, we pray Thee, the Masonic Fraternity throughout the whole world, and all others for whom we should pray. Spread, we beseech Thee, the influences of Truth, Justice and Brotherly Love. Help those who are in affliction, and comfort those who mourn; relieve those in bondage; strike off the fetters of those who are slaves to their own passions. And when we shall have finished our pilgrimage here on earth, receive us into the Grand Lodge on high, there to bask in the sunshine of Thy Orient forever. We will praise Thy name, oh Lord, for it is good. Amen.

Response: So mote it be.

[Orator reads from Isaiah xix: 25–28:]

"In that day shall five cities in the land of Egypt speak the language of Canaan, and swear to the Lord of hosts; one shall be called, The city of destruction.

"In that day shall there be an altar to the Lord in the midst of the land of Egypt, and a pillar at the border thereof to the Lord.

"And it shall be for a sign and for a witness unto the Lord of hosts in the land of Egypt; for they shall cry unto the Lord because of the oppressors, and he shall send them a Saviour, and a great one, and he shall deliver them

"And the Lord shall be known to Egypt, and the Egyptians shall know the Lord in that day, and shall do sacrifice and oblation; yea, they shall vow a vow unto the Lord, and perform it.

" And the Lord shall smite Egypt; he shall smite and heal it: and they shall return even to the Lord, and he shall be entreated of them, and shall heal them.

"In that day there shall be a highway out of Egypt to Assyria, and the Assyrian shall come into Egypt, and the Egyptian into Assyria, and the Egyptians shall serve with the Assyrians.

" In that day shall Israel be the third with Egypt and with Assyria, even a blessing in the midst of the land:

"Whom the Lord of hosts shall bless, saying, Blessed be Egypt my people, and Assyria the work of my hands, and Israel my inheritance "

[After the Orator has finished reading, the following may be sung:]

OPENING ODE.

1. EGYPTIAN MASONRY Divine,
   Glory of all ages, shine!
   Long may'st Thou reign!
   Pyramids Thy monuments stand!
   Egypt, then, had great command,
   Masonic art Divine!

2. KARNAK did then arise,
   And grace the Azure Skies;
   Thy noble ruins are
   Matchless beyond compare;
   No art can with Thee share,—
   Mystic art Divine!

3. OSIRIS, the Architect,
   Did then this Craft direct
   How cities should be built;
   Then SOLOMON, Israel's King,
   Did mighty blessings bring—
   Royal Mystic Art.

Sub. Gr. Com.—Attention, Sir Knights! This being the time for installing the officers of ——, No.—, let strict silence be observed, and when the Installing Officers shall enter this hall, let them be received in proper form.

[If the ceremonies are performed by the Grand Body, or one

representing it, and be presided over by a Grand Officer, the following should be the order of exercises:

When the Grand Officers are announced, they will be received by the whole body standing, and the Grand Master and his Deputy will be received under the Arch of Steel, and conducted to the Orient; and while standing there, the Grand Honors will be given. after which the Grand Master and Deputy will be introduced to the brethren, (presiding officer remaining uncovered,) while the Grand Master and his officers take the Orient. The other officers then vacate their places to the Grand Officers; the brethren go to their respective places, and the body is seated. The Arch of Steel is formed thus: The Conductor and Captain of the Guard each select four Sir Knights in uniform, who, with drawn swords stand on each side of the entrance door, and when the Grand Master is announced they give the order, Marshal at the head of right line, and Knight of Introduction at the head of left line: "Draw swords; present swords; cross swords, and form the Arch of Steel." When this is done, Sub. Gr. Com raps ! ! ! All being in readiness, the Grand Representative gives the alarm on the door of the room—3, 3, 3, 2, =11.]

Gd. of Sanc.—Most Wise Sublime Grand Commander, there is an alarm at the door of our Sanctuary.

Sub. Gr. Com.—Attend to the alarm, and ascertain the cause.

Gd. of the Sanc.—[Opens the door.]—Who disturbs our mysteries ? Who comes here ?

Gr. Rep.—[outside.]—The Grand Representative comes to communicate the orders of the Grand Master of the Sovereign Sanctuary in and for the Continent of America, respecting the installation of the officers of this body.

[Gd. of Sanc. closes the door, advances to the Altar, and reports, as follows :]

Gd. of Sanc.—Most Wise Sublime Grand Commander, the alarm was caused by the Right Worshipful Grand Representative, who comes to communicate the orders of the Sovereign Grand Master respecting the installation of the officers of this body.

Sub. Gr. Com.—To order, Sir Knights. Let the Arch of Steel be formed. [This is done.] Admit the Right Worshipful Grand Representative.

[Grand Representative approaches the Altar, presiding officer uncovers, Grand Representative remains uncovered, Arch of Steel keep their places.]

Gr. Rep.—Most Wise Sublime Grand Commander : It is my pleasant duty to announce to you that the Sovereign Grand Master is without, and in waiting within the vestibule of this Sanctuary, to perform the services of installation of the officers of [———— Senate, No. —, or Chapter, or Council, as the case may be.

Sub. Gr. Com.—Illustrious Patriarch Grand Representative for the Continent of America, please inform the Sovereign GrandMaster that the members of [——— Senate, No. —., or Chapter, or Council, as the case may be,] have elected their officers in due form, and at the proper time; that they are now present, and await the pleasure of the Sovereign Grand Master to perform the ceremonies of installation, and will be most happy to be honored with his presence, and be pleased to obey his orders.

[Grand Representative replies "It is well;" retires to the Ante Room, and reports as follows :]

Gr. Rep.—Sovereign Grand Master, I am informed by the Sublime Grand Commander of [——— Senate, No. —, or Chapter, or Council, as the case may be,] that the officers have been elected in due form, and at the proper time; that they are present, and await your pleasure.

[The Grand Master and Deputy and Grand Representative then enter, arm in arm ; Deputy on the right, Representative on the left of the Grand Master; the other officers two by two, in their order, thus : Orator and Prelate, Senior and Junior Wardens, Secretary and Treasurer, Conductor and Senior Master of Ceremonies, Junior Master of Ceremonies and Captain

of the Guard, Guard of the Tower and Sentinel. The Arch of
Steel is kept over the Grand Officers to the Orient, when the
Grand Master stops in front of the Altar.]

Sub. Gr. Com.—Most Worshipful Sovereign Grand
Master, we feel proud to receive a visit from you
and the Right Worshipful and Illustrious Patriarchs
of the Sovereign Sanctuary. We assure you that
we will spare no pains to make your visit a happy
one, and hope always to deserve the confidence and
esteem of your Illustrious Grand Body. We hope
and trust that you will be pleased to proceed with the
ceremony of installation. Attention, Sir Knights!
It becomes my pleasant duty to introduce to you
Most Worshipful Brother C. C. Burt, 96°, Sovereign
Grand Master; Right Worshipful Brother——,
95°, Deputy Grand Master, and Right Worshipful
Brother——, 95°, Deputy Grand Representative,
and the other Officers of the Sovereign Sanctuary
sitting in the Valley of America. Together, brethren,
give the Grand Honors.

[Three claps on the right, three on the left, and three more
on the right; at the same time stamping right foot. All stand,
while the Grand Master takes the Orient, Deputy Grand Master
on the right, Grand Representative on the left, and facing the
body.]

Gr. Mast.—Most Wise Sublime Grand Commander,
Illustrious Brethren, Sir Knights of [—— Senate,
No. —, or Chapter, or Council, as the case may be,]
and [if others are present] Ladies and Gentlemen:
It becomes our pleasant duty to perform the ceremonies of installing the officers of [—— Senate,
No. —, or Chapter, or Council, as the case may be,]
sitting in the valley of ——, and thereby renew
our assurance of friendship and brotherly love, while
we fulfill the ancient Constitution and laws of our
Order. But before we proceed in the ceremonials,

N*

let us invoke the aid of Deity to bless us and our Institution. Right Worshipful Grand Prelate, perform that pious duty.

Gr. Prelate.—[Prayer.] Supreme Architect of the Universe, inimitable Jehovah, Father of Nature, of Light and Truth, we prostrate ourselves before Thee, and to the eternal laws of Thy immaculate wisdom. Be pleased, oh Lord, to bless this assemblage. Bless the work we are about to consummate. Bless the Craft wheresoever dispersed. Bless all men and all conditions of mankind, all over the habitable globe. Grant the officers of this body strength, energy, and wisdom to combat the enemies of Masonry, and practice truth, friendship, and brotherly love, and to dispel ignorance, superstition and prejudice. Grant them strength and wisdom to support and encourage temperance, truth, fortitude, and justice—strength to practice and propagate the Divine teachings of our beloved Rite, to cultivate the social virtues and the sciences, and to practice tolerance, and to worship God in spirit and in truth; and so let their lights shine, that others seeing their good works, may glorify the great Adonai in Heaven, and say, Behold how they love each other; and that the scoffer, the skeptic, and the infidel, may be brought to a full knowledge of the light and truth as it is taught and inculcated by the teachings of our beloved Rite. Grant, oh Adonai, that our Ancient Egyptian Masonic Rite may extend itself all over the habitable globe, and that we may practice the Divine teaching of our motto, by rendering unto others that which we would others should render unto us. And unto Thy Holy Name will we ascribe all honor and praise, now and forever, world without end. Amen.

All say : Glory to Thee, oh Lord! Glory to Thy name! Glory to Thy works!

Gr. Mast.—! Right Worshipful Grand Secretary, what is the cause of this assemblage ?

Gr. Sec.—Most Worshipful Grand Master, we have assembled together this evening to install the officers of [——Senate, No. —, or Chapter, as the case may be.]

Gr. Mast.—Right Worshipful Grand Secretary, you will call the Roll of the Officers of the body (or bodies) to be installed.

Gr. Secy.—Attention, Sir Knights! I will now call the Roll of Officers of [—— Senate, No. —, or Chapter, or Council, as the case may be.] You will please rise up and respond, as your names are called.

[Secretary now calls each body to be installed, commencing with the highest. The officers rise, and remain standing]

Gr. Mast.—Right Worshipful Grand Secretary, you will now read the Charters of Constitution by which these officers are to be installed.

[Secretary does so.]

Gr. Mast.—Right Worshipful Deputy Grand Representative, have you examined the returns of the election of the officers of the several bodies, and are they regularly elected ?

Dep. Gr. Rep.—Most Worshipful Grand Master, I have examined the returns of the several elections, and find them elected at the proper time and in due form.

Gr. Mast.—Right Worshipful Deputy Grand Master, have you examined the superior officers of these bodies, to see that they are in possession of the necessary Degrees, and competent to perform the duties of their respective offices ?

Dep. Gr. Mast.—Most Worshipful Grand Master,

I have examined the several superior officers of each body; I find them trusty and true, well skilled in the mystic art, in possession of the necessary Degrees, and well qualified to fill the several stations to to which they have been, by the unanimous choice of their Brethren, elected.

Gr. Mast.—Right Worshipful Grand Conductor, you will now present at the Altar, for installation. Illustrious Brothers———, the five principal officers of each body, [Sublime Grand Commander, Senior and Junior Knights Interpreters, Orator and Prelate; Most Wise, Senior and Junior Wardens, Orator and Prelate,] they forming a circle around the Altar for Obligation. [This is done.] You will now form the balance of the officers of each body in another circle outside. [This is done.] Right Worshipful Grand Secretary, you will now call the names of all the officers of each body, and see that they are at the Altar. [This is done.] ! ! ! Brethren, you now behold at the Altar the officers you have chosen to preside over you for the ensuing year. Are you content with your choice? [They assent.] Right Worshipful Grand Prelate, you will now administer the Obligation to the officers of each body.

[The Prelate advances to the Altar.]

Gr. Prel.—Attention, Sir Knights! Present your right arm toward the Altar; the inside circle will pronounce their names and repeat after me:

I,——————— of my own free will and accord, upon the Glaive, symbol of honor, the Myrtle, emblem of immortality, and God's Holy Book of the Law, solemnly promise and swear, that I will, to the utmost of my ability, serve the body over which I am elected to preside, for the full term of my office and keep and perform my several Obligations in Masonry,

I further promise to be true and faithful to my country and just to its laws.

I further promise obedience to the laws, rules and regulations of the Egyptian Masonic Rite of Memphis.

I further promise that I will not recognize or hold Masonic intercourse in this Rite, with any person or body claiming to be of the Rite of Memphis, who does not acknowledge Illustrious Brother Calvin C. Burt, during his natural life, and thereafter his successor, and the Sovereign Sanctuary of the Egyptian Masonic Rite of Memphis, sitting in the Valley of America, as the only legal head and true body of the Rite of Memphis on this Continent.

I further promise and swear, that I will, to the best of my ability, rule and govern this body over which I shall preside or assist in the working of, in a spirit of kindness and brotherly love, and do all in ny power to inculcate the principles of harmony and brotherly love; that I will obey my superiors in office and act with kindness and consideration to my equals and inferiors, and suffer no innovations to be made in the Rituals and teachings of our Order as promulgated by the Sovereign Sanctuary, so far as the same shall come to my knowledge; that I will cause the election of officers to be held at the proper time, and when so elected, will bind my successors by the same Obligation by which I am now bound, and transmit to them all papers, Rituals, Seals and Charters which I shall be put in possession of, and bind them, also, to do the same by their successors forever, to the best of my ability. So help me God, and keep me steadfast to keep and perform the same.

Gr. Prel.—[To the officers in the outer circle.] The Obligation taken by your superior officers, you,

each of you, promise to assist them to keep and perform ? [They all assent.]

Dep. Gr. Rep.—[To officers.] Illustrious Brothers
————[naming each of the first three officers.]

1. Do you each promise to be good men, and
strictly obey the moral law. [Answer.]

2. Do you promise to work diligently, live credit-
ably, and act honorably by all men ? [Answer.]

3. Do you promise to hold in veneration the officers of the Sovereign Sanctuary and their successors,
supreme and subordinate, according to their stations,
and to submit to the awards and resolutions of your
Brethren in conclave convened, in every case consistent with the Constitutions of the Order ? [Answer.]

4. Do you promise to avoid private piques and
quarrels, and to guard against intemperance and excess ? [Answer.]

5. Do you promise to be cautious in your behavior,
courteous to your Brethren, and faithful to the body
over which you preside ? [Answer.]

6. Do you admit that the only legal Rite of Memphis contains Ninety-six Degrees, and that it is not
in the power of any man or body of men to abridge,
alter or interpolate to any less number of Degrees, or
to make any innovations in that or any other body
of Masonry ? [Answer.]

7. Do you promise a regular attendance on the
committees and communications of the Sovereign
Sanctuary and the Mystic Temple, on receiving
proper notice, and to pay due attention to your duties
as a Mason on all occasions ? [Answer.]

8. Do you admit that no new body in this Rite
can be formed without the consent and authority of
the Sovereign Sanctuary or the Grand Master, and
that no other constituted body ought to be counte-

nanced, they being contrary to the ancient charges and regulations of the Order ? [Answer.]

9. Do you admit that no person can be regularly admitted into this Order who is not a Master Mason in good standing, made in a regularly constituted Lodge, and without previous notice and diligent inquiry as to his character by a competently appointed committee at a regular conclave ? [Answer.]

10. Do you agree that no visitors shall be admitted or persons received for affiliation in the body over which you preside, without an examination and producing proper vouchers of their Masonic standing? [Answer.]

Gr. Rep.—Illustrious Brother, these are the regulations of the Egyptian Masonic Rite of Memphis. [Then to the whole body of officers he says :] Do you each and all of you consent to the same, and promise to support and sustain your superior officers in the strict observance of the same ? [Answer.]

Gr. Mast.—Brethren, I now present you with the Holy Bible, the Great Light in Masonry ; also, with the Glaive, symbol of honor, and the Myrtle, emblem of the immortality of the soul, which should always be placed upon and adorn the Altar of all the bodies of this Rite. The Holy Book of the Law will guide you in the path of duty and point to you the way to happiness on this earth, and direct your feet into the Temple of our God, Eternal in the Heaven. The Myrtle will remind you that the soul of man is immortal, and lives through all Eternity ; and the Glaive, symbol of honor, that you should always be ready and willing to draw your sword in defence of the principles of Truth and Virtue, and to stay the hand of oppression.

I also present you with the Book of Constitutions,

the Laws and Regulations of your body, together
with the Ritual of the same; which you will strictly
preserve and transmit to your successor in office, together with the Records, Papers and Seal thereof.
The Book of Constitutions you will cause to be read
in your conclaves, that none may be ignorant of the
precepts and regulations it enjoins. You will now
receive the Charter; by authority of which you will
open, rule and govern the Body over which you preside; and which you will transmit to your successors
at installation, or deliver up to the Grand Master, or
the Sovereign Sanctuary, when requested. You will
be very careful to preserve it; and remember that no
conclave can be held unless it is present. In your
absence your next inferior officer will, if in the possession of the Charter, preside, and in your and his
absence, his next inferior officer, if in possession of
the Charter, will preside. If neither of the three first
officers are present, no conclave can be held, unless
some one of the first three officers of the Sovereign
Sanctuary or their deputies, be present. But, in any
and all cases, the Charter must be present, unless the
Grand or Deputy Grand Master hold the conclave;
in which case it will not be necessary for the Charter
to be present.

Brethren, you having cheerfully complied with the
charges and regulations of this Order, you are now to
be installed in your respective offices, having full
confidence in your skill, learning and ability to govern the same, which I hope you may feel pleased to
do in such a spirit of kindness and brotherly love,
that your body and brethren may be of one mind,
and filled with a spirit of friendship and brotherly
love. Be ever watchful over the landmarks of the
Institution; see that no brother is advanced until he

has made suitable proficiency in the preceding degrees, and that no one is admitted into the Order who is not worthy. Rather have few members and worthy men than large numbers of doubtful reputation. Avoid proselyting or rivalry for members. Practice a just spirit of emulation, not only of who can best work and best agree, but who can bring the best men into the Order. Avoid contention and discussion calculated to engender strife. Speak not evil of any branch of legally constituted Freemasonry, or try to discourage brethren from entering into any other legal branch of the Order. Remember we are all brethren descended from the same common stock, and although we may not work alike, all legal work is good work, and will tend to make men virtuous and happy. Finally, brethren, live in peace with all men; revile none; slander none; but render good for evil. Be just to all. Ask nothing but what is right, and submit to nothing that is wrong. And may the God of peace be with and abide in you and your Institutions forever. Amen.

Response: So mote it be.

Gr. Mast.—Right Worshipful Grand Captain of the Guard, you will now conduct the officers to their several stations.

[The Grand Officers will now vacate the positions, and be seated near the Orient.]

Gr. Mast.—By virtue of the high power in me vested, I now declare [————Senate or Chapter, or Council, as the case may be] regularly constituted, and its officers duly installed. May the blessing of Heaven rest upon you, and may you prosper in all good works. Right Worshipful Grand Captain of the Guard, make the Proclamation.

Capt. Guard.—To the glory of the Supreme Architect of the Universe: In the name of the Sovereign Sanctuary of the Egyptian Masonic Rite of Memphis, in and for the Continent of America, I hereby declare [————Senate or Chapter, or Council, as the case may be,] duly constituted and its officers duly installed for the year 18—, and until their successors are elected or appointed, and insalled in due form.

[Grand Master now introduces the Orator, if there is one, or makes his Oration. After the Oration, the Brethren sing the following, or some other appropriate Ode.]

CLOSING ODE.

1. Almighty Father, God of Love,
   Sacred Eternal King of Kings,
   From Thy Celestial Courts above,
   Sends beams of Grace on Seraphs' wings;
   Oh! may they, gilt with Light Divine,
   Shed on our hearts inspiring rays,
   While bending at Thy Sacred Shrine,
   We offer Mystic Songs of Praise.

2. Faith, with Divine and Heavenly Eye,
   Pointing to radiant realms of bliss,
   Shed here Thy sweet Benignity,
   And crown our hopes with happiness;
   Hope! too, with bosom void of fear,
   Still on Thy steadfast anchor lean;
   Oh! shed Thy balmy influence here,
   And fill our hearts with joy serene.

3. And Thou, fair CHARITY! whose smile
   Can bid the heart forget its woe;
   Whose tread can Misery's care beguile,
   And kindness' sweetest boon bestow,
   Here shed Thy sweet Soul soothing ray;
   Soften our hearts, Thou Power Divine;
   Bid the warm gem of Pity play,
   With sparkling lustre, on our Shrine.

4. Thou, who art thron'd midst dazzling light,
   And wrapp'd in brilliant robes of gold,

Whose flowing locks of silvery white,
Thy age and honor both unfold—
Genius of MASONRY! descend.
And guide our steps by strictest Law;
Oh! swiftly to our Temples bend,
And fill our breasts with solemen awe.

[After the singing they are dismissd with the following Prayer
or Benediction by the Grand Prelate:]

PRAYER OR BENEDICTION.

Now may the blessing of Almighty God rest upon
us, and all regular Masons; may brotherly love prevail, and every moral and social virtue cement us.
Amen. So mote it be.

LECTURE.

These are the highest degrees of Masonry known
to the world, and none but those who have labored
assiduously in the Masonic Art, Symbolic and Ineffable, thereby obtaining that Wisdom. without which
our labor is useless, and our energy wasted in vanity;
giving evidence that they have been purified from
the Errors of Ignorance, Intolerance and Superstition, can ever attain to this Masonic dignity.

What can be more sacred than Masonry? What
is more binding and impressive? What cause is
purer and more philanthropic? What possible honest reason can any human being have to betray the
ceremonies and harmless mysteries of an order
founded on the grand principles of Love, Truth, Light
and Progress? Of what benefit can such treachery
be to the traitor himself or to the world at large?
None. Every effort made to injure the order, has
only made it shine brighter and nobler to the eyes of
the world.

My brethren, we can never be too cautious in our
intercourse with those who are not initiated in our

rites and mysteries, in all matters pertaining to the order. Many a light and careless word may be perverted to our prejudice, and, like the falling snow, swell into a mighty avalanche. Let it be not only our united but our individual care that such occasions for prejudice shall never occur.

In our intercourse with the world, let us carefully guard ourselves against depreciating any brother of the order, no matter what his faults may be. Let no words of ill-will fall from our lips, relating to the members of other Rites. If, from motives of jealousy, at our success and progress, they choose to be antagonistic to us, let all the aggressive acts be on their side—for if Masons disagree among themselves, and make their dissensions matters of public notoriety, what opinion of us can we expect from the outer world, and how can it believe in our professions of Brotherly Love and Friendship?

Let us in our Lodges, Chapters, Senates, and in the Sublime Council, be ever ready to yield prompt and cheerful obedience to the presiding officers of such bodies, and, when acting as such ourselves, to always consider the good of the order and the brethren, and not the gratification of our own vanity or authority. Let us be careful not to remove one of the ancient landmarks; let no ceremony be deprived of its due solemnity, and let no portion of the work be curtailed or lightly passed over, but preserved and performed in all its purity and integrity. It is this very thing which constitutes the charm and beauty of this Rite, together with its lessons of high and holy philosophy and progress.

I have dwelt on this subject at some length, my Brethren, for this is, in reality, an executive degree. You have already gained all the Masonic light and knowledge known to every Rite in existence, for ours, like the English language, combines the beauty, power, and extent of all others, for it has descended to us from the beginning.

It is an incontrovertible fact, that the *real* birthplace of the most important and sublime portions of Masonry, was that mighty land of Mystery and Wisdom—the land of Egypt. Egypt, whose very origin is obscured by the mists of countless ages—upon the banks of whose great river Nile once stood 3,000 magnificent cities, some whose populations seem almost of fabulous amount—whose gorgeous temples, and whose mighty works of art laugh to scorn the efforts of modern civilization. Their architectural works have withstood the ravages of time and the destructive hand of man, for thousands of years, and will for ages yet to come—whose gigantic pyramids rear their unbroken summits to the clouds, eternal mementos of a mighty race. Egypt! the mother of civilization—the home of wisdom and of art, when Greece and Rome were yet unsung, unheard of, and the mighty empires of the present were not.

It is the belief of many learned and accomplished Masons, that Masonry itself existed long previous to the flood, and that after that event, Noah, Shem, Ham and Japhet, re-established and reformed it; that in the very Tower of Babel were rooms set apart for Masonic purposes; that on the destruction of that building, and the dispersion of the people, they carried a knowledge of, and the precepts of the Rite with them into many countries—in which it gradually assumed different forms, but all still showing one common origin. Doubtless, this is true. Materials for everything have existed since the world commenced; but the clay must be fashioned by the potter's hand ere it becomes a vessel; the mighty monarchs of the forest must be hewn, shaped, and put together by the skill of man before the gallant ship floats upon the waters. It is the art of the sculptor that, from the shapeless mass of marble, creates a statue—a form of beauty that may endure for ages—the *stone* had existed before, but not the work of art.

So was it with Masonry; the outline, the rough material was there—the belief in and yearning for something better and more beautiful, but it lacked that which Egypt had to bestow : Wisdom, Learning, and Organization.

Yes, it was in the land of Egypt, in the Valley of Memphis, where our beloved Rite first assumed a coherent form, and gained from the greatest and best of Egypt's sages those lessons of wisdom, virtue and charity, which, with their knowledge of the arts and sciences combined, has preserved through thirty centuries or more, even through wars, famine, plagues, barbarism, and the darkness of the middle ages, the Ancient and Primitive Masonic Rite, in all its pure, unsullied beauty.

As nearly as can be ascertained, it was in the year of the world 1920, that Masonry first flourished in Egypt, and attained so strong a footing therein, that all the most learned and powerful of its population were members of the Mystic Tie. The wealth and influence of the order was almost beyond computation. Buildings of enormous magnitude were erected in which our Rites were celebrated, The greatest precautions were observed to guard our mysteries from the profane; so much so, that in the time of the Grand Hierophant Moeris (who succeeded Osymandias,) he caused a great lake to be dug around the Temple, sacred to our meetings, and called it after

his own name; but in the course of ages that lake
became choked up by the sands of the desert. The
meetings of the Rite from that time were held in the
Pyramids.

From every part of the then known world came
the most learned philosophers, the most heroic warriors, the most powerful princes, seeking admission
within the portals of our temples. Willing and
eager to submit to the rigorous examinations, the long
probations, the fasts, the vigils, the hardships, the
terrible trials of courage, strength and endurance,
which were then exacted from all candidates before
they were allowed to receive even the first degree.
The Greek and Roman mysteries were nothing but
corrupt perversions of the moral teachings of
Masonry, but the Jews, who acquired their knowledge of the craft in Egypt, were so truly imbued
with the pure doctrines of the Rite and its teachings,
that they preserved them intact, with the exception
of altering the names and locality, and, as it were,
nationalizing the earlier degrees.

The idea of *one* Supreme Being is common to all
religions, even in those which run into Polytheism
and the worship of idols. The Para-Brahmah of the
Hindoos, the Eternal Spirit of Buddha, the Zervane
Akerene of the ancient Persians; the Supreme Essence floating on the surface of the dark waters of
the ancient Scandinavian mythology; the Belus of
the Chaldeans; the Kneph of the Egyptians; the
Virococha of the Mexican, are all identical and represent the God of the Jews, Christians, and Ma
hommedans. Every faith has its two opposing
influences of good and evil—God and Satan; Brahmah and Moisasur; Ormuzed and Ahriman; Belus
and Moloch; Osiris and Typhon; the Vitzliputzli and

Tetslipuca. All have their heavens and hells, and three have purgatories, namely : The Roman Catholics, Egyptians, and the Parsees. The Brahmins have their Triune God, Brahmah, Siva, and Vishnu, three in one; and we Christians have our Trinity.

The number four seems common to all—the four elements, the four seasons, the four cardinal points, North, South, East and West; but it is almost useless to multiply instances of this. The number seven occurs so often in all religions and their ceremonies, that it almost conclusively proves a connecting link between them. Let us commence with the seven days of the week : the Jewish Rabbis describe seven hells and give their names; the Mahommedans believe in seven hells and seven heavens. Zoroaster says there are seven classes of demons; the ancients only knew seven planets; then there were the seven gothic deities; the seven Periades; the seven Titans and Titanides ; the seven Hyadel; the body of Bacchus was cut into seven pieces by the Bacchantes; there were seven holy temples in Arabia; seven lamps in the temple of Bactria. I might cite a thousand instances of its universality. To readers of the Bible I need not mention its continual recurrence in connection with all its most important events. The number twelve is another which is met with *repeatedly* in all religious rites.

My brothers, may all the blessings of our Rite be yours now and forever. Remember this—never condemn unheard. Examine, Reflect, and Tolerate !

The end of the Ceremonies known as the Forty-third Degree (Public,) styled GRAND INSTALLATOR.

GRAND CONSECRATOR (44TH) DEGREE.

DEDICATION OF A MASONIC TEMPLE.

[The invited Guests and Visitors being seated, and the Officers in their respective stations, the Hall is darkened]

Most Wise.—(*Strikes!*) Brethren, this being the time appointed for the Inauguration and Dedication of this Hall, as a Masonic Temple ; the Grand Master General (or the Grand Representative) of the Sovereign Sanctuary of the Egyptian Rite and Primitive Freemasonry, in and for the Continent of America, has arrived, and is now waiting to perform the Ceremony of Consecration. Let strict silence be observed.

[The Grand Master of Ceremonies strikes ! ! ! upon the outer door.]

Guard of Tower.—An alarm at the door of our Sanctuary, M. W.

M. W.—Sir Kt. Guard of the Tower : attend to the alarm and ascertain the cause.

G. of T.—(*Opens the door:*) The Most Wise desires to know who it is that thus disturbs ns ?

Grand Master General.—It is Calvin C. Burt, 96°, the Grand Master [or the Representative] of the Egyptian Masonic Rite, and we come to inaugurate and consecrate this place as a Temple for the propagation of the peaceful teachings and sublime morals of our Ancient Rite, under the auspices of the Sovereign Sanctuary, in and for the Continent of America, sitting in the valley of————, and of the Mystic Temple 90° for the Valley of——————, in the name and to the Glory of the Supreme Architect of the World.

o

G. of T.—Most Wise : It is the Grand Master General of the Sovereign Sanctuary [or the Representative] of our Ancient Rite, and he comes hither to consecrate this Temple to the service of God, and the Rite of Memphis.

M. W.—Admit the M. Ill. Sov. G. M. with the officers of the Sovereign Sanctuary.

[They enter, are received with the Battery as in the Installation ceremonies and remain standing between the two columns.]

M. W.—Since this edifice is to be dedicated and consecrated to such sublime and glorious purposes, I will, with the assistance of my officers, present the key.

[The Most Wise comes down from his seat. The Senior and Junior Knights advance with him to the Altar, on the cushion of which is the Sacred Book of Laws, the Sword, Myrtle, three Gavels, and a Key. They take up the cushion and convey it to the Occident, where the Grand Master (or his Representative) meets them ; he takes up the Key, and the Grand Examiner General and Grand Master of Ceremonies takes the cushion from the Most Wise and Senior and Junior Knights, who then return to their proper stations. The Grand Master and his officers stand facing the Orient.]

Grand Master.—Brethren, at the Consecration of a Masonic Temple, our first desire is, that our labor may prove welcome to the Supreme Architect of the Universe, and find grace in His eyes, that he may look with favor on our work; with that intent, let us pray.

[All kneel.]

PRAYER.

Supreme Architect of the Universe ! Soul of the World, which is filled with Thy Glory and Thy Goodness. We adore Thy Supreme Majesty. We bow down before Thy Infinite Wisdom, which has created all, and which preserves all. Deign, Being of beings, to receive our prayers, and the homage of our love. Bless the work we are now engaged in, that of consecrating this edifice to the service of universal Masonry, the propagation of the divine principles of Fraternity, Liberty and Equality, and to the Glory of Thy Name. Bless the work and the teachings here to be exemplified; make them conformable to Thy Laws; enlighten these thy servants with Thy Divine Light, that they may have no other end in view than obedience to Thee, the prosperity of Masonry, and the general good of humanity. We pray Thee, Oh Adonai, our God, which was, which is, and which will be when time shall be no more, enlighten those who are swayed by prejudice, ignorance and interest. Remove the bands of error wherewith they are blinded; and may the whole human race be benefited by the sublime truths and the divine morals hereafter to be taught in this Temple by the practice of our Primitive Laws, which we now dedicate to Thy Holy Name.

All say:—Glory to Thee, Oh Lord! Glory to Thy Name! Glory to Thy Works!

[All rise, Music plays—the Grand Master General. followed by his officers, make a tour of the Hall, and stop at the station of the Junior Knight, where there are three candles or lamps, in a triangular form.]

Gr. Master.—Sovereign Ruler of Immensity! whom we invoke by many names; Thou who reignest supreme; All Powerful; Unchangeable; Jehovah; Father of Nature; Source of Light; Supreme law of the Universe; deign to bless the lights we now enkindle; may they light the steps of the Neophyte towards the Temple of Truth, under the direction of the Ill. Bro. to whose hands I now confide this Gavel, symbol of the power of office; may prudence, zeal, and justice be his innate monitors, to guide his every action towards good, and the prosperity of our Ancient and Primitive Rite.

[G. M. gives the Gavel to the Junior Knight. The Grand Junior M. of C. lights the three candles.]

Illustrious Brother Junior Knight, what is the meaning of your three lights?

Junior Knight.—They represent the brightness of the flame of virtue, unceasingly reminding us that virtue is the support of our Ancient and Primitive Rite; and that, without virtue there would be no happiness on earth; the Divine Light of Truth, and the honor of a true Freemason, which, kept pure and unstained, will ever shine with radiant splendor.

[Music Plays.—The Grand Master and the assisting Grand Officers now proceed to the desk of the Illustrious Senior Knight in the southwest angle of the room, where are three candles, as at the Junior Knight's desk.]

Grand Master.—Omnipotent Father of Light and Love; fruitful source of knowledge, virtue and happiness; cast Thine all-seeing eye upon this, Thy servant, whose lights we are now about to kindle, and to whom we now confide this Gavel. Grant that the flame of zeal for our dearly beloved Institution may ever burn with unquenchable brightness within his breast, and that he may never use the Gavel but with discretion, wisdom and deliberate judgment; so may his labors tend towards the propagation and benefit of our Ancient and Primitive Rite.

[G. M. gives the Gavel to the Senior Knight. The Grand Junior M. of C. lights the three candles.]

Ill. Bro. Senior Knight, what is the meaning of your lights?

Senior Knight.—They represent Faith in our sublime Institution, Hope in a glorious immortality, and Charity to all mankind.

[Music Plays.—The Grand Master and the Grand Officers now proceed to the Orient.]

Grand Master.—Here, in the east of the Sanctuary, cast the rays of Thy Goodness, we beseech Thee, oh Jehovah, with a triple brightness, upon this, the chief officer, standing at the apex of the triangle in this Orient; may he tend to the elevation of Masonry, and the dignity of our Rite; and may this Gavel, wielded by his hand. with confidence and impartiality, be ever reverentially respected by the brothers.

[G. M. gives Gavel to the Most Wise. The three candles are lighted.]

Most Wise, what is the meaning of your lights?

M. W.—They are symbolical of the three-fold luminous essence of the Supreme Architect of the World—Wisdom, Justice and Patriotism, which we, members of the Ancient Rite, are enjoined to propagate among our fellow men.

Grand Master.—Sovereign Deputy Grand Master, place upon the Altar the Sacred Book of Laws, the Sword, symbol of honor, and the Myrtle, emblem of initiation.

[The Deputy Grand Master places the Sacred writings upon the Altar, then the Sword, and the branch of Myrtle on the Book.]

Dep. Gr. Master.—Ill. Brethren : behold, I place upon the Altar the Sacred Book of Laws, the guide of our conduct, the silent, but holy witness of our Masonic vows; may the inspired writings here deposited, ever admonish us to persevere in the propagation of our beloved Rite; and may our every action be as pure and unsullied as the bright blade of the Sword of honor, which, with the Myrtle, emblem of initiation, I now place in this   ; may they long remain with honor in your care, my dear Brethren, as a sacred charge.

[The Grand Master and other Grand Officers form around the Altar. The Grand Master burns a perfume, and carries it in a censer around the Hall.]

Gr. Mas. Gen.—Behold, I consecrate this hall to Universal Benevolence and to the service of Freemasonry; as practiced by the votaries of the Ancient Rite, by the purification of fire.

May no impurities enter here. Amen.—[*All respond.*]

May peace prevail. Amen.—[*All respond.*]

May all the social virtues unite us. Amen.—[*All respond.*]

May charity flow forth from this   Amen.— [*All respond.*]

May the blessings of truth, patriotism, love and charity, prevail in and around this   Amen.— [*All respond.*]

May the brethren observe and practice all these, so that our Ancient Rite shall be honored and respected by the profane, and become a blessing to humanity. Amen.—[*All respond.*]

[The Grand Master remains at the East while the Grand Orator takes a vase of water and sprinkles the different parts of the hall.]

Gd. Orator.—Be purified, and be ever as pure as the undefiled water which I now use, in accordance with the ancient customs of our venerated Rite. The consecration by water is of the highest antiquity; it was used by the Chaldeans and Egyptians, and is the origin of the "Lustral Waters of the Greeks;" and teaches us, that to be purified, man must rid himself of his evil intentions.

[The Grand Master strikes ! ! ! which is repeated by the Senior and Junior Knights. All rise.]

Gr. Mas.—Gr. Orator and Prelate, assemble the Brethren composing this body, in a triangular form about the Altar, there to pronounce the obligation of Fraternal Union, viz:

[The Grand Prelate forms the members in due position; the Most Wise at the East, the Senior Knight at the South west, and the Junior Knight at the North-west Angles. All kneel and extend the right hand towards the Altar, and the left hand upon the heart.]

To the Glory of the Sublime Architect of the Universe. In the name of the Sovereign Sanctuary of Egyptian Masonic Rite of Memphis, in and for the Continent of America. Salutation on all points of the Triangle. Respect to the Order on all good works and undertakings.

In the name of the Supreme Architect of the World, I do most solemnly promise on my faith and honor, as a true Freemason, ever to recognize and uphold this Body, as a duly and regularly constituted Masonic body, according to the Warrant received by them; to obey its By-Laws, Rules and Regulations; also the Laws, Rules and Regulations of the Mystic Temple for the Valley of———, and the Degrees emanating from the Sovereign Sanctuary of America, sitting in the Valley of America; to this we sacredly pledge ourselves; and may God keep us pure and truthful. Amen.

G. M.—Let us sing the

DEDICATION ODE.

Glorious God! on Thee we call;
Father, Friend, and Judge of all;
Holy Saviour, heavenly king,
Homage to Thy throne we bring!

In the wonders all around,
Ever is Thy spirit found,
And of each good thing we see,
All the good is born in Thee!

Thine the beauteous skill that lurks
Everywhere in Nature's works—
Thine is Art, with all its worth,
Thine each masterpiece on earth!

Yea—and foremost in the van,
Springs from Thee the Mind of Man;
On its light, for this is Thine,
Shed abroad the love divine.

Lo, our GOD! Thy children here
From all realms are gathered near.
Wisely gathered, gathering still—
For "peace on earth, tow'rds men good will!

May we, with fraternal mind,
Bless our Brothers of mankind!
May we, through redeeming love,
Be the blest of God above!

Dep. Gr, Mast.—Doth not wisdom cry; and understanding put forth her voice?

She crieth at the gates; at the entry of the city; at the coming in at the doors.

Unto you, O men, I call; and my voice is to the sons of men.

O ye simple, understand wisdom; and ye fools, be ye of an understanding heart.

Hear; for I will speak of excellent things; and the opening of my lips shall be right things.

For my mouth shall speak truth; and wickedness is an abomination to my lips.

All the words of my mouth are in righteousness; there is nothing froward or perverse in them.

They are all plain to him who understandeth; and right to them that find knowledge.

Receive my instruction, and not silver; and knowledge rather than choice gold.

For wisdom is better than rubies; and all the things that may be desired are not to be compared with it.

I, wisdom, dwell with prudence, and find out knowledge of witty inventions.

The fear of the Lord is to hate evil, pride and arrogance; and the evil way and froward mouth do I hate.

Counsel is mine, and sound wisdom; I have understanding; I have strength.

Riches and honor are with me; yea, durable riches and righteousness.

The Lord possessed me in the beginning of His way, before His works of old.

I was set up from everlasting; from the beginning; or ever the earth was.

When he prepared the heavens, I was there; when he set a compass upon the face of the deep.

Then I was by him, as one brought up with him; and I was daily his delight, rejoicing always before him.

Rejoicing in the habitable part of his earth; and my delights were with the sons of men.

Now, therefore, hearken unto me, O ye children, for blessed are they that keep my ways.

Hear instruction and be wise, and refuse it not.

Blessed is the man that heareth me watching daily at my gates, waiting at the post of my doors.

For whoso findeth me, findeth life, and shall obtain favor of the Lord.

Gr. Mast.—To your appointed places, Brethren.

[All resume stations.]

Brother Guard of the Tower, approach the Orient.

[He does so.]

The safety of this Temple is henceforth confided to your care. I deliver you the key. Be especially cautious to admit none but Masons worthy of the name. And you, officers and members, who compose this Body, bear this in mind, that any brother presenting himself for admission, *must* be clad in the proper insignia appertaining to his highest Masonic grade. All must observe the most strict decorum. The most scrupulous attention should be given to all the ceremonies; and profound silence must be observed.

2*

The Presiding Officer should remember, that on him, to a very great extent, depends the welfare of his   . His first care should be to banish any rudeness in either manners or language; to call around him brothers of ackuowledged ability, therewith to be enabled to conduct the work according to the requirements of our Ancient Rite.

If a brother fail in his duty, and is guilty of a fault, reprimand him, not too harshly; but strive to lead him back to the path of rectitude.

The *true* Freemason should lift his heart directly to the Master of all; to that Infinite and Incomprehensible Power, which, in his inmost heart, speaks for the good and just; testifying to the feelings, embracing and subduing the spirit.

Enlightened by Wisdom and Truth, the Mason diffuses the light like a man of wealth and judgment; he bestows his treasures upon those who are really in need, and not upon the *schemer*, the *flatterer* or *egotist*.

True Masons respect all forms of worship; tolerate all opinions; fraternize with all men; are charitable to all unfortunates; self-sacrificing; thinking, speaking and acting well to others.

The officers in this work should chiefly occupy themselves in demonstratiug by their example and instruction, that the moral perfection of man is the chief aim of our institution. The practice of virtue hastens its advancement, and that science enlightening the spirit, leads to that happiness to which divine wisdom destines us. The Mason nobly forgives offences and injuries.

Brethren, you have inaugurated a Temple; each of you contributing according to his means; the Rite will do you justice; your good intentions are fully appreciated. Forget not your duty to brothers less advanced; give them the example of Masonic virtue and duty faithfully performed. To your equals in dignity, manifest all that fraternity includes in its most extended sense. This task will be easy to those whose hearts are penetrated by the *true* principles of Masonry, as taught in the Ancient and Primitive Rite.

Brethren, now give your attention to the Masonic Decalogue.

Dp. Gr. Rep.—Hate superstition; adore God, who in creating thee a being, free, intelligent and capable of virtue, has made thee the arbiter of thine own destiny.

Gr. Archivist or Secretary.—Listen to the voice of reason, which cries to thee, all men are equal; all are members of one family; be tolerant, just and good.

Grand Orator.—Let all thy actions be directed to utility and goodness; judge of them beforehand; if any of thy meditated actions be of doubtful character, abstain from them.

Grand Master of Ceremonies.—Practice virtue; it is the charm of existence; it consists in mutual benefits.

Grand Prelate.—Now that thy felicity is inseparable from that of thy fellow-beings; do to them as thou wouldst wish them to do unto thee; let thy devotion to humanity involve, if necessary, even the sacrifice of thy life.

Grand Captain of Guard.—The moral law is universal; let its sacred text be graven on the hearts of men; whosoever transgresses it shall unfailingly be punished.

Grand Treasurer.—The just man, strong in his

approving conscience, is beyond the reach of misfortune and persecution; his trust is in the justice of the Supreme Being.

Deputy Grand Representative.—The wicked undergo punishment without ceasing; no "Lethean Waters" can extinguish the fires of remorse.

Deputy Grand Master.—Forget not, thy soul is not material, and, therefore, cannot perish as does the body, which dissolves into its component elements; beware of staining it with vice.

Grand Guard of Tower.—Remember unceasingly, that thy felicity is of thy own creation, and that thy place is at the head of created beings.

Grand Master.—And now, by virtue of the High Masonic dignity with which I am empowered, in the name of the Supreme Architect of the University, and under the auspices of the Sovereign Sanctuary of the Egyptian Masonic Rite of Memphis, in and for the Continent of America, sitting in the Valley of America, I declare this Temple duly consecrated to the service of true and pure Freemasonry; to Justice, Wisdom, Patriotism, Faith, Hope, Charity, Virtue, Truth, and Honor, and Universal Benevolence.

May the whole Fraternity be Benevolent, Tolerant and Just. Bless our Works. Make the walls of this Sanctuary, Salvation! and its Arch Praise! May the brothers meet in Unity! work in Love! and part in Harmony! May Fidelity guard the gate of our Sanctuary; Faith promote our duties; Hope inspire our labors; and Charity diffuse the blessings of our Ancient Rite; may Virtue and Honor distinguish the Brethren; and Masonry be honored throughout the world.

Illustrious Brethren : join me in rejoicing on this happy occasion.

[All give battery ! ! ! raise their hands, and say:]

In the name of the Most High, prosperity to this Temple of Masonry.

[All give battery ! ! !—! ! !—! ! ! raise their hands, saying]:

To Thy honor we do this, Almighty Father; to Thee we commend the whole Masonic family ; bless them, O God !

Grand Master.—Let the chain of union be formed, and the grasp of Masonic faith encircle the Temple, from the august Orient to the columns in the West.

[The chain is formed. R. H. over as in R. C. Chap.]

Father of Nature ! God of Love ! Source of all Perfection ! We, Thy children, assembled in this Temple (which we have consecrated to Thy Name, and the service of Sublime Masonry,) testify our boundless gratitude for the signal favors Thou hast lavished upon us ; continue to shed, we implore Thee, Merciful Father, over all Masons, the beneficence of Thy Divine Love ! Bless this Sanctuary, and the culture of that Mystic Science, which, in the end, will re-unite all Thy children in Thy Glorious Sanctuary above. Amen !

All.—So mote it be. Glory to Thee, Oh Lord, &c.

PUBLIC FUNERAL CEREMONIES.

GRAND EULOGIST, (45°.)

No Mason can be interred with the formalities of the Ancient and Primitive Rite, unless he has received the Degree of Kt. Rose-Croix.

The Chapter, Senate, or Council, of which the deceased was a member, must be opened in Ancient and Primitive form, and when in procession, shall be under the immediate charge of its Presiding Officer; strict decorum must be observed, and none can leave the *cortege* without his consent.

ORDER OF FUNERAL PROCESSION.

THE SYMBOLIC LODGE TO WHICH THE DECEASED BROTHER BELONGED. SENTINEL, WITH SWORD REVERSED, PRECEDING THE R C. CHAPTER.

S. K. W.   J. K. W.

BANNER OF THE

KNIGHTS ROSE-CROIX.   CHAPTER.   KNIGHTS ROSE CROIX.

GD. OF T.   CHAPLAIN.   CAPT. OF GD.

ORATOR WITH BIBLE.

ARCH.

TREASURER. CONDUCTOR. M. W. ORGANIST. ARCHIVIST.

MARSHAL.

SENTINEL OF SENATE.

S. K. I.   J. K. I.

BANNER OF THE.

SENATE.

KNIGHTS.   KNIGHTS.

G. OF S.   ARCH.   C. OF G.

ORATOR WITH BIBLE.

RECORDER.   SUB. G. COMMANDER.   TREASURER.

MARSHAL.

SENTINEL OF COUNCIL.

FIRST MYSTAGOGUE.   SECOND MYSTAGOGUE.

STANDARD BEARER.

G. OF SANC.   ARCHIVIST WITH BIBLE.   ORATOR.

GR. EXPERT.   SECRETARY. TREASURER. SWORD BEARER.

SUB. DAI.

PALL BEARERS.   (THE CORPSE)   PALL BEARERS.
WITH THE INSIGNIA OF HIS HIGHEST DEG.
THE FAMILY MOURNERS.

If the deceased is a member of the 90th Degree, the two bodies, or the members thereof, walk in the rear of the Sublime Council. Should the Grand Master of Light, his Dep. Rep. or a Gr. Rep. or M. Ill. S. G. Master be present, they will immediately precede the body, supported by their Grand officers.

[On arriving at the grave, the Most Wise, or highest actual presiding officer, stands at the head, the Senior Knight at the foot, the Orator Prelate at the right, and the Junior Knight Warden at the left.]

Orator or Prelate says: "I am the resurrection and the life," saith the Lord; "He that believeth in me though he were dead, yet shall he live; and whosoever liveth and believeth in me shall never die." All say Amen. So mote it be, so mote it be.

M. W.—Sir Knight Senior Warden, For what reason is this grave prepared ?

R. S. W.—Respect for the dead. Because the body is the dwelling and sanctuary of the soul; because the Grand Architect of the Universe made man in his own image, and because our mortal members are the fit instruments of an immortal mind. The four sides of the grave are indicative of the virtues which should adorn the person of every sublime Mason, and which we thus explain : Reverence, Truth, Justice and Purity, and are opposed to the vices of the ruffians who would destroy Masonry, namely : Ignorance, Falsehood, Envy and Egotism. The Sprig of acacia or myrtle, is the vivifying life that pervades all nature, and the urn implies the intellectual treasure, or immortal soul the body of man contains.

M. W.—What now remains to be done ?

R. S. W.—To deposit the remains of our lamented Brother in its final resting place.

M. W.—Let it be done.

[The body is now lowered by the Sir Knights into the grave.]

M. W.—Sir Knight Orator or Prelate, Let the eulogy be pronounced.

Prelate or Orator.—Even as the acacia bends before the tempest, and falls into the waters which murmur at its feet, so has fallen our beloved Sir Knight. Sorrow darkens our countenances, and our eyes are dimmed with tears, for we have lost a bright light; the Masters are plunged in sorrow ; the craftsmen lament, and even among the profane the voice of grief is heard ! ——— is no more.

All say.—No more! no more !! no more !!!

Eternal and immutable Being, whose presence fills immensity, Thine omnipotence, operating throughout nature, brings about changes without number. But nothing is lost, nothing annihilated; each atom remains and constitutes a part of the great whole. Thou hast created all men to be happy, and hast therefore bestowed upon them an intelligent mind, whose innate faculties are the evidence of its immortality, and, if well employed, capable of rendering them more and more perfect, and more fit to appreciate Thy greatness and enjoy Thy blessings. Thy infinite wisdom has so ordained nature that nothing in the universe can be lost, and our souls are not more subject to annihilation than our bodies, whose elements only suffer decomposition after death in order that they may re-assume their primitive condition.

Thanks to Thee, O Supreme Being, for the consoling ideas that Thou hast given us respecting the future existence of our souls, whereby Thou dost mitigate the grief we feel in the presence of the dead.

May our Illustrious Brother who has been taken from us, rest in peace; and his soul rise in glorious immortality. Let nature assume her empire over his inanimate remains, and may his immortal soul enjoy the happiness which his virtues have deserved. Amen.

All say.—So mote it be.

M. W.—Brethren, sing.

ODE.

Brother, thou hast gone before us,
  To the sphere whence none return
Still, fond memory shadows o'er us,
  Kind remembrance of thy form.

As we mingle with emotion,
  In our solemn, mystic rites,
Thy freed spirit's calm devotion,
  Rises where pure love invites

When, on bended knee, each brother
  Lifts his soul to God above,
Oft may memory's shadow hover,
  To refresh each soul with love.

May his bright example aid us
  Mason's duty to fulfill;
And when death in dust hath laid us,
  May Truth brightly guide us still.

M. W.—Sir Knights and Brethren : to the will and by the action of the Eternal of all ages—past, present, and to come—do we owe our origin and being; and when our earthly pilgrimage has ended, to that Parent source of all Creation must we return.

We are but infants in His mighty hands—the clay which, by the master skill, is moulded into forms of beauty and delight, the blank scrolls on which may be engrossed the golden words of Wisdom or the senseless murmurings of the profane.

We are but the creatures of His will. How then shall we presume to define, as with a line and rule, the extent of His power, His attributes of love, justice, wrath or wisdom.

We are but atoms in creation's plan, our world itself a mere speck in the immense regions of boundless space, and our very Universe but one among countless thousands.

What we are now, so once was this poor frail emblem of humanity—what he is now, shalt thou be ere many more years have sped their way into Eternity. Within this frame once beat a heart, as proud and joyous, or as humble as your own, and these limbs were endowed with the full strength of proud, exultant manhood.

From this now silent Brother once issued words of eloquence, love, devotion and friendship—and now, behold! Is this the end of all this beauty, glory, strength and intellect—this silent, lifeless form?

Believe it not, my brethren. Death is but the end of this earthly life; beyond its portal lies the land of immortality, where, fresh from the turmoils of this life, purified from all mortal passions, the enfranchised spirit ascends to the mansions of the blest, and rejoices evermore in the glorious light which emanates from the throne of the Eternal.

Shrink not, then, from these emblems of the grave, and death; what are they but the broken fragments of that mould in which the work of perfection has been cast and completed by the Great Artificer!

Captain of Guard now says: I now deposit with our departed Brother this wreath of Cypress, the emblem of Death and of Eternity. Attention, Sir Knights; draw swords.

[All draw and extend them over the grave, with hats in left hand, as 90°.]

PRAYER.

Omnipotent! Omniscient! and Omnipresent! God
of Heaven and Earth, Thou hast been pleased to call
from his earthly career the spirit of our dear Brother,
whose mortal part we now consign to the bosom of
our common mother—Earth. Grant, we beseech
Thee, that Thou, all Powerful, may receive it as pure
and virtuous as it was first sent by Thee to pass its
short probation upon earth. Pity and love those
who are left behind. Look with benign mercy upon
the widow and the orphans, who have to struggle
with the toils, troubles and tribulations of this tran-
sitory existence.

Bless our Rite and all the human family, and grant
that in Thy name, Omnipotent Being! we may
arise, and may the remembrance of the sprig of
acacia which was found on the temporary grave of
him who was truly the most excellent of Masons,
and who parted with his life sooner than betray his
trust, ever stimulate his successors to imitate his
glorious example, that virtue may enshrine our beloved Rite, and exalt our intellectual parts; and
when Death, the grand leveler of all human greatness, hath drawn his sable curtain around us, when
the last arrow of our mortal enemy hath been dis-
patched, and the bow of this mighty conqueror broken
by the iron arm of time; when Thou declarest, oh
Lord! that time shall be no more, and when, by this
victory, Thou hath subdued all things to Thyself,
then, oh God! may we receive the reward of our virtue by acquiring the possession of an immortal inheritance in those heavenly mansions veiled from
mortal eye, where every secret of Masonry will be
opened, never to be closed. Then, we pray Thee,
S. A. O. T. U. welcome us into Thy Celestial Sanc-

tuary, where peace, knowledge, and the fullness of
all that is good, eternally reigns, world without end !
Amen.

Response.—So mote it be.

M. W.—Death has inflicted a painful blow upon
our family by taking away from us a Brother whom
we loved. A secret emotion which I cannot repress,
agitates me as I stand at the head of this open grave
and think how he was so intimately associated with
our work that it is with difficulty that I can per-
suade myself that his spirit has gone to his Creator,
and that his manly form is now returning to the dust
from whence it came.

I know the mournful duty that devolves upon me,
as I mingle my sorrows with yours.

Since the Sublime Architect of the World has
called us into existence, it must, in the order of his
plans, be a blessing, and since he has allotted to it a
term, we cannot, without contradiction, pronounce
this term an evil; I would not hesitate to affirm that
the fear of death has been implanted in us as a conservative instinct; but it lessens as we advance in
years, and as we feel the bitterness of time and of
experience.

Such is the language of reason, but the heart says
more ; to suffer for our own or others is the lot of
every well-constituted being whose heart is not steel-
ed against natural affections and the sentiments of
friendship. The common lesson of experience teaches
us, that in life evil predominates over good,

Think not, my brothers, that I wish to spread
among you the gloomy doctrine which exaggerates
the evil of existence and deprives us of the energy
necessary for the fulfillment of its duties. Wherefore should I calumniate life in presence of the tomb

of a Brother who so nobly employed it; why deny
the existence of happiness when we have in memory
the image of our Illustrious Brother, who to his latest
day united it with wisdom, fortitude and probity.
What I wish to prove or rather to recall is: that
whatever the duration of our earthly journey, it is
unworthy of a true Mason to dread its inevitable end.
Be he fortunate or otherwise, the man void of reproach knows not the terrors of death; the weak
alone fear to contemplate their last abode; the wicked
only need fear to die. But though Death is no evil
to the virtuous man, how fearful it is to those loving
friends who lose the cherished objects of their affections. Alas! amid the fugitive consolations which
remain to us; amidst our sorrows, like flowers in the
desert, what treasure is more precious to us, more en-
viable than those affectionate and tender sentiments
which double our joys, and alleviate our grief. Who
could support an existence deprived of this inexpress-
ible charm. Immortality itself would seem worth-
less at such a price—for is not friendship the sweetest consolation, the brightest ornament, the loveliest
flower of life?

Friendship! my brethren, in pronouncing its sacred name at the head of this open grave, I feel the
chords of my heart unloosened, the firmness which
my duty demands seems about to leave me.

A dark cloud covers my sight, and the universal
gloom that surrounds me seems to have entered into
the deepest recesses of my soul. Yes, dear and faithful friend whom we have lost, and who will never
pass from our memory; thy brothers cannot feel that
thou art gone from among them forever; everything
reminds them of thee; every step we take in the
Temple reminds us of thy footsteps, the very walls

speak to us of thee; and this solemn moment, where, according to the Rite that was sacred in thine eyes, we are about to pronounce our last farewell, methinks thy honored shade rises from the tomb to gather the tribute of our tears, and to receive, amid the incense of flowers, the homage which Friendship renders to thy virtue.

M. W.—Sir Knights Senior and Junior Wardens, Announce in your Valleys that we are about to burn sacred perfumes, and to cast flowers upon the grave of our brother.

[First and Second Officers make above announcement. M. W. burns the perfume and says:]

May the soul of our Illustrious Brother re-ascend toward the skies.

[The M. W., followed by the First and Second Officers, pass around the grave three times, each time throwing flowers therein, and burning perfume.]

Join me in forming the chain of union, [same as in R. C.] Let us link closely this sacred chain, and let friendship console us for the only real sorrow which she can inflict upon virtuous hearts.

[They form chain. Afterwards all take their places, and the M. W. extending his hand over the grave, says, with motion of casting into the grave:]

Brother, adieu forever.

S. Kt. W.—Brother, adieu forever.

J. Kt. W.—Brother, adieu forever.

M. W.—We shall follow in the course ordained by nature, and may we one day be mourned as thou art.

[A punch bowl of colored water is brought to the M. W. M. W. dips his hand in the Lustral Water and sprinkles the grave]

You have just heard the last honors to an Illustrious Brother, whose memory will never perish in our hearts, and you have satisfed at once a debt of friendship and of gratitude; but you will stray from the spirit of an order and from the object of Masonry, if grief drives from your heart one of the most consoling truths that can awaken our meditations. Sorrow has its allusions, as have all the sentiments of the human heart; when we meet beside the remains of those who were dear, we grieve in fact but for ourselves, for they whom we loved are only relieved by death from the evils that are inseparable to human life; and when they have fulfilled their earthly duties, they enjoy in the bosom of eternal rest, the price which Divine Justice awards to virtue.

If this truth be applicable to all men, how cordially we should welcome it in our Temples.

The true Mason, who pays his ultimate tribute to Nature, accomplishes the great and last ordeal of his initiation, and the darkness of the tomb has no terror to him and is only a change to the mansion of eternal light and everlasting peace.

Illustrious Officers and Brothers, unite with us in the most solemn acclamations in celebration of the triumph of virtue, which has been gained by the Illustrious Brother.

[The Brethren give the battery ! ! !—! ! !—! ! ! Raise hands ! ! ! Battery ! ! !—! ! !—! ! ! Raise hands ! ! !]

Sublime Architect of the Universe: Father of Nature: Eternal source of all perfection and of all virtue.

We, Thy servants, are here assembled to pay the last tribute of respect to a departed Brother. May this solemn occasion teach us the importance of being ever watchful, for we know not when the silent messenger may come. And when we are called, may it find us prepared to enter Thy everlasting Chapter, where sin and death are unknown, and where we may meet those who have gone before, and with them enjoy that eternal rest Thou hast promised to all thy children. Amen.

[After the Ceremony the procession returns to the Asylum in reverse order.]

QUARREL BETWEEN THE NORTHERN AND SOUTHERN JURISDICTION.

As there has always been a desire on the part of Masons, especially Scotch Rite, or A. & A. Masons, to know how the quarrel between the Northern and Southern Jurisdictions originated, I append here a copy of the Real and Fraudulent Charter or Commission of Representation, which was handed me during the struggle of 1864 to 1866.—AUTHOR.

P

To the Masons of the A. & A. Rite:

I offer the following reason for my repudiation of the Sup.·. Council of the U. S. of America, etc., etc Late of N.·. Jurisdiction, late Sup.·. Council of the State of New York, late of (again) the N.·. Jurisdiction.

HARRY J. SEYMOUR,

Gr. Master Gen. of the A. and P.·. Rite of Memphis
Member of the Sup.·. Council of the 33° of the
Gr. Orient of Italy.

GRAND ORIENT DE FRANCE.—[No. 1.

No. 11,206.	SUPREME CONSEIL POUR LA FRANCE
Correspondance	ET LES POSSESSIONS FRANCAISES,
	O.·. de Paris, le 3 Septembre, 1862. [E. V.)

Cabinet du Grand Maitre. [Seal of the G.·. Orient.]

Addresse au Grand Orient de France, Rue Cadet, 16, Paris.

A l'Ill.·. et T.·. C.·. F.· H. J. Seymour, Souv.·. Grand Insp.·. General; Grand Maitre des Ceremonies au Sup.·. Conseil de l Etat de New York, (33° du Rite Ecos.·. A.·. et A.·.)

Ill·. F.·.

Nous avons la faveur de repondre a la Communication que vous nous avez adressee dans le but d'etablir des relations fraternelles entre le Sup.·. Conseil des.·. G.·. G.·. Insp.·. Generaux, 33 Degre du Rite Ecossais, ancien et accepte. . seant a New York, et le Grand Orient de France, Sup.·. Conseil pour la France et les possessions Francaises seant a Paris.

C'est avec une vive satisfaction, Ill·. et T.·. C.·. F.·. que nous verrions s'etablir des liens etroits entre ces deux puissances Maconniques, par la nomination de Mutuale Garants d'Amitie.

Nous acceptons apres examen des pouvoirs que vous nous avez montres a cet effet, d'etre le Representant du Supreme Conseil de l'Etat de New York, pres du Grand Orient de France, et nous proposons comme representant du Grand Orient de France pres le dit Sup.˙. Conseil l'Ill.˙. F.˙. J. Crane, Grand Maitre de la Grande Loge du Rite de York.

Ces designations Provisoires acceptees par nous en principe, seront soumises a la ratification du Sup.˙. Conseil de l'Etat de New York; elles deviendront definitives des que l'agrement de cette puissance nous sera parvenu, et elles seront ensuite officiellment notifices a qui de Droit.

Nous reposons avec confiance, Ill.˙. et T.˙. C.˙. F.. sur vos soins et diligences pour la prompte realisation de ces projets qui ne peuvent qu'ajouter a la gloire, et a la prosperite de l'Ordre en General

Agreez Ill.˙ et T.˙. C F l'assurance de notre haute et affectueuse consideration.

Le Grand Maitre adjoint de l'Ordre Maconnique en France.

HEUILLANT.

Va et approve le Marechal de France Grand Maitre De l'Ordre Maconnique en France.

MAGNAN.

TRUE TRANSLATION.—[No. 2.]

GRAND ORIENT OF FRANCE,

No. 11 206, of Correspondence.

SUPREME COUNCIL FOR FRANCE

AND THE FRENCH POSSESSIONS.

Office of the Grand Master

Orient of Paris, Sept. 3, 1862.

Address of the Grand Orient Rue Cadet, 16, Paris.

To the Ill.˙. and Most Dear Brother H. J. Seymour, Sov.˙ Grand Ins.˙. Gen˙.; Grand Master of Ceremonies of the Sup.˙. Council of the State of New York, (33.˙. Deg˙. A.˙ and A.˙. Scottish Rite.)

ILL.˙. BRO.˙.

We have the favor to respond to the Communication which you have addressed to us, with the view of establishing Fraternal rela ions between the Sup.˙. Council of Grand Inspectors General, 33d Degree, A.˙. and A . Scottish Rite, sitting at New York, and the Grand Orient of France, Sup.˙ Council for France and the French Possessions, sitting at Paris. It is with great satisfaction, Ill. . and most dear Brother, that we would see established, strict bonds between these two Masonic Powers by the nomination of mutual guarantees of friendship

We accept, after the examination of the Powers you have shown us, to this effect of being the Representative of the Supreme Council, *of the State of New York*, and we propose, as Representative of the Grand Orient of France, to the said Sup.˙. Council, the Ill ˙. Brother J. CRANE, Grand Master of the Grand Lodge of the York Rite.

These Provincial designations accepted by us in the beginning, shall be subject to the ratification *of the Sup.˙. Council of the State of New York*, they shall become definitive when the agreement of that Power shall have reached us, and shall be officially notified to whom it may concern

We trust, with confidence, Ill.˙: and most dear Brother, to your care and diligence for the prompt realization of these projects, which cannot fail to add to the glory and prosperity of the Order in general.

Accept, Ill. and dear Brother, the assurance of our high and affectionate consideration.

(Signatures.)   The Grand Master adjoint of the
Order in France,
HEUILLANT.

Seen and approved by us—

THE MARSHAL OF FRANCE.
Grand Master of the Order in France,
MAGNAN.

FRAUDULENT TRANSLATION.

By the Sub.˙. Council, formerly presided over by H. C Atwood, Edmund B. Hays, and at present by Simon W. Robinson.

Copy No. 11,206, of Correspondence.

Office of the Grand Master.

Address of the Gr. Orient Rue Cadet, No. 16.

GRAND ORIENT OF FRANCE,

SUPREME COUNCIL FOR FRANCE

AND ITS POSSESSIONS

Orient of Paris, September 3d, 1862, V. E

To the Ill.˙. and Most Dear Brother H J Seymour. Sov. Gr.˙. Ins˙ Gen.˙; Grand Master of Ceremonies of the Sub Council of the United States, 33 Deg.˙. Anc.˙. and Acc˙. Scottish Rite—Sitting in the Valley of New York.

ILL.˙. BRO.˙:

We have the favor to answer the Communication which you have addressed to us, with the view of establishing fraternal relations between the Supreme Council of Sovereign Grand Inspectors General, 33d Degree U. S A., sitting in the Valley of New York and the Grand Orient of France, Supreme Council of France, and the French Possessions. sitting at Paris.

It is with the greatest satisfaction, Illustrious and most dear Brother, that we would see strict bonds established between these two Masonic Powers, by the nomination of Mutual Guarantees of Friendship.

We accept after the examination of Powers which you have shown us, to this effect, of being the Representative of the *Supreme Council U. S. A.*, to the Grand Orient of France, and we propose, as Representative of the Grand Orient of France to the said Supreme Council the Ill.·. Bro.· JOHN J. CRANE, M. W Grand Master of the Grand Lodge of the State of New York.

These Provincial Designations accepted by us, in the beginning, shall be subject to the ratification of the *Supreme Council U. S A*; they shall have become definitive when the agreement of that Power shall have reached us, and they shall then be officially notified to whom it may concern.

We trust, with confiden e Ill ·. and most dear Brother, to your care and diligence for the prompt realization of these projects, which cannot fail to add to the glory and prosperity of the Order in general.

Accept, Ill.·. and dear Brother, the assurance of our high and affectionate consideration.

> Le Grand Master adjoint of the Masonic Order in France,
>
> HEUILLANT.
>
> Examined and approved by us—
> THE MARSHAL OF FRANCE.
>
> Grand Master of the Masonic Order in France,
>
> MAGNAN.

I certify that the Document. No. 1, is a true Copy of the Original, now in my possession; which, with other letters and acknowledgments, are open for the inspection of any Masons interested.

> HARRY J. SEYMOUR,
> 152 *Canal Street, New York.*

ROSE-CROIX CHAPTER ODES.

The following Odes are used during the conferring of Degrees in a Rose-Croix Chapter:

OPENING ODE.

Air, Hebron, L. M.

Almighty God, whose Sovereign power,
Sustains thy creatures every hour;
We would invoke thy presence here,
To guide our thoughts, our hearts to cheer.

Bless thou our solemn myst'ries here,
And fill each heart with holy fear,
Lead us aright to learn thy will,
And ev'ry duty to fulfill.

CLOSING ODE, No. 1.

Air, Home, Sweet Home.

Again round our Altar assembled we join,
In singing a parting song ere we resign,
The pleasures of social enjoyment and peace,
Where love unrestrained bids all discords cease.
  Home, home, sweet, sweet home,
  May ev'ry dear brother find peace at his home

Fond mem'ry will aid us, though absence is pain,
Until we assemble in conclave again;
For link'd in a chain, and a bond that's divine,
We each with the other, kind efforts combine.
  Home, home, sweet, sweet home,
  May ev'ry dear brother find peace at his home.

DISCREET MASTER'S ODE, No. 1.

Air, Sicily.

Brother, thou hast gone before us,
  To the sphere where none return;

Still fond mem'ry shadows o'er us,
　Kind remembrance of thy form

As we mingle, with emotion,
　In our solemn mystic rites,
Thy freed spirit's calm devotion,
　Rises where pure love invites.

When on bended knee, each brother
　Lifts his soul to God above;
Oft may mem'ry's shadow hover,
　To refresh our souls with love.

DISCREET MASTER'S ODE, No. 2.

Air, Wilmot.

Brother, thou hast gone before,
　To a peaceful state of rest,
Where no pangs of sorrow roll,
　O'er thy calm and tranquil breast.

Hope inspires our anxious minds,
　That thy change is one of gain;
And we trust thy form to meet,
　Freed from care, from grief and pain.

SUBLIME MASTER'S ODE, No. 1.

Air, Sicily.

Guided by the light eternal,
　In our hearts with truth enshrined;
Bright the virtues, ever vernal,
　Which adorned great Hiram's mind.

May his bright example aid us,
　Every duty to fulfill,
And when death in dust has laid us,
　May truth brightly guide us still.

SUBLIME MASTERS, No. 2.

Air, Old Hundred, L. M.

Unto the solemn, silent tomb,
　We've borne our brother's cold remains;

To rest 'mid solitude and gloom,
  Where darkness deep in grandeur reigns.

His spirit pure has gone where light,
  In bright effulgence meets his view;
Amid the holy seraphs bright,
  Where living scenes are ever new.

Closing Ode, No. 2.

Air, Ïon.

In peace our labors closing,
  Ere, brothers, we depart,
Your voices raise in singing,
  One song before we part.
One song of joyous gladness,
  To him who rules our days,
And soothes our ev'ry sadness,
  By love's congenial rays.

Sacred Arch Ode, No. 1.

Air, Sakara.

Almighty Father, heavenly King,
  Before thy sacred name we bend,
Accept the praises which we sing,
  And to our humble prayer attend.
    All hail, great Architect divine,
    This universal frame is thine.

On thy Omnipotence we rest,
  Secure of thy protection here,
And hope hereafter to be blest,
  When we have left this world of care;
    All hail great Architect divine,
    This universal frame is thine.

Grant us great God, thy powerful aid,
  To guide thr ugh this vale of tears;
For when thy goodness is displayed,
  Peace soothes the mind and pleasures cease.
    All hail great Architect divine,
    This universal frame is thine.

Sacred Arch. Exultation Ode.

Rejoice, rejoice, rejoice,
    The sacred word is found,
Tho' long concealed in secret arch,
    Beneath the sacred mound.
Rejoice, rejoice, rejoice,
    The sacred word is found,
Exult with heart and voice,
    Let praise and joy abound.

Knights of Jerusalem. Ode No. 1.

Go forth to the mount, bring the olive branch home,
And rejoice for the day of our freedom is come;
Bring myrtle and palm, bring the bough of each tree,
That is worthy to wave o'er the tents of the free.
From that time when the moon upon Ajalon's vale,
Looking motionless down, saw the kings of the earth,
In the presence of God's mighty champion grow pale,
Oh never had Judah an hour of such mirth.
From that day when the footsteps of Israel shone,
With a light not their own, thro' the Jordan's deep tide,
And whose waters shrink back as the Ark glided on,
    Oh, never had Judah an hour of such pride.

R. C. Ode No. 1.

Air, Bounding Billows.

Darkest shades of night dispelling,
    Light effulgent fills the mind;
Holy love within us dwelling,
    Boundless love for all mankind.

R. C. Ode No. 2. Faith.

Air, Romberg. L. M.

By Faith our souls are onward led,
    By it a steady course we steer;
By Faith our drooping souls are fed,
    Renewed and strengthened by its cheer.

*p

By Faith we pass this vale of tears.
　Safe and secure, though oft distress'd.
By Faith disarmed of all our fears,
　We go rejoicing to our rest

―――

R. C. ODE No. 3. HOPE. (L. M.)

Sweet Hope, thy peaceful influence lend,
　No more to grieve for sorrows past;
In all our thoughts, thy influence lend,
　That we may safe arrive at last

Lord, upon thee our hopes we stay,
　To lead us on to thy abode;
Assured thy love will far o'erpay,
　Our hardest toil upon the road.

―――

R. C. ODE No. 4. CHARITY. (L. M.)

Sweet Balm of peace, thy fervid glow,
　Within our hearts a sacred spark,
Makes us to feel another's woe,
　Revives the soul when all is dark.

To thee we turn, our sorrowing need,
　Imploring thy bright influence here;
When sorrows lower, we humbly plead,
　That thou wilt guide and banish fear.

―――

KNIGHTS OF THE SWORD. ODE No. 1.

Air, Adeste Fideles.

Our voices united,
Our solemn vows plighted,
In union our hearts with true love are enshrined;
　Rich is the treasure,
　Yielding us pleasure;
In purpose united. true pleasure we find.

　Around aud above us,
　Are spirits who love us,
Whose aim is to guard and to guide by a nod;
　Potent their power,
　O'er us they lower,
In love's silken bondage, to drive us to God.

Amid each commotion,
　On life's troubled ocean,
Our souls towards perfection and purity sped.
　Goodness and mercy,
　Shun controversy,
And here to secure it, we onward are led.

KNIGHTS OF SACRED VAULT.　ODE NO. 1.

Fallen is thy throne, oh Israel,
　Silence is o'er thy plains,
Thy dwellings all lie desolate,
　Thy children weep in chains
Where are the dews that fed thee,
　On Etham's barren shore,
That fire from heaven that led thee,
　Now lights thy path no more.

Lord, thou didst love Jerusalem,
　Once she was all thine own;
Her love thy fairest heritage,
　Her power thy glory's throne:
Till evil came and blighted,
　Thy long lov'd Olive tree;
And Salem's shrines were lighted
　For other gods than thee

KNIGHTS OF THE ORIENT.　ODE NO. 1.

Come not, O Lord, in the dread robe of splendor,
　Thou wor'st on the Mount in the day of thine ire;
Come veil'd in those shadows, deep, awful, but tender,
　Which mercy flings over thy features of fire.

Oh, Lord tho i rememberest the night when the nation,
　Stood fronting her foe by the red rolling stream;
On Egypt thy pillar frown'd dark de olation,
　While Israel bask'd all night in its beam.

And so when the dread clouds of anger en old thee,
　From us, in thy mercy, the dark side remove;
While shrouded in terrors the guilty behold thee,
　Oh turn upon us the mild light of thy love,

FORMS OF PETITIONS, &C.

[FORM No. 1.—*Official Letter for Archivist. The Seal should always be affixed to all Official Masonic Correspondence*]

DIXIT DEUS, ESTO LUX!

TO THE GLORY OF THE SUPREME ARCHITECT OF THE UNIVERSE:

Egyptian Rite of Memphis in and for the Continent of America.

Whatsoever ye would that men should do to you, do ye even so to them.

Masonic office of..............90° Archivist of............

Rose Croix Chapter No... sitting in the valley of ....

State of............

Illustrious Brother and Dear Sir:

[FORM No. 2 —*Petition for Membership.*]

The undersigned being a Master Mason, in good standing, and having an exalted opinion of the Egyptian Masonic Rite of Memphis, does hereby declare upon his honor, as a Mason, that he has no selfish or sinister motives in making this application to be admitted into....Rose Croix Chapter, No....., sitting in the valley of............ of the State of..............
He further states that he is now a member of ....
Lodge No ....of the State of. ....and has taken
.. .. Degrees in Masonry, and will, if elected in said Rose-Croix Chapter, conduct himself as a worthy Mason should do, and obey all the Laws, Rules and Edicts of the Order, and the By-Laws of................ so far as the same shall come to his knowledge.

Refers to ....   Signed,...............

....   Vouched for by............

This..........day of........ .....A. L. 587

Received, filed and referred to a committee consisting of Sir Knights... .... 90°, ...90°, ...90°, who were ordered to report at the next regular meeting.

.... 90°, *Archivist.*

Dated............187..

The committee to whom the foregoing application and petition was referred, would respectfully report that they have carefully inquired into the character and Masonic standing of Bro.............. ..., before named, and find him a worthy Mason, and hereby and hereon report...........favorable, and ask to be discharged from the further consideration of the subject.

$$............ ...90°,$$
$$................90°, \Big\}\ Committee.$$
$$................90°,$$

This..day of......A. D. 187..

[FORM NO. 3.—*Summons.*]

DIXIT DEUS, ESTO LUX!

TO THE GLORY OF THE SUPREME ARCHITECT OF THE UNI-
VERSE:

Egyptian Masonic Rite of Memphis in and for the Continent of America.

" Whatsoever ye would that men should do to you, do ye even so to them."

Masonic Office of Calvin C. Burt, 96°, Grand Master for the Continent of America

Postoffice address, lock box 220, Jackson, Mich.

Illustrious Brother and Dear Sir :

Whereas, At the Annual Meeting of the Sov.·. Sanc.·. for the Continent of America, held in Jackson, on the 27th day of June, A. D. 1871, a resolution was adopted to authorize the Grand Master to convene the Grand Body hereafter at such place as, in his discretion and in force of circumstances, should direct; and

Whereas, By an amendment of Article 4, Section 10, of the Constitution of this Order, passed at the Annual Meeting of the Sov.·. Sanctuary, June, 1871, it was directed that the meetings of this Body should be thereafter held quadriennially, the first of which should be held on the third Monday in June, 1874;

Therefore, Be it known, that I, Calvin C. Burt, 96°, Grand Master, by virtue of the power and authority in me vested, do hereby order and direct that the said quadriennial meeting of the Sov.· Sanctuary for the Continent of America, be held at ....in the city.... ....on............ the....day of........next, at....o'clock, for the purpose of choosing officers for the ensuing term, and the transaction of

such other business as may lawfully come before the said
Body. Hereof fail not, under penalty of a violation of your
obligation.

Done in our Sanctuary, where abide Peace, Tolerance,
Truth, and the fullness of all that is good, this....day of the
Egyptian month........answering to the....day of the month
of...... A. L. 587..

Witness our hand and the Seal of the Chapter, at the Valley
of........this.....day of.,.......Vulgar, or Christian Era,
187..

      [L. s.]   ....96°, M∴ W∴
....95°, *Secretary, or Archivist.*

To the ....*of the Egyptian Masonic Rite of Memphis
for the Continent of America, and the Most Wise*...........
96°.

Being, by force of circumstances, unable to meet with the
Body in. ......A. D. 187.. according to the command of the
above summons, I therefore authorize and empower

    Illustrious Brother........ ....9°,
To represent me as an Officer and Member of the.... ....
in said meeting, and to do every act and thing agreeable to the
Constitution and Laws of the said Body, and the craft, as fully
and completely as I myself could do if personally present.

Given under my hand, at ....in the State of.........
this...........day of.... ....A. D. 187..

                  ....95°,

[FORM NO. 4.—*Form of Record for a Rose-Croix Chapter.*]
State of ....County of.................
          Valley of . ...
At a ....Communication of...................
Rose-Croix No... ...., sitting within the Valley aforesaid.
this ....day of............... answering to the Egyptian
Month.............., year of True Light 000,000,000, E∴ V∴
18...., held at our Asylum, there were present:

Respectable Sir Knight......................95°, M∴ W∴
Respectable Sir Knight...............95°, Senior Warden.
Respectable Sir Knight........,......95°. Junior Warden.
Together with Sir Knights ....90°, Treasurer;
....90°, Secretary; ....90°, Orator;
... ...90°, Prelate; ....90°, Conductor;
.... 90°, Captain of the Guard; ....
90°, Guard of the Tower; ....90°, Sentinel.

With Sir Knights.........90°,.........90°,.........90°,
Members of this Chapter and Sir Knights....9....°,....9....°,
Visiting Brethren. (If any of the chairs are filled by substitutes,
let this so appear on the minutes.)

The Chapter was opened in due form by the M.· W.· and
Brethren.

The minutes of the last Conclave were read for information
and corrected by Sir Knight for ....

The regular order of business was then taken up. (Here let a
full record of everything of a public nature be entered) The
Chapter was about to close, when the fraternal box was passed
and the sum of .... paid over to the Archivist.
Receipts..............dollars; Disbursements, ...
dollars.

There being no further business, the Chapter was closed in
due and usual form, in peace and harmony.

....95°, M W.

(Attest:) ....*Archivist.*

[N. B —This form may be used for the record of all working
bodies in this Rite according to the facts.]

———

[FORM No 5, SENATE PETITION]

*To the Grand Master Calvin C. Burt, 96°, and to the Sublime Patri-
archs composing the Sovereign Sanctuary of the Egyptian Masonic Rite of Memphis, for the Continent of America, sitting in
the Valley of America.*

THE PETITION OF THE UNDERSIGNED RESPECTFULLY SHOWETH:

THAT your petitioners, having the most exalted opinion of
the exercise of Benevolence, the study of the Sciences, of
Philosophy, of Virtue, and Theosophy as taught by the Masonic Degrees of the Egyptian Masonic Rite of Memphis; and,
that they are Masons in good standing, having the propagation
of the Order, and the general good of humanity at heart, which
can be better consummated by having a regularly constituted
Senate in the vicinity of their immediate residences The petitioners are therefore anxious to commence and carry on their
Masonic labors under the sanction of a Senate Charter rom the
Sovereign Sanctuary of the Egyptian Masonic Rite of Memphis
for America, sitting in the Valley of Amer ca, and of the Mys
tic Temple—Sovereign Grand Council General—Princes of
Memphis, 90th Degree, for the State of.......... ....by
the name and title of................. . .Senate of Hermetic

Philosophers, No ....in the Valley of...................

And your petitioners propose the following to be the first officers of said Senate, viz:

BROTHER.......to be M.∴ W.∴ Sublime Grand Commander.
    "   ....to be Senior Knight Interpreter.
    "   ....to be Junior Knight Interpreter.
    "   ....to be Knight Recorder.
    "   ....to be Knight of Finance.
    "   ....to be Knight Archivist.
    "   ....to be Knight Orator.
    "   ....to be Knight Marshal.
    "   ....to be Knight of Introduction.
    "   ... ...to be Knight Accompanier.
    "   ....to be Knight Captain of the Guard.
    "   ......to be Knight Standard Bearer.
    "   .. .. to be Knight Sword Bearer.
    '   ....to be Knight Guardian of Sanctuary.
    "   ....to be Knight Sentinel.

May it, therefore, please the officers of the Sovereign Sanctuary, and of the Mystic Temple, to grant our petition, and constitute your petitioners into a regular Senate, and we will obey all the Statutes, Rules, Regulations, Edicts and Constitutions of the Egyptian Masonic Rite of Memphis sitting in the Valley of America, to which we pledge our honor and truth as true Free Masons.

Name | No. of Degrees taken. | Residence. | Lodge.

———

[FORM NO. 6, CHAPTER PETITION.]

To the Grand Master Calvin C. Burt, 96°, and to the Sublime Patriarchs composing the Sovereign Sanctuary of the Egyptian Masonic Rite of Memphis, for the Continent of America, sitting in the Valley of America.

THE PETITION OF THE UNDERSIGNED RESPECTFULLY SHOWETH:

THAT your petitioners, having the most exalted opinion of the exercise of Benevolence, the study of the Sciences, of Philosophy, of Virtue, and Theosophy as taught by the Masonic Degrees of the Egyptian Masonic Rite of Memphis; and, that they are Masons in good standing, having the propagation of the Order, and the general good of humanity at heart, which can be the better consummated by having a regularly constituted Chapter in the vicinity of their immediate residences. The petitioners are therefore anxious to commence and carry on their Masonic labors under the sanction of a charter for a Chapter from the Sovereign Sanctuary of the Egyptian Masonic Rite of Memphis for America, sitting in the Valley of America, and of the Mystic Temple—Sovereign Grand Council General—Princes of Memphis, 90th Degree, for the State of.. ....by the name and title of ....Chapter of Rose-Croix, No..... in the Valley of................

And your petitioners propose the following to be the first officers of said Chapter, viz:

BROTHER...... ....to be first Most Wise.
" ... .to be first Sen. Warden.
" ....to be first Jun. Warden.
" .... to be first Orator
" ....to be first Conductor.
" ....to be first Tre surer.
" ....to be first Archivist or Secretary.
" ....to be first Captain of the Guard.
" ....to be first Guard of the Tower.
" .. ..to be first Organist.
" ....to be first Sentinel.

May it, therefore, please the officers of the Sovereign Sanctuary, and of the Mystic Temple, to grant our petition, and constitute your petitioners into a regular chapter, and we will obey all the S atutes, Rules Regulations, Edicts and Constitutions of the Egyptian Masonic Rite of Memphis sitting in the Valley of America—to which we pledge our honor and truth as Freemasons.

Name. | No. of Degrees taken. | Residence | Lodge.

[FORM No 7]

To all Masons Throughout the Globe, Greeting:

TO THE GLORY OF THE SUPREME ARCHITECT OF THE UNIVERSE.

"Whatsoever ye would that men should do to you, do ye even so to them."

In the name and under the auspices of the Sovereign Sanctuary, of the Ancient Egyptian Masonic Rite of Memphis, in and for the Continent of America.

PEACE, TOLERANCE, TRUTH.

To all Masons on the face of the Globe; Union, Prosperity, Friendship, Fraternity :

Know ye, that we, the Most Wise, Senior Warden, Junior Warden, officers and brethren of Rose-Croix Chapter No.........sitting in the Valley of............in the county of...... ....and State of.......... ..... do hereby certify that our Worthy and Illustrious Brother and Sir Knight...... ....whose name is written on the margin hereof, is a ....of the.... degree in good standing, who, at his own request and by consent of this Chapter, has this day dimitted therefrom and paid all dues and demands against him to this date, and we cordially recommend him to all good, courteous and valiant Sir Knights Perfect Pontiffs and Masons generally, wherever dispersed, to render him such aid, Masonic Fellowship and assistance as he may require in accordance with the law and spirit of our beloved Masonic Rite and Institution.

Ne Varietur....

In testimony whereof, we have granted him this certificate, done in our Sanctuary where abide Peace, Tolerance, Truth, and the fullness of all that is good, this.................day of the Egyptian Month............answering to the... .... day of the month of.................A. L. 587......., Vulgar Era 187.....

By the   MOST WISE.

Witness our hand and the seal of our Chapter, at the Valley of [L. S.] ....this day of.................Vulgar, or Christian Era, 186.....

........................95°, MOST WISE.
....90°, *Archivist.*

[N. B.—This form of dimit will answer for all the Chapters or Senates.]

[FORM No. 8.—*Dispensation for Chapters and Senates.*]
To all Masons throughout the Globe, Greeting:

TO THE GLORY OF THE SUPREME ARCHITECT OF THE UNIVERSE.

"Whatsoever ye would that men should do to you, do ye even so to them."

In the name and under the auspices of the Sovereign Sanctuary, of the Ancient Egyptian Masonic Rite of Memphis, in and for the Continent of America.

PEACE, TOLERANCE, TRUTH.

To all Masons on the face of - the Globe: Union, Prosperity, Friendship, Fraternity.

Know ye, that we, the Grand Master of the Ancient Egyptian Masonic Rite of Memphis, in and for the Continent of America, having received a petition from a constitutional number of Masons, in Ancient Form, stating that they have the interests of our beloved Rite at heart, and that they desire to propagate and extend its Sublime Teachings, by forming a .... in the Valley of.................State of ....under our jurisdiction, by the distinctive name and title of....................., No........ , sitting in the Valley of ....State of............:

Now therefore, we, believing that these are good reasons for granting the prayer of the said petitioners, do by virtue of the powers in us vested, issue this our dispensation, empowering—

Our Ill. . Brother. ....to act as........ ...;
Our Ill. . Brother.............to act as............;
Our Ill. . Brother...... ......to act as............;
And Our Ill. . Brother............to act as............;
of a.................to be holden in th · Valley of........ ...
State of ...., by the name and title of............ No......... ....; and we furthermore do authorize the said Ill. . brethren to confer the several degrees of a......... ... according to the Constitutions, Ordinances and General Rules of the Sov. . Sanctuary, 95th D. ., and in no other manner. And this, our Dispensation, shall continue of force until the Sov. . Sanctuary shall issue a Constitution for the same, or until this Dispensation be revoked by us. .

In testimony whereof, we have granted this Dispensation, done in our Sanctuary where abide Peace, Tolerance, Truth, and the fullness of all that is good, this............day of the Egyptian Month............ ...answering to the.... .... day of the month of.........A L. 587...., Vulgar Era 187...

By the　　GRAND MASTER.

Witness our hand and the seal of the Sovereign Sanctuary, at [L. s.] the Valley of America this..........day of........... Vulgar, or Christian Era, 187.....

CALVIN C. BURT,
Grand Master ad Vitem 96°, *E · M · . R. . of Memphis.*
......................*Grand Secretary*, 95°.

[FORM No. 9, PETITION FOR COUNCIL]

To Calvin C. Burt 96°, Grand Master ad Vitem, and to the Sublime Patriarchs composing the Sovereign Sanctuary of the Egyptian

Masonic Rite of Memphis, for the Continent of America, sitting in the Valley of America.

To the Glory of the Supreme Architect of the Universe.

The Petition of the Undersigned Respectfully Showeth :

That your Petitioners, having the most exalted opinion of the exercise of Benevolence, the study of the Sciences, of Philosophy, of Virtue, and Theosophy, as taught by the Masonic De grees of the Egyptian Masonic Rite of Memphis; and that they are Masons in good standing having the propagation of the Order, and the general good of humanity at heart which can be the better consummated by having a regularly constituted Sovereign Grand Council General, Princes of Memphis, 94th Degree, in the State where they reside. The petitioners are, therefore anxious to commence and carry on their Masonic labors under the sanction of a charter from the Sovereign Sanctuary of the Egyptian Masonic Rite of Memphis for America, sitting in the Valley of America, by forming the Sovereign Grand Council General, Princes of Memphis, 90th Degree, for the State of ....by the name and title of....... .... Sovereign Grand Council General, Princes of Memphis. 94th Degree, in the Valley of ....

And your petitioners propose the following to be the first Offi cers of said Sovereign Grand Council General, Princes of Memphis, 94th Degree, viz:

BROTHER........to be first Sublime Dai, (Gr. Mas. of Light.)
    "   ....to be first 1st Mystagog.
    "   ....to be first 2d Mystagog.
    "   ....to be first Orator.
    "   ....to be first Treasurer.
    "   ....to be first Secretary.
    "   .... to be first Archivist.
    "   ....to be first Grand Expert.
    "   .... to be first Organist.
    "   ....to be first Messenger of Science.
    "   ....to be first Accompanier
    "   ....to be first Standard Bearer
    "   ....to be first Sword Fearer.
    "   ....to be first Guardian Sanctuary.
    "   ....to be first Sentinel.

May it, therefore, please the Officers of the Sovereign Sanctuary to grant our petition, and constitute your petitioners into a regular Sovereign Grand Council General, Princes of Memphis, 90°, and we will obey all the Statutes, Rules, Regulations, Edicts, and Constitutions of the Egyptian Masonic Rite of Memphis, sitting in the Valley of America, to which we pledge our honor and truth as Freemasons.

Name.	No. of Degrees Taken.			Residence.	Lodge.	No.Blue Lodge
	York Rite.	Scotch Rite.	Mem Rite.			

[FORM No. 10.]

To all Masons Throughout the Globe. Greeting :

TO THE GLORY OF THE SUPREME ARCHITECT OF THE UNIVERSE :

"Whatsoever ye would that men should do to you, do ye even so to them."

In the name and under the auspices of the Sovereign Sanctuary, of the Ancient Egyptian Masonic Rite of Memphis, in and for the Continent of America.

PEACE, TOLERANCE, TRUTH.

To all Masons on the face of the Globe: Union, Prosperity, Friendship, Fraternity.

Know ye, that we,...................... ....

Reposing confidence in the Integrity, Discretion and Masonic Learning of our Worthy and Illustrious Brother and Sir Knight............ ...., ...9..deg., whose name is written in the margin hereof, residing in the Valley of................State of.... .... : Have nominated, and do by these appoint and constitute him a Grand District Deputy Representative of the Sovereign Sanctuary, sitting in the Valley of America.

And we further more do authorize the said Ill∴ Brother to organize bodies and confer the several Degrees of the Rose-Croix Chapter and Senate of Hermetic Philosophers upon worthy Brethren, for the purpose of forming and organizing bodies in said district, and also to instruct them in the ritual and work according to the Constitutions, Ordinances and General Rules of the Sov∴ Sanctuary, 95th D∴, and in no other manner. And this, our Dispensation, shall continue of force until revoked by us.

Ne Varietur .. (margin)

In testimony whereof, we have granted him this Certificate, done in our Sanctuary where abide Peace, Tolerance, Truth, and the fullness of all that is good, this..... ....day of the Egyptian month................answering to the........

day of the month of..............A. L., 587 , Vulgar Era 187 .

APPROVED BY THE GRAND MASTER.

Witness our hand and the Seal of the Sov. Sanctuary, at the
[L. S.] Valley of..............this..... ....day of
..............Vulgar, or Christian Era, 187..

....
Deputy Grand Representative 95° E.·. M·. R.·. of Memphis,
for the State of.......................................

[FORM No. 11.]

To all Masons throughout the Globe, Greeting :

TO THE GLORY OF THE SUPREME ARCHITECT OF THE UNI-
VERSE

" Whatsoever ye would that men should do to you, do ye even so to them "

EGYPTIAN MASONIC RITE OF MEMPHIS.

PEACE, TOLERANCE, TRUTH.

To all Free and Accepted Masons : Know ye, that Illustrious Sir Knight...............whose name is written on
the margin hereof, has been regularly entered, passed,
raised and exalted through the degrees of Apprentice,
Fellow Craft, Master Mason, Discreet Master, Perfect
Master, Sublime Master, Just Master, Master of Israel,
Master Elect, Grand Master Elect, Sublime Grand Master
Elect, and Master of Geometry ; has also been Dubbed
and Created Knight of the Royal or Sacred Arch. Secret
Vault, Flaming Sword, of Jerusalem, of the Orient, of
the Rose Croix, and is now a member of the 18th Degree
of the said Egyptian Masonic Rite of Memphis in good
standing, and as such we recommend him to all Worthy
Brothers, and enjoin it upon all Masons to recognize him
as such, and render him such Masonic aid, assistance, and
fellowship as he may require.

In testimony whereof, we have granted him this certificate,
done in our Sanctuary where abide Peace, Tolerance, Truth,
and the fullness of all that is good, this ....day of the
Egyptian month..........answering to the........day of the
month of..................A. L. 587..., Vulgar Era, 187....

By the   GRAND MASTER.

[L. S.] Witness our hand and the seal of the Sovereign Sanctuary, at the Valley of America, this.............day
of..................Vulgar, or Christian Era, 187....

CALVIN C. BURT,
Grand Master ad Vitem, 96°, E.·. M.·. R.·. of Memphis.

[No. 12]

To all Masons throughout the Globe, Greeting:

TO THE GLORY OF THE SUPREME ARCHITFCT OF THR UNIVERSE.

"Whatsoever ye would that men should do to you, do ye even so to them "

FAITH, HOPE, CHARITY.

EGYPTIAN MASONIC RITE OF MEMPHIS.

PEACE, TOLERANCE, TRUTH.

To all Free and Accepted Masons:

KNOW YE, That Illustrious Sir Knight................ whose name is written on the margin hereof, has been regularly Entered, Passed, Raised and Exalted through the Degrees of Apprentice, Fellow Craft, Master Mason, Discreet Master, Perfect Master, Sublime Master, Just Master, Master of Israel, Master Elect, Grand Master Elect, Sublime Grand Mast ɪ Elect and Master of Geometry; has also been Dubbed and Created Knight of the Royal or Sacred Arch, Secret Vault, Flaming Sword, of Jerusalem, of the Orient, of the Rose-Croix, of the Occident, of the Temple of Wisdom, of the Key, of the Noachite, of Liban, of the Tabernacle, of the Sacrificial Fire, of the Serpent, of the Trinitarian, Knight Evangelist, of the White Eagle, of Kadosh, of the Black Eagle, of the Royal Mysteries, Knight Grand Inspector, of the Red Eagle, Knight Master of Angles, of the Holy City, Adept of Truth, Knight Elect of Truth, Chevalier Philalethe, Doctor of Planispheres, Savant Sage, Hermetic Philosopher, Adept Installator, Consecrator and Eulogist, and is now a member of the 45th Degree of the said Egyptian Masonic Rite of Memphis in good standing and as such we recommend him to all Worthy Brothers, and enjoin it upon all Masons to recognize him as such, and render him such Masonic aid, assistance, and fellowship as he may require

In testimony whereof, we have granted to him this Certificate, done in our Sanctuary where abide Peace, Tolerance, Truth, and the fullness of all that is good, this........ . day of the Egyptian month..........answering to the........day of the month of........ .. A. L. 187.., -Vulgar Era ...187..

BY THE GRAND MASTER.

Witness our hand and the Seal of the Sov. Sanctuary, at the Valley of America, this.... .. day of ....Vulgar, or Christian Era, 187 .

CALVIN U BURT,

[L. S.] *Grand Master ad Vitem, 96°, E.·. M.·. R.·. of Memphis.*

....*Grand Secretary.*

[FORM ·No. 13.]

To all Masons Throughout the Globe, Greeting :

TO THE GLORY OF THE SUPREME ARCHITECT OF THE UNIVERSE :

" Whatsoever ye would that men should do to you, do ye even so to them."

FAITH, HOPE, CHARITY.

EGYPTIAN MASONIC RITE OF MEMPHIS.

PEACE. TOLERANCE, TRUTH.

To all Free and Accepted Masons :

KNOW YE, That Illustrious Sir Knight. ....
whose name is written on the margin hereof, has been
regularly Entered, Passed, Raised and Exalted through
the Degrees of Apprentice, Fellow Craft, Master Mason,
Discreet Master, Perfect Master, Sublime Master, Just
Master, Master of Israel, Master Elect, Grand Master
Elect, Sublime Grand Master Elect, and Master of Geom-
etry; has also been dubbed and created Knight of the
Royal or Sacred Arch, Secret Vault, Flaming Sword of
Jerusalem, of the Orient, of the Rose-Croix, of the Occi-
dent, of the Temple of Wisdom, of the Key, of the
Noachite, of Liban, of the Tabernacle, of the Sacrificial
Fire, of the Serpent, of the Trinitarian, Knight Evange-
list, of the White Eagle, of Kadosh, of the Black Eagle,
of the Royal Mysteries, Knight Grand Inspector, of the
Red Eagle, Knight Master of Angles, of the Holy City,
Adept of Truth, Knight Elect of Truth, Chevalier
Phtlalethe, Doctor of Planispherea, Savant Sage, Her-
metic Philosopher, Adept Installator, Consecrator and
Eulogist, Chevalier Adept of Sirius, Chevalier Adept of
Babylon, Chevalier of the Rainbow, Chevalier Adept of
the Seven Stars, Chevalier Commander of the Zodiac,
Chevalier Barruke, Chevalier of the Luminous Triangle,
Chevalier of the Zardust, Chevalier of the Luminous
Ring, Chevalier Sublime Magi, Doctor of the Sacred
Vedas, Prince Brahmin Sublime Scalde, Chevalier Scandi-
navian, Prince of the Sacred Name, Prince of the Golden
Fleece, Prince of the Lyre, Prince of the Labyrinth,
Prince of the Lybic Chain, Prince of Truth, Prince of
the Covenant, Prince of the Sanctuary, Prince of the
Temple of Truth, Commander of the Second Series, Or-
phic Sage, Sage of Eleu, Sage of the Three Fires, Sage of
Mithra, Sage of Delphi, Sage of Samothrace,

Ne Varietur................

Sage of Eleusis, Sage of the Symbols, Sage of Wisdom, Sublime Sage of the Mysteries, Priest of the Sphynx, Priest of the Phoenix, Priest of the Pyramids, Priest of Helliopilis, Priest of Oru, Priest of Memphis, Pontiff of Serapis, Pontiff of Isis, Pontiff of the Kneph, Pontiff of the Mystic City, Perfect Pontiff, Past Master of the Great Work, and is now a member of the 90th Degree of the said Egyptian Masonic Rite of Memphis in good standing, and as such we recommend him to all Worthy Brothers, and enjoin it upon all Masons to recognize him as such, and render him such Masonic aid, assistance, and fellowship as he may require.

In teestimony whereof, we have granted to him this Certificate, done in our Sanctuary where abide Peace, Tolerance, Truth, and the fullness of all that is good, this........day of the Egyptian month..................answering to the...... day of the month of..................A. L. 587 , Vulgar Era 187 .

By the Grand Master.

Witness our hand and the Seal of the Sov. Sanctuary, at the
[L. S.]   Valley of America, this........day of.............
Vulgar, or Christian Era, 1877.

CALVIN C. BURT,

Grand Master ad Vitem 96°, *E∴ M∴ R∴ of Memphis.*

[Form No. 14.]

To all Masons throughout the Globe, Greeting :

To the Glory of the Supreme Architect of the Universe

" Whatsoever ye would that men should do to you, do ye even so to them."

Faith, Hope, Charity.

Egyptian Masonic Rite of Memphis.

Peace, Tolerance, Truth.

To all Free and Accepted Masons:

Know Ye, That Illustrious Sir Knight.............. whose name is written on the margin hereof, has been regularly Entered, Passed, Raised and Exalted through the Degrees of Apprentice, Fellow Craft, Master Mason, Discreet Master, Perfect Master, Sublime Master, Just Master, Master of Israel, Master Elect, Grand Master Elect, Sublime Grand Master Elect, and Master of Geometry; has also been Dubbed and Created Knight of the

Q

Royal or Sacred Arch, Secret Vault, Flaming Sword, of
Jerusalem, of the Orient, of the Rose-Croix, of the Occident, of the Temple of Wisdom, of the Key, of the
Noachite, of Liban, of the Tabernacle, of the Sacrificial
Fire, of the Serpent, of the Trinitarian, Knight Evangelist, of the White Eagle, of Kadosh, of the Black
Eagle, of the Royal Mysteries, Knight Grand Inspector,
of the Red Eagle, Knight Master of Angels, of the Holy
City, Adept of Truth, Knight Elect of Truth, Chevalier
Philalethe, Doctor of Planispheres, Savant Sage, Hermetic Philosopher, Adept Installator, Consecrator and
Eulogist, Chevalier Adept of Sirius, Chevalier Adept of
Babylon, Chevalier of the Rainbow, Chevalier Adept of
the Seven Stars, Chevalier Commander of the Zodiac,
Chevalier Barruke, Chevalier of the Luminous Triangle,
Chevalier of the Zardust, Chevalier of the Luminous
Ring, Chevalier of the Sublime Magi, Doctor of the
Sacred Vedas, Prince Brahmin Sublime Scslde, Chevalier
Scandinavian, Prince of the Sacred Name, Prince of the
Golden Fleece, Prince of the Lyre, Prince of the Labyrinth, Prince of the Lybic Chain, Prince of Truth,
Prince of the Covenant, Prince of the Sanctuary, Prince
of the Temple of Truth, Commander of the Second
Series, Orphic Sage, Sage of Eleu, Sage of the Three
Fires, Sage of Mithra, Sage of Delphi, Sage of Samothrace, Sage of Eleusis, Sage of the Symbols, Sage of
Wisdom, Sublime Sage of the Mysteries, Priest of the
Sphynx, Priest of the Phœnix, Priest of the Pyramids,
Priest of Helliopilis, Priest of Oru, Priest of Memphis,
Pontiff of Serapis, Pontiff of Isis, Pontiff of the
Kneph, Pontiff of the Mystic City, Perfect Pontiff, Past
Master of the Great Works Patriarch Grand Commander,
Patriarch Grand Generalissimo, Patriarch Grand Captain General, Patriarch Grand Inspector General, Patriarch Grand Orator and Prince, Sovereign Patriarch
Grand Defender of Truth, and has been duly elected,
appointed or installed to the office of..................
entitling him thereto, he now residing in the Valley of
....................and is now a member of the 95th
Degree of the said Egyptian Masonic Rite of Memphis
in good standing, and as such we recommend him to all
Worthy Brothers, and enjoin it upon all Masons to recognize him as such, and render him such Masonic aid, assistance and fellowship as he may require.

Ne Varietur..............................

In testimony whereof, we have granted to him this Certificate, done in our Sanctuary, where abide Peace, Tolerance, Truth, and the fullness of all that is good, this.............. day of the Egyptian month..........answering to the....... day of the month of.........A L. 587..., Vulgar Era, 187...

CALVIN C. BURT, 96°, *Grand Master.*

[L. s] Witness our hand and Seal, and the Seal of the Sov. Sanctuary, at the Valley of..............this........ day of the month of.............Vulgar, or Christian Era, 187..., and issued by

CALVIN C. BURT,

Grand Master ad Vitem, 96°, *E.·. M.·. R.·. of Memphis.*

[No. 15.]

To all Masons throughout the Globe, Greeting :

To the Glory of the Supreme Architect of the Universe.

DIXIT DEUS, ESTO LUX!

"Whatsoever ye would that men should do to you, do ye even so to them."
In the name and under the Auspices of the Sovereign Sanctuary,
of the Ancient Egyptian Masonic Rite of Memphis,
in and for the Continent of America.

PEACE, TOLERANCE, TRUTH.

To all Masons on the face of the Globe :— Union, Prosperity, Friendship, Fraternity.

Know Ye, That we, the Sovereign Sanctuary, sitting in the Valley of America, by virtue of the power and authority in us vested, do hereby Declare and Proclaim, That, having received a petition from a constitutional number of Masons, trusty and true, residing in the Valley of..........in the State of........ and being also assured that the interests of the Craft will be promoted by the formation of a...........................in said Valley—Therefore, we do hereby authorize and empower

CHARTER MEMBERS NAMES.

Our Illustrious Brother........to act as the first........

Our Illustrious Brother........to act as the first........

Our Illustrious Brother........to act as the first........

Our Illustrious Brother....... to act as the first........

And Sir Knights Bros to fill the other offices, viz:

Sir Knight................. ...to be first................

Sir Knight....................'.to be first................

Sir Knight....................to be first................

Sir Knight.................,....to be first................

Sir Knight....................to be first................

Sir Knight....................to be first................

Sir Knight...   ....to be first ....

Sir Knight..................to be first................

And we do hereby Declare and Proclaim, That, by virtue of these presents, we have this day constituted this a............ No....of the General number of this Sanctuary, and No....of the Special Number of the State of...............to be holden at.................aforesaid, and do hereby authorize the Sir Knights named herein, together with those named in said Petition, to become Charter Members of said...............by the distinctive name of............No....of the State of......... with full power and authority to confer the several Degrees of ....at the place aforesaid, upon Masons in good standing according to the Constitutions, Laws, Edicts, By-Laws, Regulations and General Statutes of the Egyptian Masonic Rite of Memphis, and not otherwise; also to instate and install, when duly elected, the officers of said...........annually, or before the 31st day of December in each year, and transmit this Warrant of Constitution, together with the Rituals, Records, Papers and Seal thereof, to their successors in office, and they to their successors. henceforth and forever, according to the printed and established Ritual of this Rite, promulgated by the Sovereign Sanctuary and its officers. Provided always, that the officers of the said............pay to the officers of the Sovereign Sanctuary and to the Mystic Temple Grand Council, 90th Degree, for said State, due respect and obedience, and also pay all dues due thereto, and in all respects pay due homage to the Grand Master for the time being, and otherwise obey the Constitution, Statutes, Edicts and By-Laws of the Sovereign Sanctuary sitting in the Valley of America and the Mystic Temple of said State; otherwise this Warrant of Constitution shall be void and of no effect.

Given under the hands of the Grand Officers of the Sovereign

Sanctuary, sitting in the Valley of America, on the......day of
the Egyptian month............A L. 587 , to wit:

CALVIN C. BURT,
Grand Master 96°.
WILLIAM BROWN,
Dep. Grand Master 96°.
W. B. LORD,
Dep. Gr. Rep. 95° for N. Y.
J. MABBITT BROWN,
Grand Orator 95°.

In witness whereof, we have granted this Charter, done in our
Sanctuary, where abide Peace, Tolerance, Truth, and the fullness of all that is good, this........day of the Egyptian Month
........answering to the........day of the month of.........
A L. 587 , Vulgar Era 187 .

Witness our hand and the Seal of the Sov. Sanctuary, at the
Valley of America, this........day of.............Vulgar, or
Christian Era, 187 .

Issued by the Grand Master,

CALVIN C. BURT, 96°,
[L. S.] *Grand Master ad vitem·*
FRANK E. MARSH, M. D.,
Grand Secretary, 95°, E∴ M∴ R∴ of Memphis.

[FORM No. 16]

DIXIT DEUS, ESTUS LUX !

TO THE GLORY OF THE SUPREME ARCHITECT OF THE UNI-
VERSE.

*Egyptian Masonic Rite of Memphis in and for the Continent of
America :*

,' Whatsoever ye would do that men should do to you, do ye even so to them.''

···   Masonic Office of Calvin C. Burt, 96°, Grand
Master for the Continent of America.

Postoffice Address, Lock Box 220, Jackson, Mich.

December 23d, 1878

Esteemed Fraters and Sir Knights :

The attention of the undersigned has recently been called
to a circular, or *"edict,"* issued by John W. Finch, Grand Master of this State, dated at Adrian, December 11, 1878, in which

he states that he deems it his duty to caution the brethren in
this Masonic jurisdiction, against the *pretence* of Calvin C.
Burt ; and sagely informs the brethren that there is no such
recognized Masonic body, as the Egyptian Masonic Rite of
Memphis.

What does this overwise Grand Master Finch mean by
"recognized ?" By this Grand Lodge ? It is a higher order
of Masonry. The Grand Lodge has nothing to do with it.
No more than it has to do with a Royal Arch Chapter, Council
or Commandery. Nevertheless, the E. M. R. of Memphis has
within its folds, thousands of the ablest, purest and best Masons in the United States, and they regard themselves fully
competent to judge of the propriety or impropriety of uniting
with the Rite. If this Grand Master Finch can see no beauty
in the noble and sublime teachings of this Rite, it must be the
fault of his head and heart, and not the order. He has taken
its obligations to the 90°, but is not familiar with its lectures
or work.

This "*edict*," as this Grand Master Finch calls his circular,
also states, that he has been notified by the M. W. G. M. of
the G. L. of New Jersey, that this "*person*," Calvin C. Burt,
is now under charges before that Grand Lodge for defrauding
the Fraternity of that State.

If this Grand Master Finch has any such letter, it is *not true.*
Certainly, it is false, if the records of the Grand Lodge of
New Jersey are true. In 1864, fourteen years since, without
cause, certain charges were preferred against me in the Grand
Lodge of New Jersey, but in no way connected with the E.
M. R. of Memphis. I was not then, nor have I ever been a
member of that Grand Lodge, as it will be seen by the facts
hereinafter stated, nor was I then a resident of the State of
New Jersey. I knew nothing of the charges for sometime
after they were filed. The Grand Lodge proceeded exparte, to
try me and expel me; and from what? It could only expel
me from that Grand Lodge, if a member.

I heard of the action of the Grand Lodge in 1867, when I
was a resident of Chicago, Illinois. I sent a petition to that
Grand Body, asking for a rehearing (a copy of which accom-
panies this circular;) pointing out the foolishness of the charges, and that the proceedings of the Grand Lodge were in
violation of Masonic law, and the Constitution and By-Laws
of the Grand Lodge of New Jersey. The matter was referred
to a Committee. I did not attend before the Committee, but
on the 22d of January, 1868, over ten years ago, as appears

from the proceedings of the Grand Lodge that year, page 383, a resolution was passed by that body *setting aside* and *reversing* its former action. This *reversed* its former judgment and disposed of the whole matter.

I give the foregoing as a matter of history. Not that I regard the action of that Grand Body as of any legal or binding force. It was from the beginning void. That body had no right, power or authority, under Masonic law, to entertain the charges. I was not subject to their jurisdiction.

I am informed that this same matter has been inquired into by a Committee appointed by the M. W. of Michigan Lodge No. 50, and the Committee, I am assured, found the foregoing facts to be true, and declared me to be a Master Mason in good standing.

This "edict" also states that in the matter of affiliation with any Lodge, I *remain the property* of the Grand Lodge of New Jersey! Indeed! I never was a member of that body; it had no authority to try me, no jurisdiction over my person, or Masonic standing. And such was the final decision of that body. How then can I "remain *their property!* " It is absurd; and shows a vast amount of ignorance somewhere, or a willful misrepresentation of facts and conclusions of Masonic law.

This Grand Master Finch also "forbids" all Lodges in this jurisdiction to receive or entertain the petition of the said Calvin C. Burt, and directs W. M. of Lodges to cause his "*edict*" to be read in their respective Lodges, in order to protect the fraternity against any further *imposition.*

How paternal, magnanimous and watchful is our *learned* Masonic Magnate over his "brethren." How fortunate they are to have such a "guardian " to snuff treason from áfar, and "protect" them from further "*imposition !* "

I think, however, the Masons in this State, are sufficiently intelligent and capable of judging for themselves. If any of them desire to join the "Scotch Rite," the E. M. R. of Memphis, or any other benevolent body, or even the "Independent Order of Red Men," the "edict" of the Grand Master of this State will not deter them.

Is there anything back of this? Oh, yes. A few years since I was employed by the Dental Association to defend some of its members in a suit brought against them by the Goodyear Dental Vulcanite Company. I devoted a great deal of time and money. I did not get my pay. I sued and obtained a judgment. Among the defendants was this John W. Finch.

He paid a small amount. Since that time he seems to have had no love for me, and he has since made his standing in the E M. R of Memphis quite cloudy, so much so that charges are now pending against him therein, for gross un-Masonic conduct.

But enough about this Grand Master's "Bull." Whatever motives may have prompted it, it is as absurd, ridiculous and laughable as the "Pope's Bull against the comet," and as impotent.

In conclusion, brethren, I will merely add that the Rite is in a wonderful flourishing condition, having in this State alone over fifty-four working Chapters, and numbering over two thousand members, and gaining more daily. And it will be sufficient refutation to G. M. Finch's assertion that we are not recognized, to say that its membership embraces nearly all of the prominent Masons in this State, and several of the other States, in fact, wherever it is known or been introduced, of the Blue Lodge, the Chapter, Councils and Commanderies, and as we revile none, slander none, and have only one object in view, viz: that of perfecting humanity, we shall be content with that recognition which shall always be our chief desire to make men and Masons more virtuous, honest and happy, and live in that peace of mind that surpasses riches and worldly fame.

Done in our Sanctuary, where abide Peace, Tolerance, Truth, and the fullness of all that is good, this twenty-third day of the Egyptian month Pagni, answering to the twenty-third day of the month of December, A. L. 5878, Vulgar Era, 1878, True Light, 000,000,000.

Witness our hand and the Seal of the Sovereign Sanctuary, at the Valley of Jackson, this twenty-third day of December, Vulgar, or Christian Era, 1878.

CALVIN C. BURT, 96°,

[L. S.]   *Grand Master ad Vitem E.∴ M.∴ R.∴ of M.∴*

SANFORD HUNT, 95°,

   Deputy Grand Secretary.

All Bros. Secretary: Read this at the first Regular.

CALVIN C. BURT, 96°, *Grand Master.*

TO THE READER.

And now, brethren and friendly readers, before
parting allow me to hope that you have been able to
draw from this short, imperfect history, facts and
statements enough to convince you that this Egyptian
Masonic Rite of Memphis is really what it professes
to be,—the principal key stone, pillar and foundation
of all good Masonry; and the most earnest regret I
have is that time and space forbids my treating more
at large, showing and explaining why it is that the
Mystic Brotherhood (called by the ancients the
Brotherhood of God,) has so long been allowed to
slumber, and has so long been confined in the deep
recesses of ancient and little understood languages,
when the casket contained such immense quantities of
fine and precious jewels, sparkling with truths, knowledge, and the fullness of all that is good; and it is
only till later years, the zealous Mason and searcher
after truth has had the courage to undertake the
arduous task of delving into the depths of science
and ancient history, to bring them to light, and hold
them up to the astonished eyes of a scoffing and dis-
believing, prejudiced and radically perverse mind.
But truth is mighty and must prevail; all it needs is
the ardor of Zerubbabel, the patience of Moses, the
learning of Raphael, and the appreciative sense of
true Masonry of Marconis De Negre, with the aid of
sympathizing friends and cheerful hearts, coupled
wth an indomitable will, to fight the good fight to

the end. Although the task may be laborious, the path long and weary, the crown is to be obtained at the journey's end and the goal of their ambition; for the race is not to the swift, nor the battle to the' strong, but truth is mighty and beareth the victory Hence, ask what thou will, and it shall be given unto thee, as said the faithful laborer to the end.

I am now about to submit into the hands of the Masonic Fraternity of America, this little record of our business and the doings, of the Grand Body of this Ancient Rite for twelve years, with a few samples of its work, and a brief history of its several and difficult passages; but the victory is won; we are a legal organization, a Sovereign Grand Jurisdiction, holding the scepter of truth and justice in one hand and the olive branch in the other; and we invite all good Masons into our Order. We shall always strive for the right, and will seek to establish peace, good will and harmony with all; the field is large enough for all, and really our differences, when they come to be compared, narrow down to really nothing. No one can be injured by gaining knowledge in good work, and if the degrees of the Rite of Memphis do give you *no* good, they will do you no harm. But the one fact is apparent to all Masons, that no person who has taken the pains to learn the work, or even to read, or become acquainted with its lectures or symbols, but have been pleased with them; and who can deny this fact, that no Mason can afford to do without them or the knowledg of our work? They will enable you to prove yourself in any country, among any body of men, Masons, in any part of the habitable globe. Yes, they will help you to work more fully and understand the groundwork and foundation of our noble, time-honored and ancient institution, that has for thousands of years stood the storms of all adversity; when kingdoms, cities and emperors have crumbled to dust and earth, when war (the besom of destruction,) has been seeking for its vital destruction. Although like the sun behind the stormy cloud, is obscured for a season, only to shine forth with more resplendent and refulgent beauty, it has withstood all these shocks of adversity, and to-day, like a giant (as it is,) for good deeds, neither claims or possesses the power of an infant for evil, and while all other mundane things have perished, it still lives and will live so long as man shall live,—so long as civilization and the light of science exists or continues to be the enemy of vice or war. Chapters are now forming rapidly in all parts of the country; from them spring Senates and Councils, and thus the work goes on. All Master Masons, whether affilliated or not, are eligible to these degrees. Twenty or more form a constitutional number for a Chapter, and the process of obtaining the degrees are these: First, obtain a blank petition from the Grand Master or a State Representative, on which will be instructions for obtaining the degrees. When this petition is signed, each person pays five dollars, to be held as the petition fee. When the number, twenty or more, has signed, obtain a draft on some city for the combined fees, payable to the order of C. C. Burt, 96°, Grand Master, Jackson, Michigan. Send this and draft enclosed by registered letter, on the receipt of which he will send a State Deputy, Grand Representative or some other Grand officer, or come himself, and give you each 90°, a diploma to frame, a Charter to work a Rose-Croix Chapter, and seven copies of the Secret Ritual, install the body and learn you how to work ; each member paying five

dollars *more,* which constitutes the entire charge
ten dollars, for degrees, charter, rituals, degree
and instructions, after which you will receive
candidates and manage your body the same as the
Blue Lodge does. You will also be ex-officio member of every Chapter, Senate, and the Council of your
State, and your three first highest officers will receive
the 95°; and all this for the small sum of ten dollars
each, hardly the fee of Entered Apprentice. But this
is for the express purpose of forming Chapters, as no
degrees *are sold* or given for any other purpose.
When a sufficient number of Chapters are formed,
not exceeding four Senates will be formed in a State,
and after this a State Grand Body, called a Council;
but the members and officers of each of these bodies
come from the Chapter, and a Chapter may be formed
and sustained wherever a good Blue Lodge can be
maintained. There is very little to learn, as the
work is printed out in book form, so there can be no
difference or any disagreement about its work. There
are no Grand Body dues, but each Rose-Croix Chapter
pays the Grand Body two dollars for every new member made in the Chapter. The degrees are conferred in the Chapter to the eighteenth degree; the
degrees conferred in the Senate are from eighteenth
to the forty-fifth; and the degrees conferred in the
State Body, the Council, are from the forty-fifth to
the ninetieth; the degrees of the Grand Body, the
Sovereign Sanctuary, are official, ninety to ninety-
five; the ninety-sixth degree belongs to the Grand Master and Deputy Grand Master, and can be conferred
on no other person; the first three or presiding officers of each Body, Chapter, Senate and Council, have
the ninety-fifth, and all the officers and members of
the Sovereign Sanctuary have the ninetieth degree.

They being official degrees, are communicated. No
Chapter, without express authority from the Grand
Master, (by dispensation,) can confer the degrees for
any less sum than the following, viz: The first
eighteen degrees of the Chapter, not less than $15 ;
the next twenty-seven degrees of the Senate for less
than $50; the next forty-five degrees, the degrees of
the Council, for less sum than $100. They may
charge as much *more* as they choose, which is provided for in the By-Laws of each body, the constitutional sums before named being the minimum prices,
which is the provision of the Constitution. When
bodies in this Rite are formed, the degrees are communicated to the charter members, whose names are
borne on the charter, and when the Body is installed,
all new members must come through the Chapter,
unless for the purpose of forming a new Chapter.

The officers and Grand Master of this Rite are
anxious to have the work disseminated throughout
the entire cosmos or continent of America, and are
also desirous of appointing good men who are influential Masons to become Deputy Grand Representatives, and whom the Grand Master is authorized by
the Constitution to appoint, and when so appointed
and commissioned by him, possess the power and authority to make Masons in this Rite for the purpose
of forming Chapters, they being Master Masons in
good standing in their respective Lodges, or holding
dimits in other lawful bodies; and the Deputy Grand
Representative has, when so appointed by the Grand
Master, with his consent, power to appoint deputies
under him, he·being responsible to the Grand Master
for the acts and doings of such deputies.

This Rite, acting on the principle that the laborer
is worthy of his hire, pays for Masonic services as for

any other services in forming such bodies, and any other work outside of the organized bodies in a just and liberal manner, viz : For the circulating petition, obtaining names and perfecting a Rose-Croix Chapter, fifty dollars, and other services in proportion, provided, however, that the $50 for the entire labor, including installing the Chapter, is limited to $50. And in no case will a Chapter be allowed to be installed or degrees given, unless the members be Master Masons in good standing and persons of irreproachable character. Applicants for charters in the first instance will be furnished with a grand officer to teach them how to do the work and give the degrees.

Applications for appointments, dispensations, books, charters, &c., must for the present be made to the Grand Master, C. C. Burt, 96°, Jackson, Michigan, and all letters desiring an answer, must enclose the return postage, as my time is fully taken up with such correspondence, and in the course of a year amounts to a large sum, and should be borne by those interested in it. In conclusion permit me to say, that I am very thankful to all for the very liberal manner in which the books have been subscribed for and ordered, such being the demand that a new edition is nearly ready for the press. And hoping that in my small way I have been instrumental in disseminating the light and spirit of this ancient orber of Masonry, and that it may now flourish and prosper till all good men shall be embraced within its mystic circle, and we all may know, feel and master its good morals, its teachings and precepts, is the fond hope and wish of the author.

Printed in the USA
CPSIA information can be obtained
at www.ICGtesting.com
LVHW040249011023
759788LV00033B/199